DONIA

THE SCARS WE CARRY BY DONIA

SHATTERED. FORGED. UNBREAKABLE.

First published by The Donia Effect 2025

First edition

This book was professionally typeset on Reedsy.
Find out more at reedsy.com

For the ones still holding pain in their bones.
For the ones who carry joy like it might leave again.
For the wounded. The wild. The ones still waking up.

For the nameless, the forgotten, the ones the world overlooked.

This is for you.
For your truth.
For your silence.
For your shift.

Every word in this book was built to remember you.

If no one ever wrote your story—this is your proof that you existed.

This is not a dedication. This is a resurrection.

This isn't a book.
It's a wound that speaks.
A name whispered through smoke.
You won't leave untouched.
You won't leave unmarked.
You'll feel what was lost.
You'll carry what was stolen.
Still—you rise.
Not healed.
But holy.
If you're still becoming,
if you're reaching through ruin—
welcome.
This is not the end.
This is the myth.
This is
The Donia Effect.

~The Donia Effect~

Contents

Foreword iii
Preface vi
Acknowledgments ix
1 The Birth of Donia 1
2 Chapter 1: The Roots of Resilience 5
3 Chapter 2: Embracing the Archetype: A Journey of Inner... 28
4 Chapter 3: The Power of Transformation 50
5 Chapter 4: Breaking Chains, Building Legacy 76
6 Chapter 5: Cultivating Strength Through Vulnerability 119
7 Chapter 6: Living Authentically and Fearlessly 162
8 Chapter 7: Legacy of Love and Strength 221
9 Chapter 8: The Roadmap to Empowerment 250
10 Chapter 9: Rise Again—Empowering Others 261
11 Chapter 10: The Power of Your Legacy — Living with Purpose... 273
12 Chapter 11: The Infinite Power of Faith and Belief 281
13 Chapter 12: The Infinite Power of Self-Love 292
14 Chapter 13: The Courage to Dream Big 301
15 Chapter 14: The Harmony of Wholeness — Embracing the Journey... 330
16 Chapter 15: The Phoenix Within 339

17 Chapter 16: The Final Rise — Embodying Your Legacy 346
18 Final Thoughts 351

Foreword

There are books that entertain, and there are books that inform. Then there are books that **bleed**.

Books that are **alive**, that pulse with the echoes of the human condition and burn with the fire of transformation.

The *Scars We Carry* is one of those books.

This is not just a memoir. It is not a self-help manual or a compilation of motivational quotes.

This is a **resurrection.**

A raw unveiling of truth, written not from the mountaintop, but from the trenches—from the ashes where the phoenix finds her wings.

Within these pages, Donia does something few are brave enough to do:

She tells the truth.

Not the polished truth. Not the kind meant to impress or placate.

But the truth that **trembles**, the truth that **heals**, the truth that **liberates**.

She writes for the woman who's been silenced.

For the child who was never protected.

For the dreamer afraid to believe again.

For the soul who forgot they were allowed to rise.

This book is not just meant to be read. It is meant to be **felt**—in the marrow, in the breath, in the places where words often dare not go. It is a mirror. A sanctuary. A call to rise.

Every scar she names becomes sacred. Every wound becomes a doorway. Every word, a match lighting the way back to wholeness.

And perhaps most powerful of all, The Scars We Carry does not leave you in the dark. It walks you to the light. It teaches you that survival is not enough—**you were made to thrive.**

Donia's journey is hers, yes. But as you turn these pages, you'll find it is yours too.

So take a breath.

Open your heart.

And prepare to remember who you were before the world told

you to forget.

This is not the beginning of a book.

This is the beginning of you.

Preface

This book was not written.

It was survived.

The *Scars We Carry* was never meant to be a story for the sake of storytelling—it was meant to be a mirror for the soul, a lifeline for the forgotten, a resurrection for the silenced. These words came through fire. Through ache. Through the unbearable spaces where language often fails—but God still speaks.

I did not write this book to be seen. I wrote it to see others.

To see the girl who thought her pain disqualified her.

To see the boy who was never told he mattered.

To see the woman rising from ashes with trembling hands and a quiet roar in her chest.

To see the man grieving in silence because no one ever gave him permission to break.

This is for every person who learned to function while bleeding.

Who wore strength like armor, and silence like a wound.

Who wanted to scream, but instead, smiled.

This is for the ones who kept going.

Every chapter you are about to read is a resurrection of voice. A reclamation of power. A sacred undoing of every lie that ever tried to bury you. And yes, it is my story—but it was never just about me.

It is about all of us.

The ones healing. The ones hurting. The ones becoming. The ones who don't yet know how powerful they are.

I don't offer perfection in these pages—I offer presence.

I don't offer answers—I offer **honesty**.

I don't offer escape—I offer **permission** to feel, to rise, and to begin again.

So if you're holding this book right now, I want you to know:

You're not alone.

You never were.

And you never will be again.

May this book breathe with you.

May it walk with you.

May it remind you, page after page, that your scars do not disqualify you—**they crown you**.

This is not the end of your story.

It is the turning point.

Welcome to *The Scars We Carry*.

Now, let's begin.

Acknowledgments

To God—my refuge, my reason, my resurrection.

None of this would exist without You. Every word I write, every scar I survived, every breath I take is Yours. Thank You for never letting go, even when I did. For turning ashes into art and pain into power. For saving me—over and over again.

To the two souls who give my life meaning—You are my why.

Every tear I wiped, every battle I fought, every dream I chased was with you in mind. I hope one day you'll read these pages and understand that every ounce of strength in me was poured into love. I carried these scars so you wouldn't have to.

To the broken parts of me—I see you.

Thank you for holding on when everything told you to give up. Thank you for choosing life, for daring to rise, for believing there was still more beyond the silence. This book would not exist without your courage.

To the ones who hurt me—

I forgive you. And I thank you. You gave me the fire. You gave me the fuel. And without your wounds, I would have never uncovered my wings.

To the ones who stood beside me when I was silent, shaking, or shattered—thank you.

You may never know the power of your presence, your prayers, or your patience. But I do. And I carry you with me, always.

To every soul who will find themselves in these pages—

You are the reason.

This book is not about me. It is about **us**.

Our pain.

Our becoming.

Our rise.

May you see your reflection between every line.

May you feel less alone.

And may you remember: **You are still here. And that means your story is not over.**

This is for the ones who lived through what should have broken them.

This is for you.

With all my love,

Donia

1

The Birth of Donia

Becoming the Voice

In the quiet, unspoken spaces between heartbeats and solitude, a force begins to rise—unnoticed by the world, yet destined to change it. It is not born from comfort or ideal conditions. It is born from fire. From ache. From the raw, untamed strength of a soul that has survived the fiercest storms. This is the story of Donia. A name. A spirit. A resurrection wrapped in skin.

Her story does not begin with a fairy tale. There was no charm, no safety net, no guiding hand to hold her through the darkness. Her beginning was shaped in the shadows—where love was absent, where pain was present, and where silence screamed louder than words. From a young age, life carved lessons into her like etchings in stone—deep, unrelenting, unforgettable.

She was not raised in warmth. She was raised in survival. When others were cradled in nurture, Donia was held by nothing but grit. Her father's absence was not just the missing presence of a man—it was a vacancy of identity. Her mother's presence, though physical, was hollow, leaving Donia to piece together her worth from fragments. But in those fragments, she found something the world could never take: purpose.

Donia is not a product of her past. She is the fire that survived it. Each betrayal hardened her spine. Each abandonment watered her roots. And each fall, each break, each whisper of "you're not enough" only fed the quiet rage within her to become.

Her journey was not clean or clear. It was messy, winding, and layered with missteps. But buried beneath the chaos was an unshakable truth: she was not here to crumble. She was here to rise. Every scar etched into her skin and soul became the blueprint for her transformation.

The name Donia doesn't just represent a person—it represents a becoming. A woman who didn't just heal, but chose to thrive. Who didn't wait for validation, but reclaimed her power. She realized her story was not unique—it echoed in the hearts of every soul who ever felt invisible, unworthy, or broken. And through that recognition, her pain became purpose.

But before she could ascend, she had to confront herself. No more hiding. No more pretending. The true battle was never with the world—it was with the war within. The quiet shame.

The buried rage. The internal questions that haunted her in the stillness. And yet, it was in that same stillness she met her own power.

She began to tear down the walls—brick by brick. Fear, doubt, guilt—they all tried to stay. But she stood up, looked at herself in the mirror, and for the first time, didn't flinch. She embraced the shadows. She danced with the dark. And only then did she see the light. Not outside of her. Within.

Resilience, she realized, is not about avoiding pain. It's about making peace with it. Holding it. Learning from it. Using it. Her past didn't define her. It refined her. And in the fire, she was not destroyed—she was forged.

And maybe you've felt that too—like you were burning, not to end, but to begin.

Donia's becoming was never a one-time transformation. It was a series of risings... Of shedding skins. Of walking through fire barefoot and still coming out softer. With each evolution, she got closer to her truest self—a woman who wouldn't be defined by scars, but would turn them into altars of strength.

Her healing became bigger than her. It became a call. A mission. A movement. To show others—especially the unseen and unheard—that they, too, carry the power to rise. She realized her voice was not just hers. It was ancestral. It was prophetic. It was necessary.

The name Donia became synonymous with truth. With resilience. With that quiet, sacred rebellion that says, "You will not silence me anymore."

And now, this book is your invitation. Not into a story, but into a reckoning. Into a return to yourself. Into the truth you've been afraid to say out loud. It's a mirror, a balm, a battle cry.

Donia is not just a woman. She is a movement.

She is every girl who was told to hush.

Every soul that almost didn't make it.

Every woman who learned to be her own shelter.

This is not just Donia's story.

It's yours.

So as you turn these pages, know that this is not just the beginning of a book.

*This is the beginning of **you**.*

2

Chapter 1: The Roots of Resilience

Donia's story doesn't begin with a crown. It begins in the crawl—on scraped knees, in tear-stained silence, in the spaces most people bury beneath polished smiles and practiced strength. Hers is not a tale of uninterrupted triumph. It is a descent into fire. A journey through the shadows of despair, fear, and doubt. A baptism in brokenness.

Picture her: a little girl in a dim hallway, knees pressed to cracked tile, praying for a father who never comes.And maybe—just maybe—you've been there too. Not in the same hallway, but in your own aching version of it.

And still, she rose.

Resilience wasn't gifted to Donia. It wasn't modeled or taught. It was carved into her spirit—forcefully, relentlessly—by pain. The roots of her resilience were not planted in comfort.

They were planted in absence. In anguish. In the weight of losses that should have crushed her. Where others may have withered, she grew. She did not bloom in sunlight. She bloomed in the dark.

Life gave her no easy roads. There were no maps, no handrails. Her path was paved with shattered glass and silence, betrayal and bruises. But she walked it anyway—barefoot, determined, bleeding—and with every step, she became. She learned that life does not wait for us to be ready. It demands we rise while still trembling.

Her childhood didn't cradle her. It forged her. Her earliest lessons were not of joy but survival. Dreams, for her, were not inherited—they were fought for, birthed in the trenches of "not enough" and "never yours." But even there, especially there, she found the fire inside herself.

Donia's resilience is not a shield that made her invincible. It is a muscle, torn and rebuilt. It is the echo of every moment she wanted to quit—and didn't. Her strength was not in never falling, but in getting up so many times she lost count. Her story is not a highlight reel. It is a resurrection. And every time she was knocked down, she rose different. Stronger. Louder. More whole.

What made her unstoppable was not perfection—it was her refusal to stay buried. She learned to name her pain, to look it in the eye, and to mine it for purpose. Every scar was not just survival—it was proof of a lesson learned, a fire walked through, a lie unlearned. She discovered that struggle, when embraced, becomes sacred ground. That loss clears the way for something deeper to be built.

Donia stopped waiting for someone to save her. She became her own sanctuary.

She no longer saw pain as a punishment, but as preparation. Every heartbreak, every betrayal, every moment of isolation taught her who she was beneath the noise. In the ruins of her upbringing, she began to build a different legacy—not of pretending, but of rising. Not of avoidance, but of power. She stopped measuring herself by what she lacked and started honoring what she carried.

She carried fire. And fire, when wielded with grace, becomes light.

Donia's journey is a masterclass in becoming. Not the kind that comes with applause or accolades, but the kind that strips you bare—then clothes you in your own truth. Her becoming was raw, sacred, and unfinished. But it was hers. And it was enough.

What set her apart was her belief that her story wasn't done—not even when everything inside her screamed otherwise. She didn't run from the darkness. She dragged it into the light. She used it. She turned it into fuel. She understood that her scars weren't detours; they were roadmaps. Her past wasn't her prison—it was her prophecy.

And so, she became more than a survivor. She became a vessel.

Of hope. Of healing. Of hard-won wisdom. She refused to let the fire consume her. Instead, she let it anoint her.

She learned that resilience is not hardness. It is softness that survived. It is compassion born of understanding. It is the quiet, unwavering belief that you were made for more. That your pain has purpose. That your rise will echo.

Donia's story is not about arrival—it is about movement. It is the courage to continue when the world gives you every reason to stop. It is the audacity to speak when silence feels safer. It is the decision, again and again, to choose yourself. To rebuild yourself. To become yourself.

She is the proof that we are not what has happened to us—we are what we choose to do with it.

And so, her journey continues—not with ease, but with clarity. Not with perfection, but with power. Donia does not walk unscarred. She walks unashamed. Every wound, a badge. Every tear, a truth. Every step, a reclaiming.

This is the root of her resilience: not that she was never broken—but that she bled and bloomed anyway. Not that she never lost—but that she rose from the ashes, arms open, ready to give voice to every soul still buried beneath the rubble of their own silence.

This is the beginning of Donia.

And the world has no idea what's about to rise.

The Womb of Struggle

Not the end. The beginning. The sacred soil where warriors are born.

The womb is where life begins—but not all beginnings are tender. Not all arrivals are wrapped in lullabies. For Donia, the womb of her childhood was not a sanctuary. It was a battleground. A hollow space wrapped in absence. A cradle of confusion, echoing with questions no child should carry.

She wasn't born into warmth. She was born into rupture.

From her very first breath, Donia was introduced to the ache of being unwanted. Her first lullaby was silence. Her first lesson—abandonment. Her father was a ghost in the living. Here, then gone. A presence so unreliable it became more painful than his absence. He didn't just leave—he left questions behind that clawed at her soul like thorns: Why wasn't I enough? Why didn't he stay?

He left her with a name but no voice. With blood ties but no bond. And that vacancy—that aching hollow—would stretch itself into every room she entered, every mirror she looked into. She carried it like a second skin.

Her mother was there—but not really. Not in the way a child needs. Not in the way that shelters, nourishes, sees. She was present in body but absent in spirit, burdened by her own storms. Love, for Donia, wasn't a given—it was something she believed she had to earn. With silence. With obedience. With becoming whoever she needed to be just to be seen. Just to feel safe. Just to matter.

But mattering never came. Not the way she needed it.

So she adapted. She folded herself smaller and smaller, shrinking to fit into the cracks where love should have lived. She became what the world needed—never what her soul longed for. And in that shrinking, she began to disappear from herself. Her joy faded. Her voice vanished. Her innocence cracked. All before she ever had a chance to fully be a child.

The womb she came from wasn't filled with lullabies—it was filled with silence. Long, aching silences that screamed louder than words ever could. She learned to mother herself before she was even old enough to spell the word "protection." She became her own comfort, her own confidante, her own compass. Because no one else could—or would—offer her that.

But even in this dark womb, something was being born. Not a weakness. Not a curse. A fire.

It started as a flicker. A whisper in the depths of her soul that said: There's more than this. There has to be more than this. Even when the world told her she was unlovable, that whisper stayed. Even when her reflection mirrored only emptiness, that flicker remained. A divine spark. A sacred defiance. A quiet, stubborn knowing that she was not the lie she was being raised in.

That whisper became a roar.

The womb of struggle didn't just break her. It made her. In the hollow of rejection, she began to build a different truth. One forged not by circumstance, but by resilience. One written not in trauma, but in becoming.

She began to learn that worth was not something others gave you—it was something no one could take from you. That real love wasn't performative or conditional—it started from within. It was gritty. Rooted. Sacred.

She started to see that her pain wasn't proof of her unworthiness—it was proof of her depth. That the very ache that had once silenced her was the soil where her strength was growing. That the love she longed for from others had always been inside her, waiting. Not to be handed to her. To be claimed.

And she claimed it.

Donia stopped searching for belonging in people who had no capacity to hold her. She stopped seeking validation from those too broken to see her value. She turned inward—and there, in the ashes, she found her voice. Not loud at first, but real. Not perfect, but present. A voice that said: I am here. I am worthy. I will not be undone by the ones who could not love me.

The womb of struggle became the furnace where her spirit was refined. Not erased. Not diminished. Refined.

She learned that sometimes, the people who should have loved you first are the very ones who teach you how to love yourself most fiercely. That sometimes, abandonment is not the end of love—it's the birthplace of self-reclamation. That sometimes, being denied love gives you the hunger to create a kind of love this world has never seen.

Her childhood may have been stolen, but it didn't steal her destiny. Her innocence may have been shattered, but from those shards she built a mirror that reflected the truth: She was never the problem.

She was the promise.

Donia's womb of struggle was not a place of death. It was sacred ground. A chrysalis. A holy incubation. The beginning of her becoming.

She was not buried. She was planted.

And now, she is rising.

The Burden of Silence

Some wounds scream. Hers didn't. They sat inside her like ghosts—quiet, but everywhere.

Donia's childhood was steeped in silence. Not the peaceful kind. Not the kind that comforts. This silence was suffocating. Heavy. The kind that presses against your chest and steals the breath from your lungs without ever making a sound.

It was the silence of unanswered questions. The silence of never being asked how she felt. The silence of being seen, but never truly known. No one spoke of the pain. No one acknowledged the ache. She lived in a house where emotions were swallowed, not spoken—where crying was weakness and silence was survival.

And so, she learned the language of silence. Perfected it. Wore it like armor.

She smiled when it hurt. She stayed quiet when she wanted to scream. She pretended when she needed presence. Because what other choice did she have? When no one teaches you how to hold your pain, you start hiding it. When no one holds space for your voice, you begin to believe it doesn't matter. That you don't matter.

The silence wrapped around her like a second skin. She couldn't peel it off. Couldn't run from it. Couldn't cry loud enough to break through it—because the cries never left her throat.

Inside, she was a war zone.

Every unspoken word became a bruise. Every swallowed truth became a scar. And though no one saw the blood, she was bleeding. Quietly. Constantly. Dying in pieces under the weight of everything she could never say.

And yet—even then—there was fire.

A flicker. Faint, but defiant. An ember buried deep in her spirit that refused to be extinguished. That fire whispered what no one else had the courage to say: You deserve to be heard.

It began in small ways. A journal entry. A silent prayer. A single moment where she let the truth hit the page instead of hiding in her chest. And with each word she wrote, each tear she let fall, the silence began to crack.

She discovered something sacred in that rebellion: her voice.

It didn't roar at first. It trembled. It stuttered. It questioned. But it showed up.

Her healing didn't begin with grand gestures. It began the moment she chose to stop betraying herself with silence. The moment she realized that speaking her pain wasn't weakness—it was war. And she was ready to fight.

Donia's voice was forged in silence. Hardened by it. Sharpened by it. But it would not be silenced forever.

She started to speak—not for attention, but for freedom. Not because she owed the world an explanation, but because she owed herself the truth. She stopped hiding behind "I'm fine." She stopped shrinking to make others comfortable. She stopped apologizing for existing.

And in doing so, she reclaimed her breath.

Each time she spoke her truth, she unlearned the lies the

silence taught her. Lies that said she was too much. Too broken. Too unworthy of being heard. Lies that buried her. Lies that once had power—but no longer.

Because now, her voice had become resurrection.

Donia learned that the burden of silence was never hers to carry. That her truth was sacred. That her story—raw and unfinished—was worthy of being told. Not whispered. Not hidden. Declared.

The world may have tried to mute her, but she is not quiet anymore.

She is thunder. She is wind through broken windows. She is the sound of chains breaking.

Donia's journey through silence was not a surrender—it was a gathering of strength. A slow, deliberate rise. And with every word she now speaks, she offers permission—for others to unburden, to unravel, to rise.

Because silence may have shaped her beginnings, but it will not define her becoming.

The First Step Toward Freedom

Freedom doesn't come all at once. It arrives slowly—like light cracking through the seams of a closed door. And for Donia, that light began with a whisper: "You don't have to stay here."

She didn't know what healing looked like. She had no map, no mentor, no mirror showing her who she could become. What she had was ache. What she had was exhaustion. What she had was a hunger to feel anything other than invisible.

And so, she began with what she had.

Late at night, when the world fell quiet and the silence didn't feel like suffocation but like possibility, she began to face herself. Not the version everyone else saw. Not the mask. The real her—the girl curled up in the corner of her own soul, still aching for the love she never received. The girl who had learned to survive on scraps of validation. The girl who was tired of pretending.

She didn't run from the pain this time. She sat in it. Let it speak. Let it rise. Let it tell her everything she had pushed down for years. And what she heard wasn't weakness—it was truth. It was clarity. It was her body, her heart, her spirit saying, "There's more."

That moment was not a grand awakening. It was quiet. Sacred. But it was the beginning.

Donia realized then that the first step toward freedom was not about changing her circumstances—it was about changing her response to them. It was about choosing to stop abandoning herself. About choosing to listen to the version of her that had been silenced for far too long.

For the first time, she didn't push her feelings away. She

welcomed them. She let the shame come. The rage. The grief. The longing. She let it all rise like floodwaters—and instead of drowning, she learned how to swim.

That choice—to feel—was an act of rebellion. It was the loudest "yes" she had ever whispered to herself.

She began to see that healing wasn't about perfection. It was about permission. Permission to be human. Permission to rest. Permission to grieve. Permission to take up space without apology. And most of all, permission to love herself not after she was healed, but as she was healing.

And oh, did she begin to love herself. In pieces, at first. Gently. Awkwardly. But then fiercely.

She stopped asking others to validate what God had already declared. She stopped waiting for someone to choose her, to fight for her, to save her. She became the one she was waiting for.

She chose herself.

And that choice changed everything.

Donia learned that freedom was not a finish line. It was a daily decision. A decision to forgive what cannot be undone. A decision to show up even when the weight of her past threatened to drag her back. A decision to speak life over herself, even when she didn't fully believe the words yet.

Some days, healing looked like journaling through the tears. Other days, it looked like getting out of bed when everything inside her screamed to stay hidden. But every step—no matter how small—was holy. Every act of choosing herself was sacred.

She didn't need to erase her story to find peace. She needed to face it.

And when she did, she found that freedom had been waiting for her all along. Not outside of her, but within.

Freedom wasn't the absence of pain—it was the presence of power. The kind of power that comes from knowing who you are, even when the world tries to tell you otherwise. The kind of power that says, "I've been through hell, and I'm still here."

Donia is still walking. Still choosing. Still rising. And with every step, she's rewriting the narrative.

No longer the girl hidden in the shadows.

She is the woman who stood up.

She is the woman who faced herself.

She is the woman who chose to be free.

The Strength in the Struggle

Pain never asked permission. It arrived unannounced, unin-

vited, and relentless. But Donia—she learned to make it her teacher.

She didn't choose the struggle. But she chose what to do with it. And in that choice, she found power.

For a long time, the struggle felt like a curse—something she needed to survive, something she wished away. But then she began to look deeper. To lean in. And she saw it: the struggle wasn't destroying her. It was defining her.

It was sharpening her edges. Stretching her soul. Drawing out the kind of strength that only suffering could uncover. Because there's a strength that's forged in comfort—and then there's the kind born in the trenches. Donia didn't have the luxury of the first. So she embraced the second.

She learned to use the struggle as a mirror. Every heartbreak showed her what she valued. Every betrayal revealed who she was becoming. Every setback carved out space for growth. The more she was broken, the more room there was for her to rebuild—not as who she had been, but as who she was meant to be.

She stopped seeing herself as a victim of circumstance. She became a student of it.

Each sleepless night, each unanswered prayer, each wound—these weren't detours. They were sacred appointments. Unseen initiations into the woman she was destined to become.

And she passed every test. Not always with grace. Not always without scars. But with grit. With truth. With the unshakable decision to rise anyway.

Donia's strength wasn't loud. It didn't need to be. It didn't demand applause or recognition. It was quiet. Lived. Real. It looked like getting back up when no one was watching. Like believing again after everything fell apart. Like showing up when she didn't have the energy—but did it anyway, because purpose called.

She began to understand that struggle is not the opposite of strength—it is the birthplace of it. True strength isn't about avoiding pain. It's about becoming someone through it. Not just surviving it, but letting it mold you, stretch you, refine you.

Her scars were no longer something to hide. They were her credentials.

Each one carried a story. Each one whispered: "I was there. I lived. I made it through."

And there's power in that kind of story. Power that doesn't come from escaping the fire, but from standing in it and letting it burn away everything that wasn't real. Everything that wasn't worthy. Everything that wasn't her.

Donia became a woman who honored her pain. Who stopped pretending. Who told the truth, even when it trembled in her throat.

And the more she honored her struggle, the more she honored herself.

She stopped resenting what broke her, because she saw what it built. She saw how the pain gave her depth. Compassion. Vision. And most of all—voice.

The world wants us polished. Perfect. Unshaken.

But Donia? She showed up scarred. Human. Whole.

Because her strength didn't lie in being untouched. It lay in being undone—and rising anyway.

That's the kind of strength that transforms rooms. That kind of strength shifts legacies.

And Donia—she is a legacy in motion.

Embracing the Gift of Authenticity

Authenticity doesn't ask permission. It doesn't wait for applause. It just shows up—as it is, raw and radiant. That's what Donia became.

She didn't become powerful by becoming someone else. She became powerful by becoming herself.

In a world that taught her to hide—to shrink, to mask, to perform—Donia made the most radical decision of all: to be seen. Fully. Fiercely. Unapologetically.

It began with quiet rebellion. No more pretending. No more fitting into boxes she never asked to be placed in. No more trading truth for acceptance. She peeled back the layers—one by one. The good girl mask. The perfection mask. The survivor mask. Until what remained wasn't a role, but a woman.

And when she finally stood naked in her truth, something shifted. The world around her didn't collapse—it aligned.

Because the moment Donia stopped betraying herself, the universe stopped betraying her.

Opportunities opened. Connections deepened. Her voice got louder—not in volume, but in resonance. People didn't just hear her—they felt her. Because there's a sacred gravity to someone who is fully themselves.

Her authenticity became her sanctuary.

She didn't chase love anymore—she became it. She didn't beg to be chosen—she chose herself. And in doing so, she gave others permission to do the same.

Donia discovered that authenticity isn't the absence of fear. It's the presence of courage. It's telling the truth even when your voice shakes. It's showing your scars and saying, "Yes, I bled—but I'm still here."

It's embracing every contradiction, every cracked piece, every sacred mess. And loving yourself, not in spite of them—but because of them.

Because when she stopped trying to be perfect, Donia became whole.

And in wholeness, she found power.

Not the kind built on performance—but the kind that transforms. The kind that can sit with pain and not flinch. The kind that can hold space for others because she finally made space for herself.

Her authenticity wasn't always comfortable—but it was always true. And truth has a way of lighting fires in dark places.

She became magnetic—not because she tried, but because she no longer tried at all. She simply was. And in that being, she began to bloom.

The right people found her. The wrong ones fell away. Life began to mirror the freedom she claimed on the inside. Doors opened, not because she forced them, but because they were always hers—she just had to show up as herself to walk through them.

She stopped apologizing for her presence.

She stopped softening her voice.

She stopped editing her emotions.

Because the world doesn't need another polished mask. It needs truth. It needs women like Donia—unfiltered, unshaken, unafraid.

She was no longer hiding. She was no longer waiting. She had arrived—in full. In light. In power.

Donia's authenticity wasn't just a personal breakthrough. It was a revolution.

Because when one woman decides to live her truth, she doesn't just free herself—she unlocks something eternal in everyone who witnesses her.

And now, that flame she ignited? It's spreading.

The Legacy of Resilience

Legacy isn't what you leave behind. It's what you birth through fire.

And Donia? She didn't just survive the blaze—she became it.

She stands now, not just as a woman who endured—but as a force who redefined what endurance truly means. Her story didn't end in pain. It began there. But it didn't stay. Because Donia didn't come to live small. She came to rise. To roar. To rebuild.

Every wound that tried to silence her became a well of wisdom.

Every scar she once hid became a sacred map—leading others through their own wreckage.

She didn't just heal—she transformed. She resurrected.

Now, as Donia stands at the edge of all she has become, she carries not only her own strength, but the hopes of every soul who's ever whispered, "Will I make it?"

She is their answer.

Because Donia is no longer a name—it's a declaration.

It says: You can break and still build. You can fall and still fly. You can be shattered and still become whole.

Her legacy is not one of perfection. It's one of power.

The kind forged in the darkness. The kind sung through tears. The kind that holds space for the rising of others.

She no longer walks alone. Behind her, thousands walk taller. Speak louder. Heal deeper.

Because she gave them permission.

Because she became the proof.

Because she chose to live—out loud.

Her roots run deep now. Anchored in grace. Fed by truth. Spread wide with purpose.

They do not shake. They do not break. They lift.

This is what happens when pain is not buried, but honored.

When silence is not obeyed, but broken.

When survival is not the goal—but the gateway.

Donia's life has become an offering.

To the woman still doubting her worth.

To the child still aching for love.

To the man still carrying invisible wounds.

To the soul still crawling through the ash, wondering if they'll ever stand again.

Her message is clear:

Yes, you will.

Yes, you will rise.

Yes, you are enough.

Yes, you are more powerful than the pain.

Donia didn't escape her story—she embodied it.

She didn't outrun her past—she redeemed it.

She didn't forget the fire—she became the flame that lights the path for others.

And that... that is legacy.

A legacy not written in titles, but in transformation.

Not built through applause, but through becoming.

Not sealed in stone—but etched in the hearts of those she touched.

This is what it means to rise indomitable.

This is what it means to bloom from ashes.

This is what it means to carry *The Scars We Carry*—

not as shame,

but as resurrection.

Donia's story is no longer just hers.

It's ours.

It's yours.

And it's only just beginning.

3

Chapter 2: Embracing the Archetype: A Journey of Inner Strength, Vulnerability, and Grace

The Birth of the Archetype

Maybe you've felt it too—a quiet stirring, a sacred unrest, a knowing that somewhere deep within, more of you is waiting to be born.

The journey to embracing my true self began not with external validation or superficial achievements, but with the profound realization of the feminine archetype that lives within me. To embrace this archetype was to come face-to-face with the essence of who I am—a multifaceted, deeply resilient, and powerful woman. It was a process of unearthing layers of my soul, peeling back the veils I had once hidden behind, and finding the strength to stand in my own truth.

I wasn't born knowing who I was, nor did I inherently understand the depth of my power. It took years—decades, really—

of wrestling with my own fears, insecurities, and uncertainties to unearth the true embodiment of strength that lies within every woman. The queen, the lioness, the phoenix—these were not just symbols; they were parts of me waiting to be discovered, nurtured, and embraced. And as I uncovered them, I discovered that my power wasn't a singular trait or a particular set of characteristics. It was the culmination of my experiences, my pain, my joys, and my unwavering resilience.

In the silence of my most difficult moments, I began to hear the whispers of these archetypes calling to me. The queen, regal and unwavering, who represents leadership, wisdom, and the strength to rise above adversity. The lioness, fierce and protective, embodying courage, grace, and the will to fight for what matters most. And the phoenix, a symbol of rebirth and transformation, rising from the ashes of hardship, stronger and more powerful than before. These archetypes were not separate from me; they were parts of my soul, waiting for me to awaken to them.

To truly embrace these archetypes was to face the parts of myself that I had long ignored or rejected. The parts of me that were afraid to be seen, to be heard, to step into the fullness of my power. But as I unearthed these pieces, I found the courage to stand tall, to speak my truth, and to unapologetically live in my own power. No longer did I allow the opinions of others or the weight of my past to define me. I realized that the true measure of my strength wasn't in how others saw me, but in how I saw myself.

The queen within me taught me the importance of self-respect and the power of leading with love and wisdom. She reminded me that I am worthy of honor, not just from others, but from myself. She instilled in me the belief that I am capable of making decisions that align with my truth, even when they are difficult. The lioness, with her fierce protection, showed me the importance of standing firm in my convictions and defending my values with unyielding strength. She empowered me to protect my peace, my boundaries, and the people I love, no matter the cost. And the phoenix, ever reborn, reminded me that no matter how many times I fall, I can always rise again. She taught me that transformation is not a one-time event, but a continuous journey—one that is shaped by the struggles we face and the wisdom we gain along the way.

In embracing these archetypes, I discovered that my power is not something to be feared or hidden. It is something to be celebrated and shared with the world. I realized that the greatest gift I could give myself and others was the permission to be fully, unapologetically me. The woman who is strong, vulnerable, resilient, and fiercely protective of her heart and her dreams. The woman who refuses to shrink or dim her light in the face of adversity. The woman who embraces her scars and uses them as reminders of the battles she's won and the strength she continues to carry.

This journey to embodying the queen, the lioness, and the phoenix was not about perfection. It was about embracing the fullness of who I am—flaws and all. It was about accepting that my power lies not in being flawless, but in being authentic, in standing in my truth, and in embracing my journey, with all its highs and lows. It was about recognizing that each part of me—the quiet moments of reflection, the bursts of fierce action, the moments of rebirth—are all expressions of my power and beauty.

And so, the birth of the archetype within me became the birth of my own personal revolution. It was not a sudden awakening, but a gradual unveiling of the truth that I had always known deep inside: that I am enough. That I am worthy of love, respect, and success. And that I am capable of creating the life I desire, no matter the obstacles.

In embracing the queen, the lioness, and the phoenix, I have come to understand that these archetypes are not just symbols. They are the living, breathing manifestations of every woman's strength, wisdom, and resilience. They are within all of us, waiting to be awakened. And as I stand fully in my own truth, I invite others to do the same—to uncover their own power, to embrace their own archetypes, and to rise with the same unyielding strength that lives within us all.

The journey toward embracing my true self is ongoing, but it is one I walk with my head held high, knowing that I am aligned with the deepest, most authentic parts of who I am. And as I continue to uncover the layers of my soul, I am reminded that I am not just a woman—I am a force of nature, an embodiment of strength, resilience, and beauty. I am the queen, the lioness, and the phoenix, all in one. And I will never again apologize for the fullness of who I am.

The Queen Within: Reclaiming My Sovereignty

Maybe no one ever handed you a crown—but something in you still aches to reign.

In the early stages of my journey, I struggled with the idea of sovereignty. I wasn't raised in a palace, and I certainly didn't feel like royalty. However, I soon realized that sovereignty is not confined to the walls of a castle or the trappings of wealth. True sovereignty begins within. It is the ability to take ownership of your life, your decisions, your dreams—and to claim your space in the world unapologetically.

Embracing the queen within me was a declaration to the world, but more importantly, a declaration to myself. It was a refusal to play small, to hide behind the expectations others placed upon me. The queen archetype taught me that my worth is inherent. I didn't need to prove it to anyone. No more dimming my light to make others feel comfortable. No more apologizing for my brilliance, for my ambition, for the way I choose to take up space in this world.

This was the shift: the realization that I am the sovereign of my own kingdom. And that kingdom is built on a foundation of self-love, self-respect, and unwavering belief in my own potential. No one could take that from me. No external circumstance, no hurtful words, no betrayal could strip me of my sovereignty. The queen within me was fierce, unapologetic, and unshakable. She stood tall and ruled with integrity, knowing her power was not derived from anything outside herself but from the unshakable knowing of who she was.

For too long, I had sought validation from external sources—whether it was from family, friends, or society at large. I had hoped that someone, anyone, would see me for who I truly was and give me the permission to stand in my own power. But I came to realize that no one can grant you sovereignty; it must be claimed by you, for you, and through you. The crown of sovereignty was never meant to be worn by someone else—it was mine, and it had always been mine. I simply had to remember how to wear it.

The queen archetype taught me that sovereignty is not about domination or control over others; it's about self-mastery. It's about being the ruler of my own thoughts, emotions, and actions. It's about choosing to rise above circumstances rather than being defined by them. Sovereignty is the ability to set boundaries, to say no without guilt, to walk away from situations and people that no longer serve your highest good. It is a deep understanding that my energy is precious, and I am the one who gets to decide where and how it is spent.

To reclaim my sovereignty, I had to let go of old narratives that held me captive—stories of not being enough, of being undeserving, of being too much or too little. I had to reframe my perception of myself, see myself not as a survivor of circumstance but as the creator of my reality. The queen within me doesn't ask for permission to live fully; she takes it. She demands to be seen, not out of ego, but because she understands that her presence is a gift to the world. Her voice is her power, and her strength lies in the belief that she is worthy of all that she desires.

This journey wasn't easy. There were days when doubt crept in, when the old fear tried to whisper that I was not capable of being the queen of my own life. But with each challenge, I grew stronger. I began to see that every obstacle was an opportunity to reinforce my sovereignty. Every setback was a lesson in resilience. Every judgment from others was a reminder that their opinions did not hold the power to define me.

I also learned that true sovereignty comes with deep responsibility—not to others, but to myself. It is my responsibility to honor my needs, to protect my peace, and to nurture my growth. It is my responsibility to set standards for how I expect to be treated, to refuse to settle for less than what I deserve, and to walk away from anything that compromises my integrity. The queen within me knows that she is worthy of respect, love, and loyalty, and she will not tolerate anything less.

As I embraced this sense of sovereignty, I began to notice a shift in my relationships, my career, and my life. I stopped seeking validation from others, and instead, I began to trust my own judgment. I started making decisions that aligned with my values, and I watched as my life began to unfold in ways I had never imagined. The queen within me was not just a part of me; she became the very foundation of my existence. With her guidance, I began to create the life I had always dreamed of—one that was built on my terms, not anyone else's.

Reclaiming my sovereignty has been the most liberating experience of my life. It has taught me that I do not need anyone's permission to live authentically. I am the queen of my own life, and I rule with wisdom, grace, and power. I am the architect of my own destiny, and I know that I am capable of achieving anything I set my mind to. The queen within me has awakened, and she will never be silenced again.

Now, I stand tall in the fullness of my sovereignty, unapologetically taking up space in the world. I know that I am worthy of every dream, every blessing, and every success that comes my way. And as I continue to walk this path, I invite others to reclaim their own sovereignty—to step into their own power, to recognize their own worth, and to live boldly and unapologetically, just as the queen within them intends.

The Lioness Within: Fierce and Unyielding

You were never too loud. The world was just too afraid of your roar.

But the queen is not the only archetype that defines me. Beneath the graceful crown and regal presence lies the lioness—the embodiment of fierce, unapologetic strength. She is the protector of my heart, the fierce advocate for my dreams, the warrior who will fight against anything that seeks to diminish my value or my voice.

The lioness reminds me that strength is not always loud. It's not always seen. Strength is found in the quiet moments, the ones where I choose to stand firm, to push forward, even when the world tells me to stop. It's in the moments where I rise from the ashes of past wounds, unbowed and unbroken.

There have been times in my life when I felt powerless, when I allowed others to dictate my narrative. But embracing the lioness within me has taught me to reclaim that power. The lioness within me is relentless in her pursuit of justice, truth, and personal growth. She's never afraid to face conflict or challenge. She teaches me that power isn't just about brute force—it's about strategy, resilience, and standing my ground when everything inside me wants to retreat.

The lioness reminds me that courage isn't the absence of fear—it's the ability to move through that fear, to face adversity head-on with grace and dignity. Every time I've had to step into the unknown, to confront a difficult truth, to take a leap of faith in my life or my business, it has been the lioness within me that has fueled me forward. She never allows me to shrink back, no matter how hard the journey may seem.

I've learned that the lioness within me does not wait for permission to take up space. She owns her strength, her voice, her body, and her energy. She understands that vulnerability is not a weakness, but rather, it is her raw power, revealing the depth of her humanity. The lioness stands tall, grounded in who she is, without apology.

In every battle, the lioness rises. In every trial, she finds her courage. In every setback, she discovers resilience. The lioness within me understands that the path to greatness is not a straight line, but a series of detours and challenges that serve as opportunities for growth. She doesn't flinch in the face of adversity. She embraces it, knowing that each challenge is an invitation to strengthen herself, to evolve, and to become more of who she is meant to be.

She is the one who roars with a voice that demands to be heard, who leads with compassion and strength, and who fiercely defends what she loves. The lioness within me has taught me to rise above the noise, to honor my own voice, and to trust that I have everything I need to overcome whatever comes my way.

The lioness is not afraid to stand alone when necessary, and she has taught me the invaluable lesson that solitude can be a powerful tool for growth. She has shown me that while support is essential, the true strength comes from within. She never waits for others to validate her worth; she validates herself, and that self-validation is the foundation of her power.

The lioness knows that being fierce isn't just about fighting others. It's about fighting for what matters most—fighting for my dreams, fighting for my peace, and fighting for the life I deserve. She teaches me that every battle, whether big or small, is a chance to prove to myself that I am capable. Every challenge is a reminder that I can be both tender and tough, gentle and strong, nurturing and unyielding.

As I continue to embrace the lioness within me, I stand taller, walk more confidently, and speak with greater conviction. She is my strength when I feel weak, my courage when I am scared, and my resilience when I face defeat. The lioness has taught me that power is not just the ability to protect and defend, but also the wisdom to know when to rest, when to retreat, and when to fight again.

The lioness within me has fueled my journey and helped me overcome countless obstacles. She has given me the will to never give up, no matter how overwhelming the road may seem. And she has shown me that true strength lies not in the absence of fear, but in the courage to face it and move through it. The lioness roars not just for survival, but for transformation, growth, and the unyielding belief that, no matter what, she will rise.

And so, I continue to embrace the fierce lioness within me—unapologetically, relentlessly, and with a heart full of courage. The lioness knows no limits, and neither do I. Together, we will continue to rise, to roar, and to claim the greatness that awaits.

The Phoenix Within: Rebirth and Transformation

You are not what the fire burned. You are what survived it.

If the queen represents my sovereignty and the lioness embodies my strength, then the phoenix represents my ability to transform, to rise from the ashes of my struggles, and to be reborn again and again. The phoenix within me is a reminder that nothing is ever truly lost—it is only an opportunity to evolve into something more powerful.

There are countless times in my life when I've been brought to my knees by the weight of my circumstances. There have been moments where I thought I couldn't take another step.

I've had my heart broken, my dreams shattered, and my spirit tested. But every time, the phoenix within me has risen. From the moments of despair, I have found new strength. From the ashes of my past, I have forged a new future—one that is more authentic, more aligned with my soul's purpose.

The phoenix teaches me that transformation is not just about change—it is about rebirth. It is about allowing myself to let go of the old, to shed the parts of myself that no longer serve me, and to step into a higher version of who I am. I have learned that transformation is often painful, but it is always necessary for growth. And as I shed the layers of the old version of myself, I make space for the new, for the woman I am becoming—stronger, wiser, and more aligned with my highest self.

Transformation, for me, has never been a smooth or easy path. It has been a series of trials and triumphs, each step forward accompanied by moments of doubt, fear, and uncertainty. But every challenge has been a necessary part of the process. Just as the phoenix must burn in order to rise from its ashes, I too must face the fire of my own struggles to emerge stronger and more resilient. Each challenge forces me to confront the parts of myself I've tried to hide, to face the uncomfortable truths, and to let go of the patterns and beliefs that no longer serve me.

But the beauty of the phoenix is that it doesn't remain in the ashes. It rises, more radiant and powerful than before. And so do I. With each rebirth, I learn to embrace the fullness of who I am—the light and the dark, the pain and the joy, the failures and the successes. Through it all, I continue to rise.

The process of transformation has taught me that growth is not linear. It's not a one-time event but an ongoing process of shedding, evolving, and expanding. There are moments when I feel as though I am being broken apart, only to realize that I am being pieced back together in a way that aligns more fully with my purpose. The phoenix reminds me that rebirth is not just an external process—it is an internal one, a deep and sacred journey into becoming who I was always meant to be.

And so, I rise again and again. I embrace the fire of transformation because I know that it is through this fire that I find my true strength. I welcome the ashes because I know that they are the fertile ground from which my new self will emerge. With each cycle of rebirth, I shed old beliefs, old fears, and old limitations, making space for the new, the powerful, and the infinite possibilities that lie ahead.

The phoenix is a reminder that no matter how many times life knocks me down, no matter how many times I am brought to my knees, I will always rise again. I will always find the strength to rise higher, to soar farther, and to become more than I ever thought possible.

With every rebirth, I come closer to the woman I am meant to be—a woman who knows her worth, who embraces her power, and who walks in alignment with her true purpose. And so, the phoenix within me continues to soar, a symbol of my endless capacity for transformation and rebirth, a reminder that every ending is simply the beginning of something more beautiful, more powerful, and more aligned with who I truly am.

The Power of Vulnerability

Your softness is not your shame. It is your superpower.

One of the most profound lessons I've learned through embracing my archetypes is the importance of vulnerability. For years, I saw vulnerability as a weakness—a crack in my armor, a place where others could take advantage of me. I feared that if I showed my true self, my raw emotions, my flaws, I would be judged, rejected, or seen as unworthy.

But in the process of embracing the lioness, the queen, and the phoenix within me, I've learned that vulnerability is not a weakness—it is a source of immense power. Vulnerability is the willingness to stand in my truth, even when it feels uncomfortable. It is the courage to show up as I am—flawed, imperfect, and beautifully human—and to allow others to see the real me.

When I allow myself to be vulnerable, I am not only honoring myself but also inviting others into deeper connection. I've learned that in those moments of rawness, I am at my most authentic. It's in the tears, the struggles, and the moments of uncertainty that I have found my greatest strength. Vulnerability allows me to connect with others on a deeper level, to show them that they are not alone in their struggles, and to invite them to rise with me.

I've come to realize that it is precisely through my vulnerability that I can offer the most healing. When I share my story—my pain, my triumphs, my mistakes—I am showing others that they too can be whole, despite their imperfections. I am reminding them that their journey, though sometimes messy and uncertain, is still worth embracing. Vulnerability, in this way, is a bridge. It is the pathway that connects us, that opens the door for empathy, understanding, and support.

For so long, I wore masks, hiding behind the idea of perfection, convinced that I needed to appear strong at all times. But I've learned that true strength lies not in hiding our pain or pretending to be invincible. True strength comes from the courage to be seen in our rawness, to be open to the possibility of hurt, yet still choosing to love, to give, and to show up for others.

I've also learned that vulnerability is not something that can be forced. It is a practice, an invitation to trust in myself, to trust in others, and to trust in the process of life. It's about giving myself permission to be human—to experience joy, pain, doubt, and confidence all at once. And it's about knowing that each moment of vulnerability only deepens my connection to the world around me. The more I allow myself to be vulnerable, the more I am able to show up fully, not only for others but for myself as well.

I've seen how powerful vulnerability can be in my relationships. It is through vulnerability that I've been able to form deeper, more authentic connections. I've seen how it encourages others to open up and share their truths, how it fosters an environment where people feel safe to be themselves without fear of judgment or rejection. And in turn, that shared vulnerability strengthens us all. It creates a sense of unity, a reminder that we are all part of something bigger than ourselves.

The process of embracing vulnerability has not been easy. It has required me to confront my fears and doubts head-on. But in doing so, I have found peace. I've found that I no longer need to hide behind the walls I once built for protection. I no longer need to pretend that I have it all together. Instead, I can be real, unfiltered, and fully present in every moment.

Vulnerability, I've learned, is not about weakness—it is about power. It is the power to be truly seen, to be truly known, and to fully embrace all that I am, in all my complexity. It is the power to heal, to grow, and to love with an open heart. And it is the power to inspire others to do the same.

In embracing my vulnerability, I have found freedom. Freedom from the fear of judgment, freedom from the need to be perfect, and freedom to live a life that is truly authentic. Through vulnerability, I am learning that there is strength in allowing myself to be both strong and tender, fierce and soft, unbreakable and human. In this dance between strength and vulnerability, I am discovering the power of my true self.

And so, I continue to rise, not despite my vulnerability, but because of it. Vulnerability is not something I must hide. It is the very thing that makes me whole, that makes me powerful, and that allows me to connect with others in a way that is real, meaningful, and transformational. It is in my vulnerability that I find my greatest power—the power to be seen, the power to love, and the power to rise above it all.

Grace: The Essence of Feminine Power

Grace is the thread that ties everything together. It is the soft power that emanates from within. It's not about being flawless, perfect, or untouchable. Grace is about handling life's challenges with poise, with dignity, with an open heart still willing to trust. It's about knowing that I am enough, exactly as I am, and that even in my imperfections, I hold power.

Grace is the ability to remain rooted in peace, even in the storm. It is the quiet strength that allows me to extend compassion, not just to others, but to myself. Grace is a form of love—love for the journey, love for the process, and love for the woman I am becoming. It is an ongoing practice, one that I embrace daily as I navigate the complexities of life.

When I embrace grace, I move through the world with ease. I am not constantly striving or forcing things to happen. I trust that everything I need will come to me in divine timing. Grace allows me to let go of control and to surrender to the flow of life. It's in this surrender that I find my true power—the power to be, to love, to create, and to live fully in alignment with my purpose.

Grace teaches me that true strength is not about pushing

through with sheer will, but about finding the balance between effort and surrender. It's about knowing when to step forward with determination and when to step back and trust that things will unfold as they are meant to. In moments of uncertainty, grace whispers that all is well, and I don't need to rush or force my way through. There is power in the pause, in the stillness where clarity arises and new possibilities are revealed.

What I have learned is that grace is not passive. It is an active state of being, a choice to engage with the world from a place of love, acceptance, and trust. It is not about being perfect or free from challenges. It is about how I respond to those challenges—how I choose to carry myself through them with integrity, dignity, and a heart open to learning and growth.

Grace is what allows me to rise after every fall, to smile even when life is hard, and to move forward with a sense of inner peace, even in the face of adversity. It gives me the courage to be vulnerable, to show up as I am, and to embrace every part of my journey without shame or regret. It reminds me that even in my moments of imperfection, I am worthy of love, compassion, and respect.

In the past, I believed that to be powerful, I had to be tough, unyielding, and always in control. But embracing grace has taught me that power is found in vulnerability, in softness, in the ability to flow with life instead of against it. Grace is the embodiment of strength through surrender, and it has become the foundation upon which I build every decision, every interaction, and every step I take.

Grace allows me to love myself fully—without judgment or harshness. It encourages me to honor the parts of me that are broken, to heal without guilt or shame, and to acknowledge that my worth is not contingent on my achievements or perfection. I am worthy because I am, and in that simple truth lies the deepest power of all.

Grace is the constant reminder that I do not need to strive for validation or external approval. The only validation I need is the recognition of my own worth. When I live in grace, I recognize that I am already whole, already enough, and already empowered. This is the freedom that grace gives me—the freedom to be who I truly am, unapologetically and without fear.

As I continue to embrace grace, I find that it flows into every area of my life. It strengthens my relationships, nurtures my self-love, and deepens my connection to my purpose. Grace guides my work, my creativity, and my entrepreneurial spirit. It informs how I show up for my children, my family, my friends, and even for those who may not fully understand my journey. Grace teaches me that I can be firm in my boundaries and loving in my approach, strong in my resolve and gentle in my expression.

Ultimately, grace is the key that unlocks the full potential of my feminine power. It is the balm that heals, the force that propels me forward, and the light that shines through even the darkest of times. It reminds me that no matter how difficult life becomes, I can meet each moment with dignity, trust, and love—knowing that grace is always within me, waiting to guide me through.

The Path to Embracing My Archetype

Embracing my feminine archetype has been a transformational journey. It has taken me to the depths of my soul, where I've had to confront my deepest fears and wounds. But it has also led me to the heights of my potential, where I have discovered my unshakable strength, my boundless grace, and my fierce determination.

This path hasn't always been easy. There have been moments of doubt, moments when I questioned my worth and my abilities. But each time, I have been reminded that I am more than the sum of my past experiences, more than the challenges I've faced. I have learned that the obstacles I've encountered are not roadblocks—they are stepping stones that have shaped me into the woman I am today.

And as I continue to walk this path, I know that my archetype will continue to evolve. I will continue to grow, to shed the old, and to step into new phases of my life. The archetype I embody is not fixed—it is fluid, adaptable, and always growing in alignment with my highest self. I am not static; I am in a constant state of evolution. With each chapter, I uncover new layers of my power and potential.

Through this journey, I've come to realize that embracing my archetypes is not about conforming to any rigid set of rules or expectations. It is about allowing myself to be fully authentic and to trust that my journey is unique to me. The queen within me may rise at moments when I need to step into my sovereignty and claim my space in the world. The lioness will emerge when I face challenges that require courage and resilience. And the phoenix will soar when it's time to shed the past and embrace new beginnings.

I have learned that I am worthy of everything I desire. I am worthy of success, love, and abundance. I am worthy of stepping into my power and claiming my place in the world. And I know that every woman reading this has the same potential within her. We all have the ability to embrace our inner strength, vulnerability, grace, and transformation. It is not something that is given to us by others—it is something that resides within us, waiting to be awakened.

When I look at the women around me—whether in my personal life, in my community, or across the world—I see reflections of the same archetypes. Each woman carries the potential to be a queen, a lioness, and a phoenix in her own right. It is not about comparison or competition. It is about recognizing and honoring the unique power that each of us possesses. There is room for all of us to rise and claim our sovereignty, to walk in our strength, and to transform our lives.

So I invite you, dear reader, to step into your own power. Embrace the archetypes within you—the queen, the lioness, the phoenix—and let them guide you to the life you were always meant to live. Know that your journey may not always be easy, but it will always be worth it. You will encounter moments of challenge, of uncertainty, and of pain. But in those moments, remember that you have within you the strength to rise again. You have the grace to navigate through life's difficulties with dignity. You have the courage to stand firm in your truth, even when it feels uncomfortable.

Your journey may be long, but it will also be transformational. Every step you take, every choice you make, is a part of your evolution. Trust the process. Trust yourself.

You are powerful. You are worthy. And you are ready to rise. The time is now. The world is waiting for the fullest expression of who you are. Step into your power. You've always had it within you. It's time to let it shine.

4

Chapter 3: The Power of Transformation

A Journey of Death and Rebirth

Transformation is not just about change—it is about metamorphosis. It is not merely the act of shifting from one phase to another but a deep and fundamental reshaping of who we are at our core. It is as if we die to an old version of ourselves, only to be reborn into a stronger, more authentic being. This process is often painful, as shedding our old skin means confronting parts of ourselves we'd rather keep hidden. Yet, in this very confrontation lies the power to evolve.

As we undergo this metamorphosis, we realize that transformation is not a one-time event; it's a continuous journey. There are moments where the old version of ourselves—those fears, insecurities, and self-doubts—try to cling on, pulling us backward. But each time we face these shadows, we grow more resilient, more empowered. We learn to trust in our own ability to survive, to flourish, and to rise, no matter how many times life knocks us down.

I often reflect on my personal journey and how, like a phoenix, I have risen time and time again from the ashes of my past. The ashes represent the remnants of pain, rejection, and despair—each stage of my life where I thought I had reached my limit. But just as the phoenix cannot fly without first being consumed by flames, I too could not grow without facing those fires. It was in the darkest moments, when I felt most vulnerable, that I experienced my most profound growth.

In these moments, when life felt unbearable and the future uncertain, I found myself being forced to look inward. I had no choice but to confront my deepest fears, my self-imposed limitations, and the wounds I had been carrying for far too long. These moments of death—where the old version of me was stripped away—were terrifying, but they were also the birthplace of my greatest transformation.

As I was forced to navigate through the overwhelming hardships of my life—experiencing trauma, feeling unworthy, and fighting to survive against forces beyond my control—I began to understand that transformation is not linear. It is cyclical. We must pass through repeated cycles of growth, trial, and rebirth. In each cycle, I shed another layer of fear, doubt, and limitation, and in its place, something greater emerged. A new layer of resilience. A deeper sense of compassion. A more profound understanding of my worth.

This process of rebirth is messy. It's not clean and neat, but raw and real. It requires us to be vulnerable, to expose the parts of ourselves that we have tried to bury for fear of judgment or rejection. But vulnerability is not weakness. It is the strength to show up fully, to be seen in all our complexities and contradictions, and to trust that we are worthy of love and acceptance, even in our most imperfect state.

Each time I rise from the ashes, I am reborn into a version of myself that is stronger, more authentic, and more aligned with my true purpose. And though the journey is never easy, it is always worth it. The strength, wisdom, and grace that come from facing our darkest moments are the gifts of transformation. They are the fuel that propels us forward, even when the path ahead seems uncertain.

The beauty of this journey is that it never truly ends. Just when we think we have shed it all, we are met with new challenges, new trials, and new opportunities for growth. But with each cycle, we become more capable of handling whatever life throws our way. We become more resilient, more confident, and more connected to the deepest parts of our being.

And so, I continue on this journey of death and rebirth. I continue to shed the old layers of myself, making room for the new. I continue to rise from the ashes of my past, knowing that with every challenge, I am becoming more fully myself. And I trust that no matter how many times I am tested, I will always find the strength to rise again—stronger, wiser, and more empowered than before.

In this journey of transformation, we learn that every ending is simply the beginning of something new. It is in the ashes that we find the seeds of our rebirth. And as we continue to evolve, we find that the power to transform lies within us all along.

And if you're standing in your own ashes right now...

Breathe.

Not everything that burns is meant to kill you.

Some flames are altars.

Some endings are holy.

And if you've been brought to your knees, it does not mean you've been defeated.

It means the ground is sacred.

You are sacred.

And like me, you will rise.

The Shaping of Resilience

The foundation of my transformation was built on resilience. Resilience is the ability to bounce back, not only from adversity but also from failure, disappointment, and loss. The key is not just in surviving but in learning to thrive after every setback. Life's challenges are inevitable, and yet, it is our response to those challenges that defines our strength.

Looking back on my journey, I see resilience woven into every moment, every decision I made. I see it in the quiet determination I carried as a single mother, with no clear path to success. I see it in the countless nights spent wondering how I would make it through, yet still finding the will to rise each day. I see it in the times when I had nothing but faith and sheer willpower to guide me through. I was homeless, yet I knew deep down that I would make it through, that this wasn't the end of my story. I had to learn that success doesn't come from having all the answers or the perfect circumstances. It comes from being willing to continue, to move forward despite the pain.

In those moments of struggle, I began to cultivate an inner strength that was untouchable. Resilience is not built overnight—it is formed through the repeated process of facing obstacles and learning how to rise above them. With every failure, I grew. With every hardship, I became stronger.

Resilience isn't about avoiding pain or pretending it doesn't exist. It's about allowing ourselves to experience the full weight of that pain, to feel it, and yet refuse to let it define us. We face setbacks, and sometimes we fall hard, but we always rise again, stronger than before. This is the essence of resilience—the ability to not just bounce back, but to grow, evolve, and build upon our past experiences.

There were times when I thought the challenges I faced would break me. There were moments when everything seemed like it was falling apart, and it felt as though I was drowning in the weight of it all. But in those moments, I had to dig deep. I had to remind myself that resilience isn't about enduring with a stiff upper lip; it's about being adaptable and finding creative ways to keep moving forward. It's about being gentle with ourselves when things don't go as planned and not allowing our setbacks to define our worth.

I had to face my fears head-on, staring into the abyss of uncertainty and trusting that I had the tools to pull myself back from the edge. Resilience, I learned, wasn't just about endurance; it was about adaptability and courage. It was about trusting that change, though painful, would always lead to something better if I was willing to work for it. It was about knowing that failure wasn't final, and that every setback was simply an opportunity to learn, grow, and rise again.

I had to reframe my mindset to understand that resilience isn't about resisting change but embracing it. It is about trusting the process, even when it feels uncomfortable or unknown. Every time life tested me, I had a choice: to succumb to the weight of my circumstances or to rise, transform, and create something new from it. I chose to rise. I chose to trust that each challenge would shape me into a better version of myself, even when the road ahead seemed impossible.

Now, I know that resilience is not just about the big moments—it's built in the small, everyday choices. It's in the decision to keep going when you want to give up. It's in the moments when you choose to rise from your fears, your doubts, and your failures. It's in the acceptance that setbacks are a natural part of the journey and that they do not define who you are or what you are capable of achieving.

In each of those moments of pain, loss, and struggle, I discovered a deeper layer of strength. With every hardship, I became more connected to my purpose, more aligned with who I was becoming. I came to understand that resilience isn't a destination—it is a lifelong practice. It's not about avoiding challenges, but about rising with grace every time we encounter them.

I look at the woman I've become today, and I see a warrior, a queen who has faced her battles and emerged victorious. But I also see someone who has learned the value of vulnerability, who embraces her imperfections and understands that resilience is not about perfection—it is about growth. It is about the courage to keep moving forward, even when the path is unclear, knowing that with each step, we are becoming the best version of ourselves.

Through resilience, I have learned to turn pain into power, to transform my struggles into stepping stones, and to trust that every setback is simply a lesson, preparing me for what's next. And as I continue on my journey, I carry the lessons of resilience with me, knowing that I am capable of overcoming anything that comes my way.

Maybe no one taught you how to rise.

Maybe no one told you that survival is an act of brilliance.

That getting up again—after life has broken every part of you—is a form of art.

If all you've done lately is breathe through the pain, you've already performed a miracle.

Keep breathing.

Keep standing.

You are already becoming.

The Spiritual Foundation of Transformation

A crucial aspect of my transformation was understanding the spiritual nature of my journey. For so long, I sought transformation through external circumstances—through the right job, the right relationship, the right amount of money. But it wasn't until I turned inward, seeking answers from my faith and my own inner wisdom, that I truly understood the power of personal transformation.

Faith became the core of my existence, the very thing that held me steady when everything around me was falling apart. It is the anchor that keeps us grounded in times of upheaval. Faith is the unwavering belief that everything, even the struggles, has a higher purpose. My faith has been the force that kept me moving through the storms of my life, knowing that each challenge was an opportunity to build my inner power. It is through my faith that I found the strength to rise from my lowest moments and continue walking my path with resilience and purpose. The faith I have in God, in my purpose, and in the wisdom of my own journey has been the guiding light that illuminated the darkness of my struggles.

I came to realize that transformation is not just a mental or physical process; it is deeply spiritual. It is not about achieving a goal or attaining perfection, but rather about surrendering the ego—the part of us that clings to control, to the familiar, to the illusion of security—and allowing ourselves to flow with the divine rhythm of life. Transformation is about letting go of old patterns that no longer serve us and embracing divine timing, trusting that there is a force greater than ourselves shaping us into the people we are meant to become.

Spiritual transformation is the awakening of our higher selves, the realization that we are connected to a larger purpose. It is about recognizing that our pain, our struggles, and our challenges are not meaningless—they are sacred. They are the building blocks of our spiritual evolution, the tools that shape us into the highest expression of who we are. This shift in perspective allowed me to let go of the narrative of victimhood and step into the truth that every experience in my life—no matter how painful—was part of a divine plan, a greater purpose unfolding.

In embracing this spiritual transformation, I began to view my hardships not as burdens, but as gifts—gifts that held profound lessons and wisdom. I learned to see the beauty in my scars and the strength in my wounds. I no longer feared my struggles; I began to embrace them as part of my sacred journey. This perspective shifted the way I approached every challenge that came my way. I didn't fight against the pain. I welcomed it, understanding that it was an invitation to grow and evolve. I learned that transformation, at its core, is a spiritual awakening—a return to the essence of who we are, the divine spark that lies within us all.

Each trial I faced became an opportunity to deepen my connection with the divine, to align more fully with my purpose, and to grow in wisdom and understanding. I began to understand that transformation is not a linear process—it is cyclical, like the seasons. We move through phases of death and rebirth, shedding old versions of ourselves and stepping into new ones. And with each new season of transformation, I became more attuned to the divine wisdom that flows through me, knowing that I am part of a larger, more magnificent design.

Through this journey, I came to know that true transformation requires surrender. It requires us to trust that we are being guided, even when the path is unclear. The more I surrendered to the divine, the more I let go of the need to control, the more I embraced the unknown, the more I felt the pull of my higher calling. I understood that I am not here to simply survive, but to thrive, to fully embrace the divine plan for my life, and to allow myself to be shaped into the woman I was always meant to be.

As I continue to walk this path of spiritual transformation, I have come to realize that my struggles are not obstacles—

they are opportunities to awaken to the truth of who I am. Each hardship, each trial, is a sacred part of my story, leading me to greater understanding, wisdom, and connection with my divine purpose. And as I continue to grow and evolve, I remain deeply rooted in faith, knowing that every step I take is divinely orchestrated, leading me to the highest expression of myself and the life I am meant to create.

Transformation is not just about changing who we are—it is about remembering who we've always been. It is about awakening to the truth of our divine essence, allowing ourselves to rise above the circumstances of our lives and step into the fullness of our power. And in this spiritual journey of transformation, I have come to understand that there is no end point. There is no destination. There is only the journey of awakening, growing, and evolving into the fullest expression of our divine selves. And with every step, I trust that I am becoming exactly who I was always meant to be.

And if you've been questioning your path...

Know this:

Confusion is often the doorway to clarity.

Wrestling with your faith is not the absence of it—it is the evidence that it's alive.

Even when you don't see the light, you are walking toward it.

Even when you tremble, you are still moving.

God is not far.

He's in the fire.

He's in the silence.

He's in you.

The Courage to Change

One of the greatest catalysts for transformation is the willingness to change. Change can be terrifying, especially when it means leaving behind the familiar, the comfortable, or the known. But growth is impossible without change. Transformation requires that we make difficult choices, that we step out of our comfort zones and into the unknown. For many, the fear of change holds them back from realizing their full potential. I was no exception.

There was a time in my life when I clung to what was familiar, even if it was toxic or limiting. I stayed in relationships and situations that didn't serve me, simply because they felt safer than stepping into the unknown. But deep down, I knew that if I wanted to experience true growth, I would have to let go of the old and embrace the new. I would have to allow myself to be uncomfortable, to take risks, and to trust in the process of change.

I came to understand that change is not about abandoning who we were but about evolving into who we are meant to be. It is the recognition that we are not meant to stay stagnant, but to continuously grow and expand. But that process isn't always easy. It requires us to face our fears head-on and confront the parts of ourselves we've been avoiding. It's about looking at the unfamiliar and choosing to move toward it with courage, knowing that on the other side of change, something greater awaits.

It is in the discomfort of change that we find the seeds of transformation. Every moment of fear or uncertainty is an opportunity for growth. Those moments are the breeding grounds for the strength we need to evolve. The pain of change becomes the birthplace of our future selves. It is in those moments that we must push through, knowing that the other side of change is always worth the effort.

I had to learn to embrace the discomfort of change, not as something to fear, but as something to welcome. The truth is that transformation is not for the faint of heart. It requires courage, resilience, and a deep trust in the process. It requires us to believe that there is a version of ourselves that is waiting on the other side—one that is stronger, more aligned with our true purpose, and more in tune with the divine wisdom that guides us.

When I took that first step into the unknown, it wasn't easy. The fear was overwhelming, and doubt crept in. But what I learned through the process was that the fear itself was a sign that I was on the right path. Every time I took a leap of faith, I gained a little more clarity, a little more confidence, and a deeper connection to my true self. The discomfort of change is a powerful teacher. It teaches us how to trust in the unknown, how to navigate uncertainty, and how to embrace the journey even when the destination is not yet clear.

Now, when I face moments of change, I see them as opportunities to grow and evolve. I no longer shy away from the discomfort that accompanies transformation; instead, I lean into it. I understand that growth isn't always comfortable, but it is always necessary. Each change, no matter how challenging, brings me closer to the woman I am becoming.

Transformation requires courage—not just the courage to take the first step, but the courage to continue when the path gets tough, when the doubts creep in, and when it feels like the world is working against us. It's the courage to keep going, even when we don't have all the answers, even when we're unsure of the outcome. And it is this courage that carries us through the darkest times, that lifts us up when we want to give up, and that reminds us that we are capable of more than we could ever imagine.

I invite you to reflect on the changes that have come into your life, both big and small. How have they shaped you? What has transformation taught you about yourself? And how can you continue to embrace the courage needed to step into the next phase of your journey? Remember, every moment of change is a chance to become more fully who you are meant to be. Embrace it. Trust in it. And know that on the other side of change, your greatest self is waiting to emerge.

If you're afraid to let go—

Breathe.

The ending is not the enemy.

The ending is the opening.

You are not losing yourself; you are returning to her.

The you that is brave.

The you that is whole.

The you that is not trapped by comfort, but crowned by courage.

You don't need to be fearless to change.

You just need to trust that what's ahead will never require you to shrink again.

Let go. Rise anyway.

The Alchemy of Pain: Turning Struggles into Gold

Transformation is alchemy. The struggles we face are not just burdens; they are the raw materials with which we create our most valuable treasures. Pain, hardship, and loss are the catalysts that push us toward growth. It is in the refining fires of our struggles that we find our true strength.

When I reflect on the darkest moments of my life, I realize that those were the times when I was being forged into the woman I am today. Each experience—whether it was trauma, financial struggle, or personal failure—was a necessary part of the alchemical process. I had to endure the heat, the pressure, and the uncertainty in order to emerge as something new, something better. These challenges were not meant to break me, but to shape me into a stronger, more resilient version of myself.

At the time, each struggle felt like a weight that I could not bear. The pain seemed unbearable, and the road ahead appeared too uncertain to navigate. Yet, as I moved through the fire, I began to realize that every challenge was a step toward my true self. It was in these moments of hardship that I found my inner power, my unbreakable spirit, and my capacity for compassion. I learned to see pain not as an enemy but as a teacher, showing me parts of myself that I needed to heal, strengthen, and refine.

The key to transformation lies in how we approach pain. We can choose to allow our struggles to break us, or we can choose to use them as stepping stones to something greater. I chose the latter. I chose to turn my pain into purpose, my suffering into strength. Through the alchemy of transformation, the lead of my struggles became the gold of my empowerment. It was as though each trial, each setback, and each loss added a layer of wisdom, resilience, and courage to my soul.

I began to understand that life's challenges were not a sign of my weakness but rather a testament to my strength. I realized that pain is not something to run from or avoid, but something to face with grace and courage. When we confront our struggles head-on, we learn to trust ourselves, to build resilience, and to find meaning in our experiences. It is this process of transformation that allows us to turn our pain into something of value—something that can uplift not only ourselves but others as well.

Through this alchemical process, I was able to find my purpose. What was once seen as a curse—the hardship, the loss, the pain—became my greatest gift. My struggles gave me a voice, a platform to share my story and to inspire others. They gave me the wisdom to help others navigate their own difficult paths and the strength to stand tall, knowing that I had already overcome the worst that life could throw at me.

I learned that the process of transformation is never linear. There will be ups and downs, moments of doubt and uncertainty. But just as alchemy requires time, patience, and trust in the process, so too does transformation. It is in the darkest moments that the most profound changes occur. And, when we allow ourselves to move through the pain rather than around it, we begin to see the beauty that emerges from our struggles.

I encourage you to reflect on your own journey. What challenges have you faced that, at the time, seemed insurmountable? How have those struggles shaped you into the person you are today? How can you begin to see the gold in the pain, to find the strength and wisdom hidden within your struggles?

Remember, transformation is alchemy. The struggles you face are not there to destroy you; they are the raw materials that will forge you into something greater. Trust the process. Embrace the pain. And know that, like the phoenix rising from the ashes, you too can emerge stronger, wiser, and more powerful than before.

Read this slowly:

You are not fragile because you've been through fire.

You are sacred because you survived it.

Pain didn't ruin you—it revealed you.

It showed you where your gold was buried.

You were never meant to be untouched.

You were meant to be transformed.

Every scar is an initiation.

Every ache is a forming.

Let it shape you.

Let it shine through you.

You are the alchemist now.

Empowerment Through Embracing Change

Empowerment through embracing change is a journey of self-discovery and mastery. It requires us to redefine what it means to be truly powerful—not as individuals who are immune to hardship, but as individuals who are capable of navigating life's ebbs and flows with grace and resilience. Empowerment comes from within; it is not something that can be handed to us or given as a gift, but rather something we must cultivate through our own actions, choices, and mindset.

When we embrace change, we embrace the opportunity to reinvent ourselves. Change invites us to strip away what no longer serves us—old habits, limiting beliefs, fears—and to step into a more authentic and powerful version of ourselves. It is an opportunity to shed the layers of who we thought we were, making room for who we are becoming. This process may not be comfortable, but it is necessary. The discomfort we feel is not a signal to retreat; it is a reminder that we are in the midst of transformation. And transformation, by nature, involves discomfort, upheaval, and uncertainty.

True empowerment comes when we stop seeing change as something to fear and begin to see it as an ally in our growth. It is about developing the mental fortitude to not only survive change but to thrive in it. Empowerment is not simply about navigating change with ease—it is about leaning into the discomfort and allowing ourselves to be shaped by it. When we embrace change, we tap into a deeper well of inner strength. We become more adaptable, more open to possibility, and more attuned to the wisdom that arises from life's challenges.

The key to empowerment is realizing that we are the architects of our own transformation. While external circumstances may push us toward change, it is ultimately our response that determines the outcome. By choosing to approach each change with an open heart and a positive mindset, we invite new opportunities, fresh perspectives, and the chance to grow in ways we never imagined. Empowerment is the ability to see every challenge as an opportunity for growth, to trust in the process of transformation, and to have the courage to take the steps, even when the path is unclear.

Every setback along the journey is not a failure but a necessary part of the process. It is through overcoming adversity that we discover our true strength. Empowerment is knowing that no matter what happens, we can rise again. The resilience we develop in the face of challenges becomes our greatest asset, a source of strength that continues to propel us forward. As we grow through change, we develop a deeper sense of self-worth, and we begin to trust ourselves more fully. We learn that we are capable of more than we ever believed possible.

In the end, empowerment through embracing change is about reclaiming our power to shape our own lives. It is about recognizing that we are not victims of our circumstances, but active participants in our own evolution. We have the power to choose our response to life's challenges, and in doing so, we have the power to create the life we desire. Each decision, each moment of courage, and each act of self-love builds our empowerment, making us stronger, wiser, and more capable of living in alignment with our purpose.

When we fully embrace the transformative power of change, we step into our highest selves—authentic, fearless, and empowered. The journey may be difficult, but the reward is immeasurable. The power to change is within us all, and through it, we unlock our true potential and become the powerful, resilient, and unstoppable forces we were always meant to be.

Pause here.

Ask yourself:

What am I still clinging to that no longer serves who I'm becoming?

What version of me is afraid to be left behind?

And what might happen if I let her go—not with shame, but with love?

Empowerment is not found in pretending to be fearless.

It's found in being afraid—and choosing growth anyway.

Change is not the enemy.

Stagnation is.

And you, beloved, were never meant to stand still.

You were meant to evolve.

You were meant to fly.

The Ripple Effect: Transformation Beyond the Self

The ripple effect of transformation extends far beyond our own personal journey. It is a phenomenon that we often fail to fully grasp until we realize how deeply the energy we carry can touch the lives of others. Our growth is not a solitary pursuit; it is interwoven with the people around us, and as we evolve, we invite them to evolve too. Transformation is a force that has the power to ripple outward, creating a wave of change that spreads far and wide.

When we transform, we become living proof of the power of resilience, of the strength found in adversity, and of the beauty that arises from embracing growth. Our energy shifts. Our confidence becomes infectious. The way we carry ourselves—the choices we make, the way we show up for ourselves and others—can inspire others to reconsider their own lives and their own potential for change. What once may have seemed impossible to those around us now becomes tangible, achievable, and real.

As we step into our own power, we serve as a mirror for others, reflecting what they too could be if they chose to embrace change. Transformation becomes a shared experience, one that binds us together as we walk our individual paths while encouraging one another to rise to our fullest potential. This interconnectedness is a testament to the fact that our lives are not separate from one another. The impact we have on others, whether intentional or not, is immeasurable. It is a reminder that transformation, though deeply personal, is never a solitary experience—it ripples outward, creating a legacy of change.

In the process of my own transformation, I've seen how it has impacted those closest to me. My family has watched me grow, and in turn, they too have been inspired to embrace their own paths of growth. Our shared experiences have become a catalyst for open conversations, for healing, and for pushing each other to evolve into the best versions of ourselves. It's been a journey of mutual growth—where the transformation of one person serves as a model for the transformation of others.

It's not just family and friends who are touched by this energy; even strangers, witnessing my journey from the outside, feel the effects of this transformation. Whether through small interactions or through sharing my story, I've seen how my growth can encourage others to confront their own challenges and transform their lives. The message is simple: If I can rise, so can they. The courage it takes to embrace change is contagious, and it encourages others to take the leap toward their own growth.

The ripple effect also goes beyond inspiring others to change—it creates a community of transformation. As we evolve, we attract others who are on a similar path of growth, creating spaces where collective healing and empowerment occur. These spaces become havens for growth, for sharing wisdom, and for encouraging each other to continue rising, no matter how difficult the journey may seem. We realize that we are not alone in our struggles, and that by sharing our transformation, we are not only helping ourselves but helping others step into their own power too.

Transformation, when embraced fully, becomes a movement—a movement that spreads through our families, our communities, our workplaces, and beyond. It shows others that change is possible, that growth is inevitable, and that it is never too late to evolve. The power of transformation is not just in how it changes us, but in how it transforms everyone and everything we touch.

The ripple effect of our transformation can be felt in ways we may never fully understand, but that doesn't lessen its impact. We are all connected, and as we rise, we raise others with us. It is this interconnectedness that makes our personal journeys so powerful, for in embracing our own transformation, we become the catalyst for the growth of those around us. And in doing so, we create a world where transformation becomes the norm, where growth becomes inevitable, and where our collective power is limitless.

The Phoenix Rises, Again

The Phoenix symbolizes resilience, rebirth, and the unyielding power to rise from the ashes, no matter the devastation it faces. It does not shrink from the flames that threaten to consume it, but instead, it thrives in them. For the Phoenix, the fire is not a force of destruction but a necessary part of its transformation. Similarly, we too face our own fires—our struggles, losses, fears, and challenges—but with each one, we are granted the opportunity to emerge renewed, more radiant, and more powerful than before.

Every trial, every test, every setback in life is an invitation to step into the fire and allow it to purify us. The flames of hardship are not a sign that we should shrink back in fear; they are a call to evolve. They challenge us to become something more than we were before. Just as the Phoenix must burn before it can rise again, we too must experience moments of intense heat, pressure, and pain to forge the strength, wisdom, and courage necessary for our own rebirth.

The process of transformation is cyclical, much like the Phoenix's perpetual rise from its ashes. Each time we face adversity, it feels as though we are being torn apart, but in reality, we are shedding the old layers of who we once were to reveal something more powerful within us. We are not being destroyed by the fire, but rather, we are being refined. We are shedding our fears, doubts, and limitations, making space for the person we are becoming.

Just as the Phoenix rises from its ashes, so too do we rise from our challenges. The ashes represent the past, the pain, the struggles we've endured. But the rising is symbolic of hope, strength, and renewal. With every challenge we face, we have the chance to rise higher, to evolve, and to become a stronger version of ourselves. And this process is continuous—it doesn't end with one transformation, because life will always present new challenges, new fires. But each time we emerge from the flames, we are not the same. We are better. We are more equipped. We are more prepared for the next stage of our journey.

Embrace your inner Phoenix. Welcome the flames, for they are the crucible in which your true power is forged. Know that no matter what you face, you are not being broken. You are being remade, reshaped into the person you were always meant to become. The power of transformation lies in our willingness to embrace change, to face challenges head-on, and to trust that each trial is an opportunity for growth.

Remember, the Phoenix does not rise only once—it rises again and again, becoming more magnificent with each ascent. So too will you. Your transformation is not a one-time event but an ongoing journey, and with every rise, you will become more of the person you are destined to be. The struggles of today will serve as the foundation for your strength tomorrow. You are becoming something greater than you ever imagined.

So, when life's challenges come, do not shrink back in fear. Do not shy away from the fire. Instead, walk boldly into it, knowing that, like the Phoenix, you are destined to rise—stronger, bolder, and more powerful than ever before. Embrace the struggle, trust in the process, and know that each time you rise, you become more magnificent than the last.

5

Chapter 4: Breaking Chains, Building Legacy

The Chains of the Past: A Heavy Burden and the Path to Freedom

Every path toward greatness begins with an undeniable truth: the chains we carry, whether visible or invisible, shape our lives in ways we often don't realize. These chains are the burdens of our history—personal, familial, and cultural. They are the traumas, the failures, the inherited fears, and the scars passed down from generation to generation. For too long, I lived with these chains wrapped tightly around my spirit. They were the remnants of a past filled with pain, disappointment, and rejection, but they were not solely my burden to bear—they were the weight of my ancestors, the broken promises and unmet dreams of those who came before me.

As a child, I was taught to carry these chains without ever

knowing how heavy they truly were. I didn't realize that the cycles of trauma, the unhealthy patterns, and the self-limiting beliefs I inherited were not a reflection of who I was, but rather a reflection of who I had been conditioned to believe I was. There is a deep, spiritual inheritance that comes with generational pain—one that compels us to hold onto the past, to repeat the mistakes, and to feel stuck in cycles that prevent us from becoming our highest selves.

The first step to breaking these chains is awareness. You have to understand that the chains are not your fault, and yet, you are the one with the power to break them. They are part of your story, but they are not your destiny. For me, this awareness came through painful introspection, difficult conversations with myself, and the courage to confront the reality of my past. I had to acknowledge the hurt, the fear, and the anger that lived within me, recognizing that I was not destined to carry the weight of those chains forever.

It's easy to blame others for the pain we carry. For me, it was about blaming the people who had hurt me—those who had abandoned me, betrayed me, and belittled me. But as I grew, I realized that healing wouldn't come from blaming others. It would come from understanding that the chains were not meant to hold me back forever; they were simply part of the journey. These chains were reminders, not of my failures, but of the lessons I had yet to learn and the strength I was destined to reclaim. It was only through breaking them that I could step into my true power.

The power to break the chains comes through emotional

ownership. It requires not just awareness, but a willingness to feel the discomfort of what has been hidden away, to look into the eyes of your deepest pain, and to reclaim your birthright of freedom. Breaking these chains demands courage—courage to confront and accept the past, courage to forgive those who wronged you, and most importantly, courage to forgive yourself. The process of healing involves letting go of the old stories, narratives that no longer serve you, and releasing the emotional weight of inherited pain.

Once I began the process of letting go, I realized that breaking these chains wasn't just about the past—it was about embracing a new future, one free from the limits of old beliefs. I had to let go of self-doubt, the belief that I was unworthy of success or love, the fear that I would never be enough. I had to shed those layers that kept me small and kept me stuck in familiar patterns. Every time I faced my fear, every time I chose healing over bitterness, I took another step toward breaking free from the chains that had once bound me.

But breaking the chains was not just about healing. It was about reclaiming my sovereignty, my power, and my voice. I was no longer willing to be defined by my past. Through action, self-compassion, and deep introspection, I began to emerge as a woman reborn. I began to see myself not as a victim of my circumstances but as the architect of my future. No longer weighed down by inherited fear or outdated beliefs, I began to take ownership of my life, stepping boldly into the truth of who I was meant to be.

Breaking the chains required action. It required setting

boundaries, walking away from toxic relationships, and making choices that aligned with my highest vision for myself. But most importantly, it required the profound act of forgiveness—not for the sake of others, but for my own liberation. By forgiving, I freed myself from the hold of past pain and made space for new blessings to enter my life. Forgiveness wasn't about excusing harm—it was about giving myself permission to let go and move forward.

As I continue to grow, I realize that breaking these chains is an ongoing journey. It is a constant process of letting go of what no longer serves me and embracing what I am becoming. I am no longer bound by the past, but I honor it. I carry forward its lessons, but I am no longer chained to its weight. I am free.

Now, I carry my own chains—not the chains of my past—but the chains of my own making. Chains forged through choices, through the power of knowing who I am and what I deserve. These chains are not burdens; they are the symbols of my freedom, of my sovereignty, and of the strength I have gained through breaking the old ones. I am free to walk into my future, no longer bound, but empowered by the lessons of my past and the infinite possibilities of my future.

Breaking Free from the Past: A Journey of Transformation

Breaking free from the chains of the past is not a singular moment of liberation—it's an ongoing process, a continual journey of unlearning, reprogramming, and reclaiming what was always mine to begin with. The chains I carried were not always visible, but they were suffocating. They were invisible to most people, but to me, they were as real as the air I breathed. Fear, shame, guilt, and self-doubt had been my silent companions for so long that I hadn't even known how to live without them. These chains kept me in the past, anchored in pain, and unsure of what life could look like if I dared to break free.

To begin the process of breaking free, I had to turn inward. I had to be brave enough to ask myself the hard questions that I had avoided for years: *Why do I feel unworthy? Why do I carry the pain of others, even though I'm not the one who inflicted it? Why do I feel trapped in cycles that I know no longer serve me?* These were not questions I could answer with ease. They demanded honesty and introspection. They forced me to confront parts of myself that I had long buried, parts that felt too painful or too shameful to face.

Healing began with those questions—and it was uncomfortable. There were no easy answers, no quick fixes. The trauma I had endured had woven itself into the very fabric of who I was, coloring my beliefs and shaping the choices I made. But I was learning that I wasn't bound by that trauma. I was learning that I was more than my past. That the pain I had carried for so long wasn't the end of my story, but rather the beginning of my healing. But to believe that, I had to actively choose to let go of the pain. I had to make the conscious decision to stop being defined by my wounds, to stop identifying myself with the experiences that had hurt me.

This part of the journey is not for the faint of heart. It is a battle—one fought in the deepest corners of the soul. It's a battle where the enemy is not a person, but the pain itself. It is about tearing down the false identities that have been built up over the years, identities forged by the judgments, expectations, and disappointments of others. It is about stripping away the layers of self-doubt, guilt, and fear that have bound me, and rediscovering who I am underneath it all.

Breaking free from the past isn't always pretty. It's messy, painful, and often lonely. There are moments when I wanted to give up, when the weight of the past felt too heavy to bear. There were days when the urge to retreat into the familiar chains of fear and shame seemed too strong to resist. But the truth is, those moments of discomfort were not the end. They were the beginning of my transformation. As each layer of the past was peeled away, I began to see the light that had always been inside me. The light that had been obscured by the darkness of my past. I began to realize that the chains were not meant to break me; they were meant to show me how strong I really am.

The chains were not there to destroy me—they were there to teach me. To show me that I could endure pain and still emerge stronger. That I could carry the weight of my past, but I didn't have to be defined by it. I could use the lessons from my past to shape the woman I was becoming. And the moment I understood that, the chains lost their power. They were no longer symbols of my weakness; they became symbols of my strength.

Healing is not a destination—it is a process. It is a constant journey of letting go of the past and stepping into the future. Each day is an opportunity to break free from the cycles that have held me captive, each moment an invitation to step more fully into my power. But breaking free doesn't mean erasing the past. It means learning to live with it, to integrate the lessons, and to rise above it. It means accepting that the pain of the past does not define me, but the strength I've gained from it does.

There is power in the act of letting go. When you choose to release what no longer serves you—whether that's old pain, old beliefs, or toxic relationships—you make space for something greater. You create room for healing, for growth, and for joy. Letting go is not about forgetting; it is about understanding that what lies ahead is far more important than what lies behind. The past may have shaped me, but it does not have to limit me.

As I began to break free from the chains of my past, I began to see myself with new eyes. I started to see my worth, my beauty, and my potential. I began to realize that I am worthy of love, success, and happiness—not because of anything I've done to earn it, but simply because I exist. I am worthy because I am a child of the universe, deserving of every good thing life has to offer.

Each victory along the way—each chain I broke, each lie I let go of, each moment I chose healing over bitterness—was a step toward reclaiming my true self. The more I reclaimed my power, the more I realized that I was never truly bound by the chains of my past. They were only as powerful as I allowed them to be. By choosing to heal, by choosing to rise above my pain, I took back my power. I took back my freedom.

And so, I continue to break free. Every day is a new opportunity to step further into the person I was always meant to be. A person who is free from the weight of the past, a person who embraces change and transformation, and a person who knows that the chains of the past no longer have any hold over me.

Breaking free is not an event—it is a journey. It is an ongoing process of shedding the old and embracing the new. And every day, I am becoming more and more the woman I was always meant to be: strong, powerful, and free.

The Role of Forgiveness in Breaking Free: A Liberation of the Soul

One of the most profound and difficult aspects of breaking free from the chains of the past is the act of forgiveness. For many, forgiveness is seen as a gift we give to those who have wronged us—an act of kindness or compassion that lets them off the hook for their actions. But as I embarked on my own journey of healing, I learned that forgiveness is not about absolving others of their wrongs. It's not about making excuses for their behavior or pretending that their actions didn't hurt me. Instead, forgiveness is about releasing the hold that the wrongdoers have on my life. It's about taking back my power, my peace, and my joy.

For years, I struggled with the idea of forgiveness. I believed that by forgiving those who had hurt me, I would be somehow weakening myself. I thought that if I let go of my anger, if I allowed myself to forgive, I was in some way condoning what had been done to me. It felt like an impossible choice, as if forgiveness was a sign of weakness or submission. But as I walked deeper into my healing journey, I realized that my refusal to forgive wasn't hurting the people who had wronged me—it was hurting me. I was holding onto anger and resentment, letting those feelings fester within me and shape my present. I was allowing my pain to continue to control my life.

The truth that emerged from this realization was both liberating and humbling: forgiveness is not for them—it is for me. It is an act of self-liberation. It is the key that unlocks the chains of resentment, anger, and bitterness that hold us hostage to the past. Without forgiveness, we remain tethered to our wounds, unable to move forward, unable to experience true peace. The longer we hold onto grudges, the more power we give to the people who hurt us. The more we carry those grudges, the more we allow our past to dictate our future. Forgiveness is not about excusing the hurtful actions of others—it's about reclaiming our ability to move forward, to heal, and to live with freedom.

When I began to forgive, it wasn't an immediate or easy process. It was slow, deliberate, and often painful. The wounds I carried ran deep, and the scars were still fresh in my heart. But with every act of forgiveness, I felt lighter. The weight that had burdened me for so long—anger, hatred, and pain—began to dissipate. As I let go of the hold these emotions had on me, I felt the freedom that comes from no longer being controlled by them. I felt the power of choosing peace over pain, freedom over imprisonment. It was as if I was shedding a layer of myself that had once been bound by the chains of my past, and with each layer I shed, I revealed a deeper version of who I was meant to be.

Forgiveness is not an event—it is an ongoing process. It is not a one-time decision that can instantly erase the scars of the past. It is a continual act of choosing to release the power that anger, resentment, and bitterness have over us. And each time we forgive, we step closer to the person we are meant to become. The journey of forgiveness is long and at times grueling, but it is one of the most powerful steps we can take toward healing and freedom.

What I learned in this process is that forgiveness does not mean that I have to forget what happened, or even that I have to continue to allow the person who hurt me back into my life. Forgiveness does not excuse the behavior or make the pain go away. But what it does is free me from being defined by the actions of others. It means that I no longer allow the person who wronged me to have a hold on my life. I no longer allow their actions to control my present or my future. By forgiving, I take back my power. I take back my peace. I take back my joy. And with every act of forgiveness, I heal a little more.

The beauty of forgiveness is that it has a ripple effect. As I began to forgive others, I realized that I also needed to forgive myself. I needed to let go of the guilt, the shame, and the self-blame I had carried for far too long. I needed to forgive myself for the mistakes I had made, for the ways in which I had allowed myself to be hurt, and for the times when I had failed to stand up for myself. Self-forgiveness was just as essential as forgiving others. It was the final piece of the puzzle, the key that unlocked my own heart and allowed me to move forward with grace.

Through this process of forgiveness, I discovered that true healing is about accepting both the beauty and the pain of the past. It's about acknowledging the wrongs done to me, feeling the weight of that hurt, but not allowing it to define who I am today. It's about choosing to rise above the past and choosing to let go of the emotional baggage that weighs us down.

Forgiveness is about making space—space for healing, space for growth, space for peace. When we forgive, we create room in our hearts for love, compassion, and joy. We make room for new experiences, new relationships, and new opportunities. The act of forgiveness is an investment in our own well-being. It is a gift we give ourselves, a decision to stop letting the past hold us hostage, and to step fully into the freedom and power that is rightfully ours.

I've learned that forgiveness doesn't mean that everything will be perfect. It doesn't mean that all the pain will magically disappear, nor does it mean that I won't still have moments of hurt. But it does mean that I no longer carry the burden of resentment and anger. It means that I no longer let my past dictate my future. And it means that I am no longer a prisoner to the chains of bitterness. Through forgiveness,

I have reclaimed my power, and in doing so, I have taken another step toward breaking free.

So, I choose forgiveness. I choose to release the past. I choose to heal. And in doing so, I choose freedom. Because the truth is, no one can hurt me unless I allow them to. No one can hold power over me unless I give it to them. And the moment I forgive, I take back my power. I take back my peace. I take back my joy.

And that is the greatest liberation of all.

Reclaiming My Power: The Path to Personal Liberation and Collective Healing

Breaking free from the chains was more than just letting go of past hurts—it was about reclaiming the personal power I had long abandoned. For so many years, I had allowed external factors—other people, circumstances, and societal expectations—to dictate my sense of worth, my actions, and even my identity. I sought validation in the wrong places, always hoping that someone or something outside of myself could fill the emptiness I felt within. But as I journeyed through my healing process, I came to the profound realization that the power I had been seeking had always resided inside of me.

This realization was both liberating and terrifying. On one hand, I felt an incredible sense of empowerment. I was finally coming into the truth of who I was, and for the first time, I could see that my worth was not contingent upon external approval. I could see that the power to shape my destiny lay within my own hands. On the other hand, this newfound awareness was overwhelming because it also meant I could no longer hide behind excuses or blame. I had to confront the reality of my life, take full responsibility for the choices I had made, and accept that the power to change was entirely mine.

Reclaiming my power meant stepping into full ownership of my life and choices. It meant acknowledging that I had allowed myself to be a victim of circumstances for far too long, to the point where I had lost sight of my own strength. It was about understanding that while the pain I had endured was real and the injustices I had faced were undeniable, I had the power to shape my future, regardless of what had happened in the past. I could no longer look to others for my sense of validation or to circumstances for my happiness. I had to stand in my own truth, recognizing that the ability to create the life I desired resided solely within me.

In reclaiming my power, I also had to confront my mistakes. It wasn't enough to simply take ownership of my life; I had to accept that I was not perfect and that I would make mistakes along the way. But instead of allowing those mistakes to define me, I began to see them as opportunities for growth. I realized that mistakes were not failures; they were lessons, guiding me toward becoming a better, more resilient version of myself. Owning my story meant embracing the full spectrum of experiences—both the triumphs and the setbacks. It meant recognizing that my imperfections didn't make me weak; they made me human.

The process of reclaiming my power was also an act of self-love and self-respect. For so long, I had allowed others to define my worth and my capabilities, often sacrificing my own desires and needs in the process. I had given away pieces of myself in the hopes of gaining acceptance or avoiding conflict. But as I healed, I began to see the beauty in standing firm in my own truth, regardless of others' opinions. I learned to honor my boundaries, to protect my peace, and to value myself in ways I had never done before.

Once I embraced my power, I realized that my journey wasn't just about me. Yes, it was a personal awakening, but it extended beyond my individual experience. I understood that the power I had reclaimed wasn't just for my own personal success—it was for the collective healing of those I loved and for the generations that would come after me. I wasn't just breaking chains for myself—I was breaking them for my children, my family, and my community.

By reclaiming my power, I was no longer trapped in the cycles of pain, trauma, and limitation that had once defined my life. I was no longer bound by the expectations or limitations placed upon me by others. I was forging a new path, one where I could live fully in my truth, where I could embrace my flaws and strengths alike, and where I could take responsibility for the legacy I was creating. The choices I made, the actions I took, and the healing I pursued were not only for my own growth but for the collective well-being of everyone I cared about.

I began to see that my transformation was part of a much larger story—a story that would impact the lives of my children and the generations to come. By breaking free from the chains that had bound me, I was laying the foundation for a new future, one where my children could grow up knowing their own worth and power, unburdened by the same struggles and limitations that I had faced. I wanted them to see me as a model of resilience, of strength, and of unwavering self-love. I wanted them to learn from my mistakes, not just from my successes.

But this power I had reclaimed wasn't just for my immediate family. It was for my broader community as well. I realized that when we heal, we heal not only ourselves but also those around us. Our healing has a ripple effect, touching the lives of everyone we encounter. The more we reclaim our power, the more we empower others to do the same. It is through our own transformation that we can help others recognize their own strength and begin their own journey of healing.

Reclaiming my power also meant understanding the importance of community. Healing is not a solitary endeavor—it's a collective one. We are all connected, and our individual journeys of reclaiming power are intertwined with the journeys of others. As I healed, I became more aware of the ways in which my growth was linked to the growth of those around me. I began to see the value in sharing my story, in being vulnerable, and in offering support to others who were walking similar paths.

In embracing this collective healing, I realized that breaking free from the chains is not just about personal success or individual freedom—it is about creating a legacy of empowerment and healing for everyone we love and serve. Reclaiming my power was not just for me; it was for my children, my family, my community, and for the generations that would follow.

By reclaiming my power, I was not only transforming my own life—I was transforming the lives of those who would come after me. I was breaking the chains of the past, not just for myself, but for the future. And in doing so, I was creating a legacy of strength, resilience, and empowerment that would reverberate for generations to come.

Building a Legacy: The Gift of Freedom

A legacy is not merely something we inherit—it is something we actively create. It is not the material wealth, the possessions, or the accolades that we leave behind that define our true legacy. Rather, it is the values we instill, the lives we touch, the love we give, and the stories we leave behind for the next generation. A legacy is an expression of the life we lived, the lessons we learned, and the way we chose to impact the world around us.

For me, building a legacy was deeply personal, as it meant showing my children and future generations that they are not bound by the limitations of our past. It meant teaching them that no matter the struggles, no matter the scars, they could rise above the challenges they faced, heal from their pain, and create a future that was brighter and freer than anything they had known before. I wanted them to understand that their identity is not shaped by the hurt they endured but by the strength they carry inside of them. The story of their lives does not have to be a continuation of the past—it can be a new chapter, one written with the ink of their own dreams, hopes, and aspirations.

The legacy I wanted to build was not one of personal success alone. Yes, I wanted to achieve my goals, to see my dreams realized, but the true depth of my legacy lay in the generational healing I sought to foster. I wanted to leave behind more than just tangible assets or recognition; I wanted to leave behind a blueprint for healing, growth, and empowerment. I wanted my children to see that they are worthy of love, success, and peace, no matter their beginnings or the obstacles they face. I wanted them to know that the challenges they encounter do not define them; rather, it is how they rise from them, how they embrace the healing process, and how they continue moving forward with hope and resilience.

I didn't want my legacy to be defined by the accumulation of wealth alone; instead, I wanted it to be rooted in the wealth of spirit—resilience, love, courage, and the deep knowledge that we are capable of transcending our circumstances. These were the gifts I sought to pass down to my children—the understanding that life's greatest treasures are not material, but spiritual. I wanted them to learn the importance of self-love and the power of forgiveness, both of which are key to breaking free from the chains of the past. In teaching them these lessons, I wanted to give them the tools to heal, to find peace, and to navigate life's challenges with grace and strength.

But the gift of freedom in building a legacy isn't just about passing wisdom down to our children. It extends far beyond our immediate families—it's about our contributions to the broader world. I found myself asking some profound questions: What kind of impact do I want to make in this world? What will my legacy be in the lives of others? What do I want people to say about me when I'm no longer here? These were not just questions about material success; they were about how I showed up in the world, how I served others, how I loved, and how I stayed true to my authentic self.

I wanted my legacy to be defined by the ways I touched others' lives, by the way I served my community, by the authenticity I embodied, and by the love I extended to those around me. It was never about the tangible things—how much money I made, the titles I earned, or the recognition I received. True fulfillment, I realized, would come from the way I showed up for others in the most meaningful ways. It would be defined by the way I gave from my heart, by the way I used my voice, my strength, and my power to serve and uplift those in need.

Building a legacy requires intention. It's about being deliberate in our choices, actions, and words, knowing that each decision contributes to the future we are crafting. Every step we take, every action we make, has a ripple effect. It's about understanding that the legacy we leave behind is the sum of our small, consistent actions, the quiet moments of kindness, the words of encouragement, and the impact we have on the lives of others. Building a legacy is not a single, grand gesture—it is a life lived with purpose, with love, and with integrity.

I learned that creating a lasting legacy means leaving a trail of light that others can follow. It means living a life that inspires and empowers others to live authentically, to heal, and to reach their fullest potential. We all have the ability to make the world a better place simply by choosing to live in alignment with our values, by using our unique gifts and voices to contribute to something greater than ourselves. Our legacy is not just about what we have done—it's about what others take from our lives and the way we inspire them to live their own truth.

I have come to realize that every action, every decision, every word I speak, has the power to shape the world around me. The choices I make today impact the generations to come. I understand that the love, wisdom, and lessons I share today will be carried forward by my children and those who witness my life. And though I may not be able to control the future or predict the impact my life will have, I can live with the intention of leaving behind a legacy of love, strength, and freedom.

I think about the world I want to create for my children, for my community, and for future generations. The world I envision is one where love, healing, and forgiveness are at the core. It's a world where people are free to be their authentic selves, unburdened by fear, shame, or guilt. It's a world where we lift each other up, where we create safe spaces for healing, and where we acknowledge that we are all part of a much larger story—a story of collective transformation.

By being intentional with my actions, by living my truth, and by choosing to contribute to the world in meaningful ways, I am building a legacy that will outlast me. It's not about what I accumulate or how much I achieve in my lifetime—it's about the love I give, the peace I create, and the healing I inspire. My legacy will not be measured by the things I leave behind, but by the lives I touch, the hearts I heal, and the ways I inspire others to find their own freedom. And this gift of freedom, this gift of love, will live on in the stories told by those whose lives were touched by my journey.

In the end, building a legacy is the ultimate gift of freedom—not just for ourselves, but for the generations that will carry our stories forward. It is the freedom to be authentically ourselves, to live in love, to heal from the past, and to create a future that is filled with possibility. This is the legacy I am building—the legacy of freedom, of love, and of healing that will continue to grow long after I am gone.

Family: The Foundation of Legacy

At the very heart of legacy-building lies family. Family is the first place where our legacy begins to take root. It is the first environment in which we are nurtured, shaped, and taught the values that will guide us through life. However, family is not merely defined by bloodlines. It is also composed of the people we choose to walk alongside us—the mentors who challenge us, the friends who uplift us, the partners who support us, and the community members who offer us strength, wisdom, and encouragement. These individuals, although not bound by blood, are integral to the fabric of our lives and, ultimately, to the legacy we create.

True legacy-building within a family means fostering a culture of love, respect, and support. It requires more than just providing for our children or offering them material things—it's about teaching them values that will guide them through their own journeys. It's about instilling in them the importance of kindness, honesty, and resilience. These values are the pillars upon which strong families and strong legacies are built. It's about showing our children that the most important thing in life is not what we accumulate, but how we treat others, how we care for ourselves, and how we approach life's challenges with grace and courage.

I've come to understand that family is a place where love is unconditional, and support is unwavering. It's not always about being perfect, but about showing up for one another with authenticity, empathy, and compassion. Legacy-building within the family is not just about leaving behind wealth or possessions; it's about nurturing relationships, creating memories, and imparting wisdom. It's about teaching the next generation how to be resilient in the face of adversity and how to cultivate love and compassion within themselves and toward others.

The foundation of my legacy is built on the lessons I impart to my children—the values I share with them, the examples I set, and the love I give. These are the things that will shape their futures. I want them to understand that their worth is not determined by their circumstances, but by the strength and power they carry within themselves. I want them to know that they are capable of achieving anything they set their minds to and that they can overcome any obstacle. I want them to believe, without a shadow of a doubt, that they are worthy of love, respect, and success—not because of their external accomplishments, but because of who they are at their core.

As a mother, I want my children to recognize that they, too, have the ability to break free from any chains that may bind them. The chains of fear, shame, guilt, or past trauma do not define them. They are not bound by the mistakes of others or by the limitations of their environment. They have the power to heal, to rise above, and to build lives filled with purpose, passion, and fulfillment. By teaching them this truth, I empower them to create their own destinies, to write their own stories, and to live lives of meaning and joy.

Legacy is about creating a ripple effect that extends beyond our immediate family. It is about creating a culture that transcends generations, one where each individual feels empowered to contribute to the collective well-being. It's about teaching my children to be not only strong but also kind, to be resilient but also compassionate, to be independent but also humble. A legacy isn't just about what we leave for our children—it's about what we leave *in* them. It's about the seeds of wisdom, strength, and love we plant in their hearts and minds, and the ways they carry these seeds forward into the world.

Building a legacy within the family is also about creating spaces for growth and healing. Family should be a sanctuary where we are allowed to show up as our true selves, where we are accepted and loved despite our flaws, and where we are encouraged to grow, learn, and evolve. It means providing a safe environment where mistakes are seen as opportunities for learning and growth, not as failures. It's about showing my children that it's okay to make mistakes, that they are not defined by their missteps but by how they rise from them, how they learn from them, and how they continue moving forward with grace.

I also want to teach my children the importance of community. Family extends beyond our blood relatives—it includes the people who walk beside us in life, the mentors who guide us, the friends who offer us their support, and the community members who give of themselves to help us grow. We are all interconnected, and the legacy we build is not just for our immediate families but for the greater good of society. It's about teaching my children that the greatest legacy we can leave is not just the impact we make within our homes but the ways we serve others, the love we share, and the lives we touch along the way.

The culture of love, respect, and support that I want to create within my family is not something that happens overnight. It requires consistent effort, intentionality, and patience. It's about being present with my children, listening to their needs, and showing them that they are valued for who they are, not for what they can achieve. It's about being a role model who shows them the importance of self-love, forgiveness, and humility. It's about making sure they understand that the greatest power in life is not external—it's internal. It's the power to choose, to change, and to create a life that reflects the deepest values of who we are.

I also recognize that creating a family legacy is not just about the future; it's about healing the past. It's about breaking generational cycles that no longer serve us, acknowledging the hurts that may have been passed down, and working to heal and transform those patterns. I want my children to understand that healing is a lifelong process and that it's okay to seek help when needed. I want them to know that they are not alone in their struggles, that they have a family that will always stand beside them, supporting them through every challenge they face.

In this way, family becomes both the foundation and the manifestation of the legacy we create. It is the fertile ground where love, respect, resilience, and healing take root, allowing the next generation to grow and thrive in ways we can only imagine. Through the lessons we impart and the love we give, we build a legacy that lasts far beyond our lifetime—a legacy that not only transforms our immediate families but also has the power to impact the world. And by teaching our children the power of self-love, forgiveness, and resilience, we give them the tools to break free from any chains that would seek to hold them back.

A Legacy for the World

Our legacy extends far beyond the boundaries of our immediate families; it is a gift we offer to the world, shaping the future in ways that transcend time and space. The legacy we leave behind is measured not by what we acquire or accomplish for ourselves, but by the impact we have on others—the lives we touch, the communities we serve, and the changes we inspire. True legacy isn't simply about personal success; it is about contributing to the broader human experience and inspiring others to rise above their struggles and create something of profound value in their own lives.

I want my legacy to be one of empowerment—empowering others to break free from the chains that bind them, to shed the limitations of their past, and to fully embrace who they are at their core. It is about offering people the permission to live authentically, to be unapologetically themselves, and to create lives that are filled with purpose, passion, and fulfillment. I want to leave behind a legacy of love—a love that transcends generations, a love that speaks to the hearts of people, no matter where they come from or what they have been through. This love is not conditional or based on what people do for us, but is rooted in the belief that every person deserves to be seen, valued, and loved for who they truly are.

A legacy is not something that happens overnight. It is the result of years of conscious decisions, actions, and struggles, culminating in a life that reflects our highest values and deepest purpose. It is something we cultivate day by day, through the way we show up for ourselves and for others, through the lessons we teach, and through the way we live out our truth. The impact we make on the world is the sum of every decision we make, every struggle we endure, every victory we celebrate, and every lesson we learn. These experiences form the foundation upon which we build our legacy, and the way we carry ourselves through life becomes the model for others to follow.

Building a legacy, for me, is not solely about achieving external success or financial gain. It is about creating a life of fulfillment—living in alignment with our true purpose, living in accordance with our deepest values, and staying committed to the things that matter most. A legacy of fulfillment is one that is marked by joy, peace, and a deep sense of meaning. It is not about chasing after accolades or recognition, but about living a life that leaves an indelible imprint on the hearts and minds of others. The ripple effect of our actions—whether through simple acts of kindness, standing up for what is right, or empowering others to rise—is what forms the true measure of our legacy.

I want to build a legacy that fosters freedom—the kind of freedom that goes beyond physical liberation to include emotional, mental, and spiritual freedom. This freedom is not just about breaking free from the chains of our own past, but about liberating future generations from the limitations they've inherited. I want to inspire others to transcend their struggles, to heal from their wounds, and to transform their pain into power. I want the next generation to understand that they are not defined by their circumstances or the challenges they face, but by their ability to rise above them and create lives filled with meaning, purpose, and fulfillment.

This legacy of freedom will be one that teaches future generations that they are capable of anything they set their minds to. They will know that their worth is not tied to their past, to their mistakes, or to the negative experiences they have endured. They will understand that their true power lies in their ability to choose—choose how they respond to life's challenges, choose how they shape their future, and choose how they show up in the world. This sense of freedom is what I hope to impart to my children and to all those I encounter along my journey. It is the freedom to live authentically, to dream big, and to pursue one's purpose without fear or hesitation.

The world needs a new kind of legacy—a legacy that is rooted in empowerment, love, resilience, and self-transformation. The next generation must understand that they are not bound by their circumstances, nor are they defined by the struggles they face. Rather, they are defined by their capacity to transcend those struggles, to rise above them, and to create something extraordinary. I envision a world where people no longer see their challenges as insurmountable, but as opportunities for growth and evolution. A world where individuals embrace their imperfections, knowing that they are worthy of love and success, and where every person is empowered to create a life that is meaningful and aligned with their highest self.

As I reflect on the legacy I wish to leave, I am reminded that it is not about what we accumulate in this lifetime—it is about the impact we have on others and the way we inspire change in the world. A true legacy is one that empowers others to break free from their chains, to rise above their limitations, and to create something beautiful, not just for themselves, but for the world. I want my legacy to be a beacon of hope, love, and empowerment, guiding others on their own journeys of healing and self-discovery. It is about showing people that they are not alone, that their struggles are not in vain, and that they have the power to create lives filled with purpose and passion.

Ultimately, the legacy we leave behind is the gift we give to the world. It is the mark we make, the lives we touch, and the change we inspire. It is the culmination of every decision we make, every lesson we learn, and every person we help along the way. A legacy is not just about us; it is about the way we use our lives to make the world a better place for those who come after us. And in that, we find the true measure of our success—the lives we touch, the hearts we uplift, and the change we inspire in the world around us.

The Power of Resilience: A Legacy in the Making

Resilience is the very heartbeat of legacy-building. It is the essential force that enables us to face life's storms, to withstand the pressures and pains, and to rise time and time again. Without resilience, we cannot overcome the obstacles that life throws at us, and without overcoming these obstacles, we cannot create something that stands the test of time. Resilience is the strength that allows us to rebuild, reimagine, and redefine ourselves after every setback, and it is the cornerstone of the lasting legacy we are building.

For me, resilience became my lifeline. It was the constant thread that pulled me through the darkest times of my life, the force that kept me going when all seemed lost. The challenges I faced were not easy, and at times, they seemed insurmountable. There were moments when I felt as though I would never make it out, when the weight of everything I was going through threatened to crush me. But with every setback, I discovered a deeper strength within myself, a strength that I had not known existed until those very moments of adversity.

Resilience is not just about bouncing back from failure; it's about using that failure as a springboard to propel us forward. It's about growing stronger with each challenge, with each loss, and with each moment of doubt. I began to understand that every hardship, every struggle, was not a roadblock but an opportunity for growth—a chance to build character, to learn new lessons, and to become more of the person I was always meant to be. Every hardship I faced became a teacher, showing me what I was truly capable of. And as I embraced resilience, I realized that I wasn't just surviving; I was thriving.

Resilience means continuing to move forward even when the path ahead is unclear, even when the weight of the world feels unbearable. It's about refusing to stay down, refusing to accept defeat, and instead, choosing to rise—again and again. I discovered that resilience isn't about avoiding the hard times or pretending that life doesn't throw curveballs; it's about facing those challenges head-on and learning to adapt, evolve, and persist in the face of them. Resilience is about standing tall in the midst of the storm, not just waiting for it to pass, but learning to dance in the rain.

With each challenge I faced, I added another layer to my

foundation. I built resilience not just in my actions, but in my mindset. I learned that true resilience is cultivated from within—it is a choice we make every day, a mindset we adopt, and a practice we continue to develop throughout our lives. It's about recognizing that adversity doesn't define us; it refines us. The more we face, the more resilient we become, and the more capable we are of handling whatever comes next.

The resilience I have cultivated is not only for my own survival—it is for the future. It is the foundation of the legacy I am building, not just for myself, but for my children, my family, my community, and even the world. The legacy I am creating is rooted in resilience—the resilience to rise above adversity, to keep moving forward no matter the cost, and to build something that lasts far beyond my own lifetime. Resilience is what gives us the strength to keep going when the road ahead seems impossible. It is what allows us to transform pain into power, loss into learning, and struggle into success.

As I look to the future and to the legacy I am building, I realize that resilience is the key to everything. It is the trait that will ensure that my children, my family, and those who come after me will have the strength to overcome the challenges they face. I want my children to see that resilience isn't just a skill to be learned; it is a way of life. It's about showing them that no matter how many times they fall, they can always get back up—stronger, wiser, and more capable than before. I want them to know that life may not always be easy, but it is always worth living with resilience and strength.

In building my legacy, resilience becomes the anchor that holds everything together. It is the force that enables me to rise above my own struggles and to move forward with purpose and passion. It is the source of my courage, the foundation of my success, and the driving force behind every action I take. Resilience is not just about enduring—it's about thriving, about expanding, and about achieving greatness, even in the face of adversity.

When I think about the legacy I am leaving, I understand that resilience is not just a personal trait—it is a gift I offer to the world. It is something that can inspire others, something that can help lift them up and empower them to face their own battles with courage and strength. By embracing resilience, I am not only building a better life for myself and my family, but I am also creating a ripple effect of strength, courage, and empowerment that will touch the lives of others for generations to come.

Resilience is the heartbeat of my legacy. It is the fuel that drives me to keep going, to keep pushing forward, and to keep building something beautiful. And it is the foundation upon which I will continue to build my legacy—a legacy that is not defined by my struggles, but by my ability to rise above them and to inspire others to do the same. With resilience as my guide, I know that the legacy I am creating will be one of strength, hope, and lasting transformation for all those who come after me.

A Legacy of Healing and Empowerment

Healing is the foundation upon which any lasting legacy is built. It is impossible to create something meaningful, something that will stand the test of time, without first tending to the wounds of the past. Healing is not simply about letting go of the pain we carry; it is about transforming that pain into power, wisdom, and resilience. It is about turning our scars into symbols of strength and using our experiences—no matter how painful—as fuel to propel us forward into a future filled with purpose.

For me, healing has been one of the most profound, and at times, painful journeys I have ever undertaken. I have spent years mending the broken pieces of my past, confronting the trauma that has shaped my life. There were times when the weight of these experiences felt unbearable, when the pain seemed too much to bear. But through this process of healing, I have come to understand that the very act of facing the darkest parts of ourselves is what enables us to create the brightest futures. Healing is the work of turning wounds into wisdom, and pain into purpose. It is the process of turning our tragedies into the raw material from which we can build something extraordinary.

The road to healing has not been linear. It has been filled with setbacks, detours, and moments of doubt. Yet, with every step I took, no matter how small, I found more strength within me. I discovered that healing is not an event, but a continuous process. It is not something that happens overnight; it is something that requires patience, self-compassion, and a willingness to face the parts of ourselves that we would rather hide. It is a journey that requires us to peel back the layers of our pain, to confront the beliefs and patterns that no longer serve us, and to make the conscious choice to let go of the things that hold us back.

Through my own healing journey, I have learned the importance of embracing my truth—no matter how difficult or uncomfortable it may be. I have learned that authenticity is the key to healing. When we allow ourselves to be vulnerable, to show up in our lives as we truly are, we create the space for deep, transformative healing. And through this healing, we are empowered—not just to live for ourselves, but to show up in the world in a way that inspires others.

As I heal, I am able to give more of myself to others. Healing has empowered me to show up fully in my life, to be true to who I am, and to pass on the lessons I have learned along the way. My legacy is not defined by the material things I leave behind, but by the empowerment I offer to others. It is about helping others discover their own strength, their own resilience, and their own capacity for healing. It is about showing others that no matter how deep the wounds, they have the power to heal, to rise, and to create something beautiful out of their pain.

When we heal, we break free from the chains that bind us—not just for ourselves, but for those who come after us. Healing is a gift we give to ourselves, but it is also a gift we pass on to future generations. By healing, we create a ripple effect that spreads through our families, our communities, and beyond. As I heal, I am breaking generational curses, undoing the patterns of trauma and pain that have been passed down through the years. And as I do this, I am creating a new legacy—one that is free from the shackles of the past, one that is filled with hope, empowerment, and possibility.

My legacy is a legacy of healing—a healing that goes beyond personal transformation and extends to the world around me. It is about breaking the cycles of pain and trauma, about showing others that they can overcome their own struggles and create a future that is defined not by their past, but by their strength, their resilience, and their ability to heal. It is about empowering others to take control of their own healing journeys, to reclaim their power, and to create lives that are not only survivable but are filled with joy, purpose, and fulfillment.

The empowerment that comes from healing is profound. It is the recognition that we are not victims of our circumstances, but warriors of our own fate. We are the creators of our stories, and when we choose to heal, we are choosing to write a new chapter. This empowerment is what I hope to pass on to others—to my children, my family, and my community. I want to show them that healing is not just a process; it is a way of life. I want them to understand that they are not defined by their wounds, but by their ability to rise above them, to heal, and to build something greater than what they have experienced.

The legacy of healing I am building is one that transcends time. It is a legacy that will continue to impact future generations, not just through the wisdom I impart, but through the healing that I embody. It is a legacy of breaking free from the pain of the past and creating a future that is not only brighter but more compassionate, more resilient, and more empowering.

Healing is the most powerful gift we can give ourselves and the world around us. When we heal, we become beacons of hope, light, and strength for others to follow. We inspire them to begin their own healing journeys and to create lives that are filled with meaning, purpose, and joy. The legacy of healing is a legacy of empowerment—empowering others to heal, to rise, and to transform their lives. It is the ultimate gift we can give to the world, and it is the gift I strive to leave behind—a legacy of healing, empowerment, and transformation for generations to come.

A Legacy of Love, Faith, and Purpose

At the deepest core of everything I do, at the very heart of the legacy I am building, lies love. Love is not just an emotion or a fleeting sentiment; it is the very foundation of our existence, the force that connects us all. It transcends time, distance, and circumstance. It is the energy that fuels everything I do—behind every decision, every action, every word, every choice. Love is the spark that ignites my passion, the fire that drives me to continue when the road gets tough, and the glue that binds all of my endeavors into something greater than myself. It is the motivating force that pushes me to give of myself, to pour into others, and to create a world that is filled with compassion, connection, and kindness.

Love is not always easy, but it is always worth it. In a world that can sometimes feel fractured and divided, love is the glue that holds us together. It is the power that heals, the force that transforms, and the ultimate antidote to fear, hatred, and resentment. It is the power to forgive, the capacity to move forward in spite of the past, and the willingness to give of ourselves, even when it feels like we have little left to give. Love is the foundation of everything I strive to build and the ultimate legacy I want to leave behind. It is the energy that inspires my purpose, and it is the legacy I wish to pass on to my children, my family, my community, and the world.

And faith—faith is what sustains me. It is the invisible force that carries me through the darkest moments and the most difficult trials. It is the unwavering belief that, no matter what obstacles I face, no matter how many challenges lie ahead, I will overcome them. I am not walking this journey alone; I am guided by a higher purpose, a divine hand that leads me and a greater plan that unfolds in the most beautiful and surprising ways. My faith is the foundation of my legacy. It is the compass that directs me, the anchor that keeps me grounded when the winds of life threaten to pull me off course, and the light that illuminates the path when the road ahead feels unclear. Faith is what reminds me that there is always hope, that I am always supported, and that no matter what I face, I can overcome it.

Faith is also the wellspring of resilience. It is the belief that even in moments of uncertainty, I am being shaped and prepared for something greater. Faith is not just about believing in the unseen; it is about trusting that the journey I am on has purpose, even when I cannot see the destination. It is the certainty that every challenge, every setback, and every triumph is part of a greater story—one that I am privileged to be a part of. My faith is the pillar of my strength, and it is the force that sustains me as I build this legacy. It keeps me going, even when the road gets hard, and it fuels my belief that my life, my work, and my contributions to the world have meaning.

Purpose is the third and final pillar of my legacy. Purpose is what gives my life meaning. It is the reason why I wake up every morning, the driving force that propels me forward, even when the journey feels impossibly long or overwhelming. Purpose is what pushes me to do the hard work, to make sacrifices, and to keep moving forward when everything inside of me wants to stop. It is the light that guides me through the darkest days, the thread that weaves together all of my experiences, and the foundation upon which my legacy is built.

My purpose is not just about personal success or achievement; it is about something far greater. My purpose is about serving others, lifting others up, and helping them break free from the chains that bind them. It is about empowering others to live lives of freedom, joy, and fulfillment. It is about showing people that they are capable of more than they ever imagined, that they have the strength within them to overcome any obstacle, and that they can create a life that is not only fulfilling but meaningful.

Through my purpose, I seek to inspire others to discover their own sense of purpose and to live lives that are aligned with their own values, passions, and gifts. I want to leave behind a legacy that is not just about the things I have achieved, but about the impact I have made on others. I want to create a legacy that speaks to the heart of who I am: a person who values love, who believes in the power of faith, and who is driven by purpose.

The legacy I strive to leave is a legacy that transcends time and place. It is a legacy that will continue to impact the lives of others long after I am gone. It is a legacy of love that will ripple through generations, a legacy of faith that will inspire others to trust in the divine guidance that leads them, and a legacy of purpose that will empower others to live lives of significance and meaning.

I want to leave behind a world that is better because I was here. A world where people have the courage to love deeply, to trust in their faith, and to pursue their purpose with passion and determination. I want to show the world that it is possible to overcome the darkest of days, to heal from the deepest wounds, and to create a life that is not only fulfilling but impactful.

In every action I take, in every word I speak, in every decision I make, I want to be guided by love, sustained by faith, and propelled by purpose. And in doing so, I want to build a legacy that not only reflects the best of who I am but also inspires others to create their own legacies of love, faith, and purpose. Together, we can build a world that is filled with meaning, purpose, and love—a world that continues to grow and flourish long after we are gone. A legacy that is greater than ourselves, greater than our struggles, and greater than anything we could ever imagine. This is the legacy I hope to build—a legacy that is not just for me, but for the world, for the future, and for all those who will follow.

A Legacy That Lives On

The legacy I am building is far more than the choices I make today—it is a vision of something that endures, that continues to touch lives and inspire long after I am gone. It is about creating an imprint on this world, a ripple that spreads outward, transcending time and generations. It's about crafting a legacy that ignites change, uplifts spirits, and empowers individuals to step into their own potential, transforming their lives and the world around them. In the deepest sense, the legacy I want to leave is not just a story of my life but a story of empowerment—one that lives on, impacting others long after my own journey ends.

Building a legacy is a journey, a process of continuous growth, healing, and transformation. It's not something that happens overnight. It's not a destination with a fixed end, but a lifelong commitment to living with purpose and passion, to embodying the principles of love, faith, strength, and resilience in every moment. And the beauty of this journey is that it's not just about the destination—it's about the lives we touch along the way, the change we catalyze, and the impact we make in the present moment that sets the foundation for the future.

Legacy-building is deeply rooted in the understanding that we are part of a much larger story. It's not just about creating something for ourselves, but about leaving a gift for those who come after us—our children, their children, and every soul that encounters the truth we live by. The choices we make today create the foundation for tomorrow. Our actions, words, and beliefs have a ripple effect on future generations, shaping the world they inherit and the mindset they carry. Through every step I take, every challenge I face, and every triumph I achieve, I know that I am contributing to a future that will be brighter, more hopeful, and more empowering than the one I was given.

My legacy is not about material possessions or external achievements. It's not about the wealth I accumulate, the accolades I receive, or the recognition I garner. It is defined by the lives I touch, the hearts I heal, and the change I inspire in others. What matters most is the depth of the impact I have on the lives of those around me. It's about the moments when I've uplifted someone when I've been the source of hope in their darkest days, when I've shown them that they, too, have the power to overcome, to rise, and to create the life they desire. It's about the healing I've experienced and the healing I pass on, the resilience I model, and the strength I share.

Legacy is not only about what we build, but also about how we live. It is defined by the love we give, the grace we extend, and the compassion we show in every action. It is about standing tall in the face of adversity, lifting others up, and empowering them to believe in themselves. It is about facing life's challenges with unwavering determination, and, in doing so, showing others that they too can rise above any circumstance. My legacy will be written in the stories of those whose lives I've touched, whose futures have been altered because they believed in their own power to change, because they witnessed what is possible when one dares to break free from the chains of fear, doubt, and limitation.

The foundation of my legacy is resilience. Resilience is what allows us to rise after every fall, to find strength in the face of adversity, and to continue moving forward despite the challenges. It is the heartbeat of legacy-building, the force that pushes us to overcome, to transform, and to keep fighting for what is rightfully ours. In each setback, I find the seed of a greater triumph. Every difficulty becomes an opportunity for growth and expansion. And through every obstacle, I lay the groundwork for a future that is brighter, more powerful, and more empowering than the one I inherited.

A legacy of hope is another cornerstone of what I wish to leave behind. Hope is the light in the darkness, the promise of a better tomorrow. It is the belief that, no matter how difficult the journey may be, there is always a way forward. A legacy of hope is a beacon that guides others, even when the road ahead seems unclear or insurmountable. It reminds people that their struggles do not define them, that their pain is not permanent, and that healing is always possible. It is the reminder that, even in our most challenging moments, there is always the potential for transformation, for growth, and for a brighter future.

Purpose also plays an integral role in the legacy I am building. Purpose is the force that drives me, the compass that keeps me aligned with my true calling. It is the reason why I wake up every day, why I push through the hard times, and why I continue on this path even when it feels impossible. Purpose is what keeps me grounded and focused, reminding me that everything I am building is bigger than myself. It is about creating a life that is aligned with my deepest values and passions, and that leaves a positive impact on the world. Through purpose, I create a legacy that is not just about my individual achievements but about the collective impact I have on the lives of others.

In the end, the legacy we build is not just what we leave behind—it's the mark we make on the world while we are here. The true measure of a legacy is not in the material things we acquire or the accolades we collect, but in the lives we transform and the positive impact we have on those around us. When we live with intention, when we embrace our own power, and when we break free from the chains that have held us back, we create a legacy that is much greater than ourselves. It is a legacy that lives on through the lives of others, through the change we inspire, and through the positive ripples we send out into the world.

Every action we take, no matter how small, has the potential to change the course of someone's life. And when we live with intention, when we consciously build a life that aligns with our deepest values, we lay the foundation for a legacy that will outlive us, that will continue to shape the world long after we are gone. We all have the ability to create something that transcends time, something that lives on in the hearts and minds of future generations. This is the legacy I aim to build—a legacy of empowerment, healing, resilience, hope, and transformation—a legacy that is built not just for me, but for the world, for the future, and for the generations to come. And in doing so, we leave behind a legacy that will never be forgotten, a legacy that will continue to inspire, uplift, and empower those who come after us.

6

Chapter 5: Cultivating Strength Through Vulnerability

Redefining Strength: The Power in Imperfection

In a world that often glorifies invincibility, we are led to believe that strength is synonymous with toughness, resilience without cracks, and an exterior that never bends. From a young age, many of us are conditioned to suppress emotions, avoid vulnerability, and hide the wounds we carry, because vulnerability is perceived as a weakness—something to be ashamed of, something to overcome. We are told that to be strong means to be impenetrable, unyielding, and unwavering. But what if we've been living in a myth all along? What if true strength isn't found in invulnerability, but in the ability to embrace vulnerability and imperfection?

True strength is not defined by the absence of fear, failure, or pain. In fact, it is defined by our willingness to face these challenges head-on, to walk through them with courage, authenticity, and openness. It is the decision to show up, despite the fear, despite the uncertainty, despite the pain. True strength lies in our ability to face the most vulnerable parts of ourselves and still choose to keep going. It's about choosing to rise each time we fall, about finding the courage to stand tall even when we feel fragile. It's not about being perfect, but about showing up imperfectly, embracing our flaws, and moving forward anyway.

Vulnerability is the birthplace of strength. It requires a willingness to expose our deepest fears and insecurities. It asks us to surrender the illusion of control, to step into discomfort, and to trust that even in our realest moments, we are enough. Vulnerability is not weakness—it is the foundation upon which authentic strength is built. When we allow ourselves to be vulnerable, we tap into a well of courage that we never knew existed. In those moments, we realize that our greatest strength is not in being unbreakable, but in being willing to be seen for who we truly are, flaws and all.

In a society that often values perfection and flawless appearances, it's easy to believe that our imperfections make us less worthy, less valuable. But the truth is, there is incredible power in imperfection. Our imperfections are not what make us weak—they are what make us human. They are what make us relatable, authentic, and real. They are what connect us to others on a deep, emotional level. It's our struggles, our scars, and our brokenness that give us the ability to understand and empathize with others. They are the threads that weave our shared human experience together.

One of the most beautiful representations of the power of imperfection is found in the Japanese art of kintsugi. Kintsugi is the art of repairing broken pottery with gold or silver lacquer, transforming the cracks into a part of the piece's beauty rather than hiding them. The cracks are celebrated, not concealed, and in doing so, the object becomes more unique, more valuable, and more beautiful because of its flaws. Kintsugi teaches us that the broken parts of us are not things to be ashamed of or hidden away—they are what make us more valuable, more resilient, and more authentic.

Just like the broken pottery, we too are more beautiful and valuable because of our cracks. It is in our imperfections that we find our strength. When we embrace our flaws, we embrace our true selves. We stop hiding behind facades and start showing up authentically. And in doing so, we give others permission to do the same. By embracing our vulnerability and imperfection, we become living testaments to the power of authenticity and self-acceptance. We show others that it is okay to be broken, to be flawed, and to be imperfect—because in those very imperfections, we find our true power.

We live in a world that often tries to tell us that our value is tied to our perfection—to our ability to present an image of invincibility, to always be strong and unyielding. But the truth is, true strength comes from embracing the parts of ourselves that we are often told to hide—the fear, the doubt, the pain, the vulnerability. It is through these cracks that our light shines brightest. It is through these cracks that we can truly connect with others, build deeper relationships, and create meaningful change in the world.

When we stop trying to hide our flaws and imperfections, we give others the courage to do the same. We create spaces where authenticity is celebrated, where vulnerability is seen as a strength, and where imperfections are acknowledged as part of the beautiful, messy journey of being human. Our scars become symbols of our resilience, our strength, and our growth. They tell the story of how far we've come, how much we've endured, and how much we've overcome.

The power in imperfection lies in the freedom it offers. When we embrace our imperfections, we release ourselves from the need to be perfect. We stop measuring our worth against impossible standards and start measuring it against the things that truly matter—our kindness, our courage, our authenticity, and our ability to love and be loved. We free ourselves from the chains of perfectionism and start living a life that is fully aligned with who we truly are.

In embracing vulnerability, we begin to redefine what strength looks like. We see that strength is not about never being broken, but about rising after each fall. Strength is about being authentic, about showing up for ourselves and others, even when we are uncertain, fearful, or hurting. Strength is about embracing the cracks, the scars, and the brokenness, knowing that they are what make us whole.

Ultimately, the true power in imperfection lies in its ability to set us free. When we stop hiding behind the facade of perfection, we free ourselves to live with more joy, more connection, and more love. We step into our power as perfectly imperfect beings, embracing all of who we are. And in doing so, we give others permission to do the same. The world doesn't need more flawless, unbreakable people—it needs more people who are willing to be vulnerable, to be authentic, and to embrace their imperfections as sources of strength. In doing so, we become living testaments to the power of embracing our raw, authentic selves and letting our imperfections shine.

A Personal Reckoning: The Cost of Guardedness

For many years, I wore my strength as a shield—an impenetrable barrier I believed would protect me from the wounds of the world. I convinced myself that by fortifying my heart with walls so high, I could navigate life without the risk of being hurt. It felt safer to hide my emotions, to guard myself against the pain of vulnerability. I believed that if I kept my feelings locked away, I could prevent myself from getting hurt. I didn't need anyone, I told myself, because I could handle things on my own. I didn't need to rely on others for comfort or support.

But as time passed, I began to realize something profoundly unsettling: the very walls that I had constructed to protect myself were the same walls that isolated me from the people I loved the most. My armor, which I thought was a symbol of strength, became a cage that kept me distant from real connection, from the deep relationships I secretly longed for but never allowed myself to embrace. I thought I could protect my heart from pain, but in doing so, I deprived myself of the richness of true intimacy, of the warmth and joy that comes from allowing others to love and be loved in return.

It wasn't always so clear to me. The disconnect, the isolation, crept in slowly, like the gentle tide of an ocean that slowly rises, unnoticed until you realize that the shore has been engulfed. The process of becoming aware was gradual, not a singular life-altering event. It began with small fractures: the subtle fading of a friendship I once cherished, the increasing pressure I put on myself to appear perfect in every way, and the quiet, almost deafening nights where I was surrounded by people but felt as though I was utterly alone. The realization that I was living in a self-imposed prison was not immediate; it built up over time, in the stillness of those long, empty hours spent within my own thoughts.

I had fooled myself into thinking that my guardedness was a form of strength, that by withholding pieces of myself from others, I was somehow invincible. But the truth began to reveal itself slowly, in moments of stillness and introspection. What I had mistaken for strength was, in reality, fear. Fear of being vulnerable, of exposing the parts of me that might be deemed unworthy or flawed. Fear of rejection, judgment, and failure. I feared that if I let down my walls, I would be too much for others to handle, that my imperfections would cause people to walk away, leaving me more alone than before.

I thought that by guarding my heart, I was controlling my narrative, protecting myself from the unpredictable twists and turns of life. But by clinging to that fear, I was limiting myself in ways I hadn't yet fully understood. The walls I built to protect myself from the world were also the very same walls that kept out love, joy, and connection. The price of my self-protection was loneliness. I was shutting myself off from the very things that make life meaningful—relationships, connection, love, and growth. I was hiding my authentic self, afraid that the real me wasn't enough.

The turning point came when life forced me to confront the emptiness behind my armor. It was no longer enough to simply survive; I longed to live fully, to experience the depth of human connection, and to feel the freedom that comes with embracing vulnerability. The more I sat with my own fear, the more I realized that my guardedness was not the answer. It was a crutch, something I had leaned on for far too long out of habit and comfort.

The walls I had built were an illusion of safety, a lie I had told myself in order to avoid the discomfort of being seen, of being known. I had convinced myself that my self-reliance was enough, that I didn't need others to complete me or support me. But the truth was, I was missing out on something far more powerful—the healing that comes through authentic connection.

I began to understand that true strength doesn't lie in avoiding pain or guarding against hurt. True strength is found in the courage to be vulnerable, in the willingness to open up to others, to expose the raw, unpolished parts of ourselves and trust that, even in our brokenness, we are worthy of love and acceptance. True strength is in knowing that, yes, there is risk in being vulnerable, but the reward is worth it. The reward is connection, intimacy, and the freedom to be fully yourself without fear of judgment.

When we live behind walls, we deny ourselves the opportunity to experience the richness of life in all its forms. We miss the chance to be truly seen, to be loved for who we are, and to love others in return. We deprive ourselves of the joy that comes from sharing our hearts and souls with those around us. I had spent so much of my life thinking that being guarded was the answer, but in reality, it was the problem. It was a barrier to living fully, to embracing the fullness of life's blessings.

It wasn't easy to dismantle those walls. It took time, patience, and a willingness to trust that the world, and the people in it, could be trusted with the real me. But as I began to tear down the walls, piece by piece, I felt a sense of liberation that I hadn't known before. I started to allow myself to feel deeply, to express my emotions openly, and to ask for help when I needed it. I began to lean into the discomfort of vulnerability, knowing that it was in those moments of openness that I would find the deepest connection, the most meaningful relationships.

I realized that the true cost of my guardedness wasn't just the isolation or loneliness—it was the missed opportunities for growth, love, and transformation. By hiding behind my walls, I had been denying myself the chance to truly connect with others and to experience the fullness of life. But by letting go of that fear and embracing vulnerability, I was opening myself up to a world of possibility.

Through this reckoning, I learned that strength isn't about building walls to protect yourself from the world. It's about having the courage to let those walls come down, to face the world with an open heart, and to trust that, even in your brokenness, you are worthy of love and connection. Strength is found in vulnerability, and vulnerability is the key to building the kind of life that is rich with meaning, depth, and fulfillment. The cost of guardedness is high, but the reward of living authentically, with an open heart, is priceless.

The Liberating Power of Vulnerability

When I first allowed myself to be vulnerable, it felt like stepping into the unknown, unarmed, and exposed. It was like standing on the edge of a cliff, looking down into the vast unknown, unsure of what would happen if I let go of the safety I had held onto for so long. Vulnerability is something I had spent years running from, hiding behind the walls I had so carefully constructed around my heart. I told myself that if I let anyone see the real me—the raw, unpolished, imperfect version of myself—I would be judged, rejected, or worse, abandoned.

But, in a moment of profound need, when the weight of holding everything in became too much to bear, I made the decision to take that leap. I shared parts of myself I had long kept hidden: my deepest fears, my insecurities, the pain I thought I had buried so far beneath the surface that it couldn't possibly surface again. It felt uncomfortable, terrifying, and almost unnatural. But it was also liberating, like breathing fresh air after suffocating in a confined space for too long.

To my surprise, instead of being met with judgment or ridicule,

I was met with understanding, compassion, and empathy. People responded with kindness, offering their support and letting me know that they, too, had their own struggles. They showed me that vulnerability was not a sign of weakness; it was, in fact, a sign of strength. At that moment, I realized that vulnerability is not about being broken or fragile—it is about courage. It takes immense bravery to stand in the truth of who we are and say, "This is me—flaws, fears, and all."

That experience opened my eyes to the transformative power of vulnerability. It revealed to me that hiding behind the facade of perfection and strength only isolates us from others. We may think that by keeping our vulnerabilities concealed, we are protecting ourselves, but in reality, we are only preventing ourselves from forming deep, meaningful connections with those around us. Vulnerability invites others in; it creates a space where we can show up as our authentic selves and where others can do the same.

There is an unparalleled freedom in embracing vulnerability. It liberates us from the constant pressure to be perfect, to have it all together, and to present a version of ourselves that we think others will approve of. When we allow ourselves to be vulnerable, we give ourselves permission to be human—to make mistakes, to experience joy and pain, to grow and evolve. We no longer have to live under the crushing weight of trying to maintain an image of flawlessness. Instead, we can simply be who we are, unfiltered and unashamed.

In sharing our vulnerabilities, we open the door for others to do the same. It creates an environment of mutual understanding, where people feel safe to share their own fears, doubts, and struggles. When we allow ourselves to be vulnerable, we give others permission to be vulnerable too, and in doing so, we create deeper, more authentic relationships. Vulnerability fosters connection, compassion, and empathy. It enables us to relate to others on a deeper level, understanding that we are all navigating life's challenges in our own unique ways, but we are never truly alone in our struggles.

Vulnerability also allows us to heal. When we release the burden of carrying our pain in isolation, we give ourselves the opportunity to process, release, and transform it. Holding on to pain and fear, pretending that everything is fine when it's not, only prolongs our suffering. But when we open up about our struggles—whether to a friend, a therapist, or a loved one—we allow ourselves to begin the process of healing. In sharing our pain, we often discover that others have walked similar paths and can offer wisdom, support, and comfort.

Another powerful aspect of vulnerability is the way it deepens our sense of self-awareness. When we allow ourselves to be honest about our fears, weaknesses, and imperfections, we are not only opening up to others but also to ourselves. We come to terms with the parts of us we have tried to hide or deny, and in doing so, we can begin to accept ourselves as we truly are. This self-acceptance is a crucial step in personal growth. It frees us from the inner critic that tells us we are not enough and allows us to step into our own power, knowing that we are worthy of love and acceptance, flaws and all.

Through vulnerability, we also begin to experience a shift in perspective. Instead of seeing vulnerability as something to fear, we begin to see it as a source of strength. It becomes a tool for growth, transformation, and connection. The more we practice vulnerability, the more we learn to trust ourselves and others, and the more we create a life filled with genuine love, deep relationships, and true fulfillment.

I have come to believe that vulnerability is the key to living an authentic and meaningful life. When we allow ourselves to be vulnerable, we free ourselves from the shackles of perfectionism and self-doubt. We give ourselves the gift of being fully present in our own lives, embracing the beauty of our imperfection. Vulnerability doesn't make us weak—it makes us human, and it is through our humanity that we find the greatest strength.

By sharing our truth, we begin to unravel the shame and fear that hold us back. We begin to rewrite the stories we've been told about ourselves—stories that say we are not enough, that we need to hide our flaws, or that we must keep up appearances at all costs. Instead, we embrace the truth: that we are worthy of love and connection just as we are, flaws and all.

So, let us not be afraid to show up in our full humanity—vulnerable, messy, and imperfect. Let us not be afraid to share our fears, our hopes, and our dreams. In doing so, we invite others to do the same, and together, we can create a world where vulnerability is seen as a strength and not a weakness. A world where we are all free to be our authentic selves, without fear of judgment, rejection, or shame. That is the power of vulnerability—the liberating power to live fully, love deeply, and be true to who we are.

The Myth of Perfection

Perfection is a myth that has been woven into the fabric of our society for generations. It is an ideal that we are told to strive for, something that promises acceptance, success, and happiness. We are bombarded with images of flawless people, perfect lives, and impeccable achievements, both in the media and in our daily interactions. We internalize this message from a young age, and it becomes the standard by which we measure our worth.

But perfection is a lie—a dangerous one. It keeps us trapped in a never-ending cycle of self-doubt and shame. We believe that if we just try hard enough, if we work long enough hours, if we put on the right smile, we can avoid criticism, failure, or pain. We think that by perfecting every aspect of our lives—our appearance, our careers, our relationships—we will be invincible, immune to the discomforts of life. But perfection is not a shield that protects us; it is a cage that confines us.

This cage of perfection is made up of expectations—expectations that are often unrealistic, out of touch with reality, and ultimately harmful. These expectations create a space where we cannot breathe freely. We are constantly striving to meet standards that are impossible to attain, and each time we fall short, we feel like a failure. Instead of embracing our progress, we focus on our perceived flaws, constantly measuring ourselves against an unattainable ideal.

The harder we try to achieve perfection, the more we distance ourselves from our true selves, hiding our imperfections in shame.

But what if, instead of striving for perfection, we chose to embrace our imperfections? What if we stopped running from the parts of ourselves we thought were unworthy, broken, or flawed? What if we recognized that our imperfections are not something to hide or fix, but something to celebrate?

In truth, people are not drawn to perfection. They are drawn to authenticity. It is our authenticity, not our perfection, that connects us to others. We connect with people not through their polished exteriors, but through their shared humanity. It is in the moments of vulnerability—when we show our raw, unpolished selves—that we forge deep, meaningful connections. Our imperfections, our struggles, our scars, and our realness are what make us relatable and human. They are the threads that weave us into the fabric of community, the moments that allow us to say, "I see you. I understand you. I am just like you."

Perfection is a performance, and we all know that performances are scripted. They are designed to impress, to deceive, to create an illusion. But authenticity is not a performance. It is the raw, unscripted version of ourselves—the version that is messy, complicated, and beautiful in its own unique way. It is the version of ourselves that doesn't need to hide behind masks or put on airs. When we embrace our authentic selves, we invite others to do the same.

Brené Brown, a researcher and storyteller who has devoted much of her work to studying vulnerability, courage, and shame, once said, "Vulnerability is not winning or losing; it's having the courage to show up when you can't control the outcome." This quote encapsulates the essence of living authentically. Authenticity is not about presenting a flawless image to the world; it is about showing up, even when we feel exposed, unsure, or afraid. It is about being brave enough to face the world with all of our imperfections and trusting that our humanity is enough.

Living authentically means accepting that we are not perfect and that we never will be. It means embracing the messy parts of our lives—our mistakes, our failures, our flaws—and using them as opportunities for growth. Authenticity means being willing to show up for ourselves and others, even when we feel vulnerable. It means owning our story, regardless of how uncomfortable or imperfect it may be.

When we let go of the myth of perfection, we open ourselves to a life that is more genuine and fulfilling. Instead of chasing an ideal that keeps moving further away from us, we can focus on the present moment, on living with purpose and intention. We can take pride in the journey rather than fixating on a destination that doesn't exist.

Moreover, when we choose authenticity over perfection, we create a safe space for others to do the same. The more we allow ourselves to be vulnerable, the more we invite others to be vulnerable with us. We create a culture of honesty, acceptance, and support, where people are no longer afraid to show up as their true selves.

Embracing our imperfections also allows us to cultivate self-compassion. Perfectionism often comes hand-in-hand with self-criticism. When we fail to meet our own unrealistic standards, we are quick to condemn ourselves, to point out our shortcomings, and to believe that we are not enough. But when we embrace our imperfections, we allow ourselves the grace to learn from our mistakes rather than berate ourselves for them. We begin to see ourselves not as failures, but as works in progress—constantly evolving, constantly learning, and constantly growing.

The truth is that perfection is a moving target. No matter how hard we strive to meet it, we will never arrive at that ideal place where everything is flawless. Life is inherently imperfect, and that imperfection is what makes it so beautiful. It is in the struggle, the messiness, and the rawness of life that we find our strength. It is through our imperfections that we discover what it means to be truly alive.

So, let us abandon the myth of perfection. Let us stop trying to be flawless and start embracing our true selves—our authentic, imperfect, and beautiful selves. Let us show up with courage, knowing that vulnerability is the key to connection, growth, and freedom. When we let go of perfection, we open ourselves to a life that is rich with love, meaning, and purpose. And that, in the end, is far more valuable than any polished image we could ever present.

Vulnerability in Relationships: Bridging the Gap

Relationships are the lifeblood of our emotional well-being. Whether with romantic partners, family members, or close friends, our bonds are shaped by the depth of our connection to one another. At the heart of these relationships lies vulnerability—the willingness to expose the parts of ourselves that are raw, unpolished, and imperfect. However, despite its importance, vulnerability in relationships can often feel like the most terrifying thing we can do. It requires us to let go of control, to trust others with the most intimate pieces of our hearts, and to risk the possibility of being hurt. Yet, it is this very vulnerability that is the key to deep, meaningful, and lasting connections.

The Fear of Vulnerability

For many of us, vulnerability feels like a threat. It is easy to see it as weakness, to associate it with being exposed, judged, or abandoned. We live in a world that often celebrates strength, resilience, and invulnerability. We are taught to put on a brave face, to keep our struggles to ourselves, and to never show signs of emotional fragility. The belief that we must be perfect, unshakable, and self-sufficient can make it difficult to open up to others. There is an inherent fear that if we allow ourselves to be seen—truly seen—people might reject us. We might be perceived as flawed, unworthy, or unlovable.

This fear of vulnerability has a profound impact on the way we interact with those we love. We hold ourselves back, maintaining a distance even from those closest to us. We conceal our true emotions, thoughts, and desires, opting instead to present only what we think others want to see. Over time, this guardedness becomes a barrier, separating us from the deep connection we crave. And though we might feel safe behind these walls, we also feel isolated, lonely, and disconnected.

The Cost of Guardedness

I've experienced this myself, and I know how easy it is to fall into the trap of guardedness. There were years when I believed that if I kept my walls high enough, no one could hurt me. I thought that if I kept my vulnerabilities hidden, I could avoid rejection and preserve my sense of control. But the more I kept people at a distance, the more I began to realize that I was losing something invaluable in the process—authentic connection.

It wasn't just about romantic relationships; it was about every relationship in my life. The walls I built around my heart didn't just protect me from pain—they also kept me from experiencing love, intimacy, and understanding. I feared that if others truly knew me—the real me, the imperfect, flawed, and sometimes broken version of myself—they might walk away. And so, I kept quiet about my fears, my dreams, my past, and my struggles. I created an illusion of strength and self-sufficiency, when in reality, I was yearning for deeper connections.

But the more I stayed guarded, the more I felt the emptiness of isolation creeping in. I missed out on the joy of being seen for who I truly was, flaws and all. I longed for the kind of relationship where I didn't have to hide behind a façade, but could show up authentically, without fear of judgment or rejection. I knew I had to make a change.

The Turning Point: A Leap of Faith

The turning point came when I decided to take a leap of faith. I realized that if I wanted my relationships to evolve and grow, I had to allow myself to be vulnerable. I began by sharing my fears—those deep-rooted, often irrational fears that I had kept locked away for so long. I admitted when I was wrong, instead of always trying to appear perfect or infallible. I allowed myself to ask for help, to show my need for others, and to express my doubts and insecurities.

What I discovered was nothing short of transformative. Each small act of vulnerability brought my relationships to new depths. I felt a sense of liberation in letting go of the need to control every aspect of how I was perceived. And in return, others responded with empathy, understanding, and compassion. People didn't judge me for my imperfections—they celebrated them. They saw me as I truly was and, instead of pushing me away, they embraced me even more deeply. I found myself opening up more and more, and in doing so, I built stronger, more authentic connections.

One of the most profound realizations I had during this

process was that vulnerability is not just about revealing our weaknesses—it is about being open to the full spectrum of human experience. It is about sharing our fears, our dreams, our doubts, and our hopes. It is about acknowledging our pain and our joy, and allowing others to do the same. Vulnerability is a two-way street; it is not just about us exposing ourselves, but about creating space for others to do the same.

The Power of Vulnerability

Vulnerability is not a one-time event; it is a continuous practice, a choice we make each time we interact with others. It is the decision to show up as our true selves, without the masks, without the pretenses. It requires courage—courage to be imperfect, courage to be uncertain, and courage to face the unknown.

In relationships, vulnerability is the bridge that closes the gap between isolation and connection. It is the force that allows us to see each other clearly, without the filters of judgment or expectation. When we are vulnerable, we allow others to see us in our entirety—not just the parts that are easy to love, but the parts that are messy, broken, and unfinished. And in doing so, we create space for others to be vulnerable as well.

There is an immense strength in vulnerability. It is not weakness; it is the most courageous thing we can do. When we allow ourselves to be seen, when we take the risk of being vulnerable, we open ourselves to deeper relationships, more meaningful connections, and a sense of belonging. We move from a place of isolation to one of communion. And in doing so, we find that the very thing we feared the most—the possibility of rejection—becomes the gateway to the love and acceptance we have longed for.

A New Way of Being in Relationships

Vulnerability does not guarantee that we will never be hurt. It doesn't promise that every relationship will thrive or that we will always be understood. But it does promise that we will experience relationships in a new, richer way. It promises that we will be seen for who we are, loved for who we are, and that we will find the connection we seek. Vulnerability is the foundation of authentic relationships, and it is through these relationships that we experience the fullness of life.

By embracing vulnerability, we begin to break down the walls that separate us from each other and from ourselves. We allow ourselves to be human, to be imperfect, and to be loved in spite of—or perhaps because of—our flaws. And in this process, we create relationships that are not only deeper but also more real, more fulfilling, and more enduring.

Vulnerability is not about showing weakness; it is about showing strength—the strength to be seen, to be heard, and to be loved as our true selves. It is the key that unlocks the door to intimacy, connection, and understanding in all of our relationships. It is the bridge that brings us closer to one another and to the fullest experience of what it means to be human.

Leadership Through Vulnerability: Redefining Success

In a world where leadership is often associated with power, authority, and unshakable certainty, vulnerability is frequently seen as a weakness. Leaders are expected to maintain a facade of infallibility—always having the right answers, showing unwavering confidence, and steering their teams with precise control. This image of leadership—rigid, invulnerable, and distant—can be a compelling illusion, but it is also deeply flawed. The truth is that the most effective leaders are not those who hide behind masks of perfection; they are those who lead with authenticity, empathy, and courage. They understand that vulnerability is not a liability but a powerful tool for growth, connection, and transformation.

The Power of Vulnerability in Leadership

Vulnerability in leadership is often misunderstood. It is not about showing weakness or fragility. It is about embracing authenticity and acknowledging that, as humans, we are all imperfect. Leaders who embrace their vulnerability are those who understand that growth doesn't come from pretending to have all the answers, but from the willingness to learn, to fail, and to evolve. By showing their true selves, leaders create an environment where others feel safe to do the same. This openness fosters trust and collaboration, which are critical elements of effective leadership.

When I first started embracing vulnerability in my role, I was unsure of how it would be received. I feared that admitting my struggles, mistakes, or uncertainties would undermine my credibility or authority. But as I began to open up about my own challenges—whether it was navigating difficult decisions, managing personal setbacks, or admitting when I didn't have all the answers—I noticed a shift in the people around me. Instead of feeling disconnected or unsure of my abilities, my team began to see me as more approachable, more relatable, and more human. This shift didn't diminish my leadership; it enhanced it.

Building Trust Through Vulnerability

One of the most significant impacts of vulnerability in leadership is the trust it builds. Trust is the foundation of any successful team or organization. Without trust, people are less likely to be honest, share their ideas, or take risks. Leaders who hide their vulnerabilities create an environment where employees feel like they cannot be open, either out of fear of judgment or the belief that their struggles will be seen as failures. On the other hand, when leaders embrace their own imperfections, they send a powerful message to those around them: "It's okay to not have all the answers, and it's okay to struggle. What matters is that we learn and grow together."

By being vulnerable, leaders create a culture of psychological safety—an environment where team members feel comfortable expressing their thoughts, admitting mistakes, and asking for help. This openness allows for deeper collaboration, better problem-solving, and stronger relationships. When people feel that they are trusted and supported, they are more likely to take initiative, contribute their ideas, and go above and beyond in their work.

The Myth of Perfection in Leadership

The myth of the perfect leader is a trap that many fall into. Perfection is an unattainable and often unrealistic standard, and yet so many leaders feel pressured to present themselves as flawless. This drive for perfection can be paralyzing—it leads to overthinking, indecision, and an unwillingness to take risks. Perfectionism also stifles creativity and innovation because it fosters an environment where mistakes are seen as failures rather than opportunities for learning.

Leadership is not about being perfect; it is about being human. It is about embracing our flaws and using them as a source of strength. When leaders accept their own imperfections, they give others the permission to do the same. This creates a culture where growth is valued over perfection, where mistakes are seen as stepping stones, and where innovation is encouraged because it is understood that failure is part of the process.

Rather than demanding perfection from ourselves and our teams, we should focus on progress and development. Leadership should be about leading with integrity, being open to feedback, and showing resilience in the face of challenges. It is about having the humility to admit when we don't know something, the courage to learn, and the wisdom to guide others through uncertainty.

Connection Over Control

At its core, leadership is about connection. It is not about exerting control over others or maintaining a facade of authority; it is about building relationships based on trust, respect, and mutual understanding. Leaders who embrace vulnerability are able to create deeper connections with their teams because they are willing to share their authentic selves. This creates an atmosphere where people feel seen, heard, and valued—not just for their work but for who they are as individuals.

When we show up as our true selves, we invite others to do the same. This creates a space where people feel safe to express their ideas, challenges, and emotions. It fosters a culture of inclusivity, where everyone's voice matters, and every person is encouraged to bring their full selves to the table. Connection, rather than control, becomes the driving force of effective leadership.

The most successful leaders are not those who dominate conversations or make decisions from a place of power; they are those who listen, collaborate, and empower others. They recognize that leadership is not about having all the answers; it is about creating an environment where everyone feels valued and supported in their journey of growth and development.

Redefining Success in Leadership

Traditional definitions of success in leadership often focus on achieving results, driving performance, and maintaining control. But I believe that true success as a leader goes beyond metrics and outcomes. It lies in the relationships we build, the trust we foster, and the growth we facilitate in others. Success as a leader is not about being perfect—it is about being present, authentic, and courageous in our vulnerability.

When we lead with vulnerability, we create a ripple effect that extends far beyond our immediate teams. We inspire others to be brave, to speak their truth, and to show up as their authentic selves. We redefine what it means to succeed, moving away from the illusion of perfection and embracing the power of connection, empathy, and authenticity.

Leadership through vulnerability is not just about what we give; it is also about what we receive. By being open, we not only foster a culture of growth and trust, but we also deepen our own understanding of ourselves and others. We learn from our mistakes, build resilience in the face of challenges, and become more compassionate and effective leaders.

The Courage to Lead Authentically

True leadership requires the courage to be authentic. It requires the willingness to embrace imperfection and to lead from a place of openness and vulnerability. When we do this, we not only become more effective leaders, but we also create a legacy of compassion, empathy, and growth.

The most effective leaders are those who are not afraid to

show their humanity—who are willing to admit when they don't have all the answers, who are open to feedback, and who lead by example in creating environments where others feel safe to do the same. This type of leadership fosters deeper connections, stronger teams, and a more authentic and fulfilling sense of success.

In the end, leadership through vulnerability is not just about what we accomplish; it is about how we make others feel. It is about creating spaces where people can thrive, grow, and be their true selves. When we lead with vulnerability, we redefine success as the ability to build meaningful connections, foster trust, and inspire others to embrace their own authenticity. And in doing so, we change not just the way we lead, but the way we live.

The Healing Journey: Turning Pain Into Power

Pain is a universal experience, an inevitable part of the human condition that transcends all boundaries—whether physical, emotional, or mental. It comes for all of us in various forms: the grief of losing someone we love, the heartache of a broken relationship, the weight of unmet expectations, or the quiet suffering that lingers in the depths of our own minds. In those moments of pain, it is easy to feel as though we are alone, as though no one else could possibly understand the depths of what we are going through. Pain, especially when it feels overwhelming, has a way of isolating us, making us feel like we are trapped in a world where our suffering is uniquely our own.

But here's the truth: pain is not an isolating force; it is a shared experience. It is a part of life that connects us all. We may not always see it, but in our collective struggles, there is an unspoken bond that holds us together. And it is through facing pain with courage and vulnerability that we can transform it into something powerful. It is through this process that we begin to see pain not as a curse, but as a catalyst for growth, healing, and transformation.

The Weight of Pain

There was a time when I thought my pain defined me. I believed it was a weight I had to carry with no end in sight, a constant reminder of my failures, losses, and the wounds that seemed to never heal. In the past, I would hide behind distractions—busyness, numbness, and denial—to avoid confronting the deep ache within me. It was easier to put on a brave face, to keep moving forward, to act as though everything was okay when inside, I was falling apart.

At the time, I saw my pain as something that held me back, something that kept me stuck in a perpetual state of sorrow and regret. I didn't know how to let go of it or what to do with it. All I knew was that it hurt, and I longed for it to end. But over time, as I faced my pain head-on, I began to understand that it didn't define me—it was simply a part of my journey. I learned that my pain was not a mark of failure or weakness, but rather a doorway to something deeper.

Pain as a Catalyst for Growth

Slowly but surely, I began to see my pain differently. I realized that it wasn't just something to endure or escape—it was a powerful teacher. Pain had the ability to shake me to my core, to strip away the masks I had worn for so long, and to force me to confront the parts of myself I had been avoiding. It became a mirror, reflecting the areas of my life that needed healing, growth, and change.

Rather than seeing pain as an obstacle to my happiness, I began to understand that it was an invitation to grow. Pain, when faced with openness and vulnerability, became a source of strength. It taught me resilience. It pushed me to face my fears, to confront my demons, and to look inward for the healing I had long been seeking. It urged me to stop running from the hurt and to lean into it, to sit with it, and to allow it to transform me.

Healing, I learned, is not a destination but a journey. It is a continuous process that unfolds in unexpected ways. There are no shortcuts or quick fixes. It is messy, unpredictable, and often painful. But it is in that messiness that we find the beauty of transformation. It is in the discomfort of healing that we discover our inner strength and resilience.

The Messiness of Healing

Healing is not linear. It is not a simple, straight path from pain to peace. Instead, it is filled with twists and turns, setbacks, and moments of doubt. There are days when the pain feels unbearable, when the progress we've made seems to unravel, and when we question whether healing is even possible. There are days when we feel like we're taking two steps forward and five steps back. But this, too, is part of the journey.

It is easy to become disheartened when healing doesn't happen as quickly as we'd like, when the wounds don't seem to heal as neatly as we expect. But it is precisely in these moments that our resilience is forged. Healing teaches us patience, and it teaches us grace. It shows us that it is okay to not have everything figured out, that it's okay to stumble, to fall, and to feel lost at times. What matters is that we keep going, even when it feels like we're not making any progress. Every small step forward, no matter how insignificant it may seem, is a victory. Every moment we choose to rise above the pain, to keep showing up for ourselves, is a testament to our strength.

Turning Pain Into Power

What I've come to realize is that pain is not something to be feared or avoided. It is not a force that diminishes us; it is a force that has the potential to empower us. When we allow ourselves to fully experience our pain, without running from it or numbing it, we unlock the power within ourselves to heal. We learn that we are stronger than we thought, that we are capable of enduring more than we imagined, and that our pain does not define us—it refines us.

Through my own healing journey, I have learned that our greatest power often comes from the places we are most afraid to go. The pain we try to avoid is the very thing that can set us free. By leaning into our pain, we learn the lessons we need to learn and emerge stronger, wiser, and more compassionate. We become more connected to ourselves and to others. Our scars become symbols of our resilience, not signs of defeat.

In my journey, I've discovered that healing isn't just about the end result. It's about what we learn along the way. It's about the person we become as we navigate through the darkness, as we face our fears, and as we allow ourselves to feel the full range of our emotions. Healing is not just a process of repairing what's broken—it is a process of becoming who we were always meant to be. Pain, in its rawest form, holds the power to awaken us, to help us step into our full potential.

The Power of Resilience

Resilience is not about never feeling pain; it is about finding the strength to rise in the face of it. It is about choosing to continue moving forward, even when life feels heavy. It is about understanding that we are not defined by our pain, but by how we respond to it. Resilience is about learning to transform our wounds into wisdom, our struggles into strength, and our fears into courage.

As we move through the healing journey, we must remember that we are not alone. Our pain connects us to the collective human experience. Every person we meet is carrying their own struggles, their own pain. And in this shared experience, we find solidarity. We find the courage to be vulnerable, to lean on others, and to offer compassion in return. The power of healing is not just in the individual process but in the way we support one another, lifting each other up as we move toward wholeness.

The healing journey is one of transformation. It is about turning pain into power, about using our experiences to fuel our growth, and about emerging from the darkness with a renewed sense of purpose and strength. It is not easy, and it is not quick, but it is worth every step. Because in the end, healing is not about perfection—it is about embracing our scars, owning our journey, and celebrating the strength we've gained along the way.

The Ripple Effect of Vulnerability

Vulnerability is a force that ripples outward, touching not just our lives but the lives of those around us. When we choose to step into the unknown, to expose our true selves, to embrace our flaws and fears, we unknowingly create a space for others to do the same. Vulnerability, when practiced authentically, becomes contagious. It invites others to lower their walls, to shed their masks, and to show up in their most raw, unguarded forms. The ripple effect of vulnerability is profound—it not only deepens our connections with others but also transforms entire communities, cultures, and societies.

The act of being vulnerable is revolutionary. In a world that often celebrates perfection, control, and self-sufficiency, vulnerability stands in stark contrast. It challenges the notion that strength is found in the ability to be flawless, unshakable, and invulnerable. Instead, vulnerability teaches us that true strength lies in our willingness to be seen as we truly are, to embrace our imperfections, and to share our struggles with others. It is a bold act of courage, and it has the power to change the way we interact with one another, the way we view ourselves, and the way we engage with the world.

Breaking Down Walls

When we allow ourselves to be vulnerable, we break down the invisible walls that separate us from others. These walls are built over time, often out of fear, shame, or a desire to protect ourselves from judgment or rejection. But these walls also isolate us, preventing genuine connection and understanding. They create an illusion of safety, but in reality, they only serve to keep us further apart.

Vulnerability shatters these walls. It creates a space where authenticity can flourish, where people can come together in their shared humanity. When one person dares to be vulnerable, others feel invited to do the same. They no longer need to hide behind facades or pretend to be someone they're not. They can show up as they are, flaws and all. This openness allows for deeper, more meaningful connections—connections that transcend surface-level interactions and move into the realm of true understanding and empathy.

The power of vulnerability is that it creates a sense of belonging. When we let others see our struggles and vulnerabilities, we invite them to see us for who we truly are. This invitation to authenticity creates a shared space of trust and compassion, where judgment is replaced by understanding and support. Vulnerability fosters a sense of safety, a space where people feel that they are not alone in their struggles, and where they can begin to heal.

Inspiring Others to Share Their Stories

The beauty of vulnerability is that it inspires others to share their stories as well. We all have stories, experiences, and struggles that we carry with us. But often, we hesitate to share them because we fear rejection, ridicule, or judgment. We fear that by exposing our true selves, we will be met with criticism or misunderstanding. But when one person steps forward and chooses to be vulnerable, it gives others permission to do the same. It shows them that they, too, can speak their truth, without fear of being silenced or dismissed.

Every time we choose to be vulnerable, we break the silence surrounding the things we often hide—our pain, our fears, our insecurities. And in doing so, we create a culture where others feel safe to share their own vulnerabilities. The act of vulnerability becomes a catalyst for healing, not just for ourselves but for others as well. It creates a space where people feel supported, seen, and heard. And this is where the ripple effect begins.

When we share our vulnerabilities, we give others the opportunity to connect with us on a deeper level. They see that they are not alone in their struggles. They realize that their pain, their challenges, their fears are not unique to them but are shared by others. This realization has the power to heal—not just ourselves but others. It creates a sense of solidarity, a sense of shared humanity that transcends differences and unites us all in our common experiences.

Changing the Narrative of Strength

One of the most profound ways that vulnerability creates a ripple effect is by challenging the traditional narrative of strength. For so long, we have been conditioned to believe that strength means being invulnerable, that true strength is found in the ability to hold everything together and never show weakness. Vulnerability, however, redefines what it means to be strong. It teaches us that strength is not about perfection or invincibility; it is about the courage to be seen, to show up, and to stand tall in the face of our fears and insecurities.

Vulnerability is the truest form of strength. It requires immense courage to be vulnerable, to let down our defenses and allow others to see our most authentic selves. In a world that often rewards stoicism and emotional suppression, choosing vulnerability is an act of defiance. It is a refusal to conform to the expectations placed upon us by society, a refusal to hide our true selves behind a mask of perfection.

When we embrace vulnerability as a strength, we not only

redefine what it means to be strong—we also create a space for others to do the same. We show them that it is okay to be imperfect, to struggle, to not have all the answers. We remind them that their worth is not defined by their ability to appear strong or invulnerable, but by their willingness to be authentic, to show up as they are, and to share their struggles with others.

Creating a World Where Authenticity is Celebrated

In a world where superficiality often reigns, vulnerability is a radical act of authenticity. When we allow ourselves to be vulnerable, we invite others to do the same. We create a space where authenticity is celebrated, where imperfections are embraced, and where people are free to be themselves without fear of judgment or rejection. This is the world we have the power to create—a world where vulnerability is not seen as a weakness, but as a source of strength.

Vulnerability has the power to change the way we see ourselves and others. It invites us to stop hiding behind masks and to show up as our true, unfiltered selves. It challenges us to move past the façade of perfection and to embrace the beauty of our imperfections. In a world that often values surface-level appearances, vulnerability calls us to look deeper, to connect on a soul level, and to see the humanity in everyone we encounter.

When we choose vulnerability, we are not just changing our own lives—we are changing the lives of those around us. We are creating a culture where people feel safe to be their authentic selves, where they feel supported in their struggles, and where they are encouraged to embrace their imperfections. We are building a world where vulnerability is not feared, but celebrated. A world where authenticity reigns, and where we are all empowered to show up as our true selves.

Becoming Change-Makers Through Vulnerability

Ultimately, vulnerability is a tool for change. When we choose to be vulnerable, we become change-makers. We challenge the status quo, disrupt the norms, and pave the way for a new way of being. We redefine what it means to be strong, and in doing so, we create a space for others to do the same.

Vulnerability has the power to transform not just individuals but entire communities. It brings people together in their shared humanity, creating connections that are deep, meaningful, and healing. It breaks down the walls that divide us and creates a sense of unity, of togetherness, of belonging. And it is through this shared vulnerability that we can begin to change the world.

So, let us embrace vulnerability, not just as an individual practice but as a collective force. Let us choose to be open, to be real, to be authentic. Let us create a world where vulnerability is celebrated, where our shared struggles become a source of strength, and where we all have the courage to show up as our true selves. Because in the end, it is through vulnerability that we can begin to heal, to connect, and to create the change we wish to see in the world.

The Indomitable Spirit: Rising From the Ashes

Vulnerability is not something to shy away from or conceal—it is the very essence of our strength. It is the gateway to authenticity, the bridge that connects us to others, and the catalyst for profound transformation. In a world that often values perfection, control, and invulnerability, we may be led to believe that vulnerability is a flaw. Yet, it is vulnerability that reveals our deepest humanity, and it is through this authenticity that we find our true power.

Vulnerability is a double-edged sword: on one hand, it exposes our wounds, our fears, and our scars. But on the other, it provides us with the opportunity to heal, to connect, and to evolve. It is the moment we take the leap to face our deepest truths, acknowledging our fragility and embracing it, that we unlock a wellspring of resilience, strength, and courage. It is only by stepping into our vulnerability that we can rise from the ashes of past pain and heartache, transforming into the indomitable beings we are meant to be.

The Power of Vulnerability

Vulnerability is the opposite of weakness. It is not an admission of defeat, nor a sign of fragility. Instead, it is a recognition of our humanity, an acceptance of the messy, beautiful complexity that makes us who we are. When we embrace vulnerability, we stop running from our fears, our imperfections, and our past mistakes. Instead, we allow ourselves to show up, to be seen, and to be heard for who we truly are. And in doing so, we not only heal ourselves but also inspire others to do the same.

It is through vulnerability that we tap into our true power. The journey to self-discovery, to healing, and to transformation begins when we accept that we are not defined by our failures, our scars, or our struggles—but by how we choose to rise in the face of them. Each time we fall, each time we face hardship or setback, we have the choice to stay down or to rise again. And in every rise, we become stronger, more resilient, and more authentic.

Embracing the Messy, Imperfect Truth

In a society that often prizes perfection, it can be easy to fall into the trap of thinking that we must always present a flawless, unshakeable image. We strive to maintain control, to project an image of success and invulnerability, fearing that any cracks in our facade will make us appear weak or inadequate. But the truth is, perfection is an illusion. It does not exist in the real world, and it certainly does not exist within us.

The beauty of vulnerability is that it invites us to embrace the messy, imperfect truth of who we are. It is only by shedding the expectation of perfection that we can truly be free to be ourselves. The power lies not in crafting a perfect version of ourselves, but in accepting and loving the version that is real—the version that carries both light and shadow, triumphs and failures, joy and pain.

Our scars, our mistakes, and our imperfections are not flaws to hide but badges of honor that reflect our journey, our growth, and our resilience. They are a testament to the battles we've fought, the tears we've shed, and the strength we've gained along the way. When we embrace these parts of ourselves, we give others permission to do the same. We create a culture of authenticity, where people are no longer bound by the expectations of perfection, but are free to be their true selves.

The Courage to Rise

The most powerful aspect of vulnerability is not in our ability to endure pain, but in our capacity to rise every time we fall. Life is full of challenges, setbacks, and heartache, and it is easy to become discouraged. There are times when the weight of the world feels unbearable, and it seems like the pain will never subside. Yet, it is in those very moments that our true strength is revealed.

Rising from the ashes is not about pretending that the pain does not exist. It is not about denying our struggles or minimizing our wounds. Rather, it is about acknowledging our pain, feeling it fully, and then choosing to rise despite it. Every time we choose to stand up, to keep moving forward, we are embracing our power. Every time we choose to face our fears, to speak our truth, and to move beyond our comfort zone, we are growing stronger.

Rising is not a one-time event—it is a continual process. It is the decision to keep going, even when the path seems uncertain. It is the willingness to fall, to stumble, and to fail, and then to rise again, learning from each experience. It is in the act of rising that we discover the depth of our resilience and the breadth of our strength.

Healing Through Vulnerability

When we embrace vulnerability, we open ourselves up to the possibility of healing. Pain is a natural part of the human experience, but when we suppress it or hide from it, we only prolong the healing process. Vulnerability allows us to face our pain head-on, to acknowledge its presence, and to process it in a way that leads to growth.

Healing is not linear—it is a messy, unpredictable process. It involves facing uncomfortable truths, allowing ourselves to grieve, and giving ourselves permission to feel the full range of human emotions. But in this messiness lies the beauty of healing. Each tear shed, each painful step taken, is an act of bravery. It is a reminder that we are alive, that we are human, and that we are worthy of healing.

Through vulnerability, we can also heal others. When we share our pain, our struggles, and our journeys, we invite others to heal with us. We create a space where it is safe to be vulnerable, where people can connect through their shared humanity. In this shared vulnerability, we discover the power of collective healing. Our pain no longer feels isolating—it becomes a bridge that connects us to others and reminds us that we are not alone.

The Superpower of Vulnerability

At its core, vulnerability is a superpower. It is the strength to be real, to face our fears, and to embrace our imperfections. It is the courage to show up, even when we are uncertain, exposed, or afraid. It is the resilience to keep going, even when the world feels heavy, and the faith to rise every time we fall.

Vulnerability is the key to unlocking the fullest expression of ourselves. It allows us to live authentically, to connect deeply with others, and to experience the beauty and richness of life. When we embrace our vulnerability, we unlock our true power. And in doing so, we become unstoppable—indomitable, like a phoenix rising from the ashes.

A Call to Action: Embrace Your Vulnerability

To those who fear vulnerability, I offer this: Your strength lies not in hiding your scars but in wearing them proudly. Your courage lies not in being unbreakable but in choosing to rise every time you fall. And your power lies not in perfection but in the beautiful, messy, and imperfect truth of who you are.

Embrace your vulnerability. It is your superpower. It is through your vulnerability that you will find your strength, your authenticity, and your purpose. And as you rise, you will inspire others to rise with you. Together, we can create a world where vulnerability is not seen as a weakness, but as the ultimate strength. A world where we all embrace our scars, our stories, and our humanity—where we rise from the ashes, stronger than ever before.

7

Chapter 6: Living Authentically and Fearlessly

The Call to Live Authentically

At some point in our lives, many of us are confronted with a powerful realization—a moment of reckoning that demands our attention. It's the undeniable truth that the life we are living, although it might appear successful to the outside world, is not fully ours. It's as if we are going through the motions, playing a role in a script that was never written by us. This script is handed down by society, by our families, our peers, or by the cultures we inhabit. It defines who we are supposed to be, how we should behave, and what success should look like. The problem, however, is that as we follow this script, something feels off, like we're wearing a mask that doesn't fit or walking a path that doesn't truly resonate with our soul.

I've experienced this profound shift firsthand. I've walked

through periods of my life where I felt like I was living according to a version of success that wasn't truly mine. For years, I tried to meet the expectations of others—being the daughter who always made everyone proud, the nurse who never showed weakness, the mother who seemed to have it all together. I wore those roles with pride, and yet, inside, I often felt a gnawing emptiness. It was a feeling that no amount of accolades, achievements, or praise could fill. I was doing what I thought I was supposed to do, but deep down, I was not fully living my truth. I was pretending to be someone I wasn't, trying to fit into a mold that others had shaped for me, and I realized I was sacrificing parts of myself in the process.

This is where the call to live authentically begins. It's a call that speaks to the core of our being. It's the pull that urges us to stop pretending, to stop conforming to the expectations of others, and to step into the fullness of who we truly are. It's a radical shift—a decision to stop hiding behind the masks we've been taught to wear, to unlearn the scripts that no longer serve us, and to stand proudly in our own truth. Living authentically doesn't mean we will be perfect, nor does it require us to have every area of our lives figured out. Instead, it's about showing up as we are, flaws and all. It's about embracing every part of ourselves—the parts we love and the parts we struggle with—and allowing ourselves to be seen in our most genuine form.

Living authentically means making the brave choice to let go of the need to please everyone or to fit into someone else's idea of who we should be. It's about giving ourselves the grace to be imperfect, to make mistakes, and to learn along the way. It's about understanding that we are worthy of love and acceptance *exactly as we are*—not for the roles we play, the accolades we accumulate, or the standards we meet, but simply for the unique and beautiful person that we are at our core.

The Struggle to Be Authentic

The process of stepping into authenticity requires courage. It means unlearning the patterns we've been taught and shedding the layers of identity that no longer serve us. There were times when I struggled with the idea of releasing these roles, especially when they had defined my self-worth for so long. The thought of being "less than" or "not enough" without these external validations haunted me. What I didn't realize then was that the very essence of who I am lies beneath those roles.

Living authentically doesn't mean that we abandon responsibilities or the values that are important to us. Instead, it's about approaching life from a place of self-acceptance and honesty. It's about aligning our actions, words, and choices with what feels true to our core. It's realizing that we don't need to fit a mold to be worthy of love, respect, or success. And that we can find beauty in the messiness of life, knowing that imperfection is part of our human experience.

In my journey, I came to understand that living authentically is not a destination, but rather a continuous practice. It's an ongoing process of checking in with myself, questioning where I might be playing small or hiding out of fear, and consciously choosing to stand in my truth, even when it feels uncomfortable. It's understanding that the fear of rejection or failure will always be present, but that it doesn't have to control my actions. I had to learn to lean into the discomfort, knowing that the rewards of living authentically far outweigh the temporary discomfort of stepping outside of my comfort zone.

The beauty of authenticity is that it allows us to connect more deeply with others. When we stop hiding behind masks and start showing up as our true selves, we create space for others to do the same. It fosters genuine connections, rooted in vulnerability, understanding, and shared experiences. And this is where the magic happens—the space where healing, growth, and transformation occur.

Being authentic is about trusting that we are enough, just as we are. It's about embracing all parts of ourselves—the light and the dark—and understanding that we are worthy of love, success, and happiness, regardless of how perfectly we measure up to society's standards. It's about reclaiming our power and our voice, and letting go of the need for validation from external sources.

The journey to authenticity isn't easy. It's messy, uncomfortable, and often filled with doubt. But it's also deeply rewarding. It leads us to a life that is truly ours—a life that is filled with purpose, passion, and a deep sense of fulfillment. And in embracing our authentic selves, we find the strength to rise above the fears and limitations that once held us back. We discover that the power to shape our own narrative lies within us, and that, no matter what we've been through, we are more than enough.

So, if you're feeling stuck, unsure, or overwhelmed by the thought of living authentically, know that you are not alone. It's okay to take small steps, to stumble along the way, and to embrace the imperfections that come with this journey. The struggle is part of the process, and in the end, it will lead you to the most powerful version of yourself. Don't be afraid to let go of the roles that no longer serve you, and allow yourself the freedom to be who you truly are. Because in the end, your authentic self is the one that deserves to shine the brightest.

Breaking Free from Conformity

Choosing authenticity over conformity is not about rejecting societal norms or the values of others; it's about recognizing the importance of honoring your own truth, even when it's different from what the world expects. The pressure to conform often stems from a desire to fit in, to be accepted, and to avoid standing out. It's easy to fall into the trap of thinking that our worth is tied to meeting external expectations. But what I've come to understand is that true fulfillment doesn't come from adhering to a predefined standard; it comes from breaking free from those constraints and creating your own definition of success and happiness.

Living authentically means questioning the assumptions that have shaped your life. It's about looking at the beliefs, habits, and patterns you've adopted over time and asking yourself: *Are these truly mine? Or have I been living according to someone else's script?* For me, this was one of the most powerful shifts I made—becoming the author of my own story, instead of letting others dictate how I should live it. It meant confronting the fear of judgment, the fear of rejection, and the fear of not being good enough. But as I leaned into those fears, I realized that they were only holding me back from the life I was meant to live.

The process of breaking free from conformity doesn't happen overnight. It's a gradual journey of shedding the layers of expectation and pressure that have been placed upon us, and allowing ourselves to breathe and grow. It's about embracing our imperfections and flaws, recognizing that they are part of what makes us unique and beautiful. And it's about realizing that we don't have to be perfect to be worthy of love, success, and happiness.

There were times in my journey when I doubted my decision to live authentically. The temptation to fall back into the comfort of conformity was strong, especially when I faced criticism or disapproval from others. But each time I chose to stay true to myself, I grew stronger and more confident in my ability to navigate the unknown. And with each step, I realized that the discomfort I was experiencing was not something to be feared; it was something to be embraced. It was in that discomfort that I found the courage to keep going, to keep evolving, and to keep pushing forward.

Living authentically requires a deep sense of trust in yourself and in the process of life. It means letting go of the need for external validation and choosing to trust that you are enough, just as you are. It means choosing to prioritize your own happiness and well-being, even when others may not understand or approve. It means recognizing that your path is your own, and that you have the power to shape it in a way that aligns with your deepest values and desires.

In my own life, breaking free from conformity has opened up doors I never thought possible. It has allowed me to step into a version of myself that is stronger, more resilient, and more connected to my true purpose. And while the journey has not always been easy, it has been incredibly rewarding. Each step I take towards authenticity brings me closer to the person I am meant to be, and each step I take away from conformity brings me closer to the life I am meant to live.

So, if you're feeling the pull to break free from conformity, know that it's okay to take it one step at a time. It's okay to be uncomfortable. It's okay to make mistakes along the way. What matters is that you stay true to yourself and your journey, no matter how difficult it may seem. The world may try to pull you in different directions, but remember that your voice, your truth, and your happiness are worth fighting for. Don't let the pressure to conform dim your light. Trust in your own path, and know that as you embrace your authenticity, you will find the peace and fulfillment you've been searching for.

The Freedom of Authenticity

The freedom that comes with authenticity is one of the most liberating experiences we can have in this life. It's the freedom to let go of the masks we wear, the roles we've been conditioned to play, and the expectations others have placed upon us. It's the freedom to stop pretending and to fully embrace who we are—flaws, quirks, strengths, and all. Living authentically means giving ourselves permission to exist without the constant need to fit into a mold, to meet a certain standard, or to seek approval from anyone but ourselves.

In this space of authenticity, we stop measuring our worth by external benchmarks. We stop comparing ourselves to others, and we stop chasing after things that don't align with our true desires. Instead, we begin to measure our success by how aligned our actions are with our values. We find satisfaction not in pleasing others or meeting their expectations, but in knowing that we are living according to our own truths. This shift in perspective allows us to experience a deeper sense of peace and fulfillment, because we are no longer driven by fear or the need for validation.

As we embrace our authentic selves, we also become more resilient. Life becomes less about avoiding failure or seeking perfection and more about embracing growth and transformation. Mistakes are no longer seen as setbacks but as opportunities for learning and evolution. We begin to trust ourselves more, knowing that we have the strength and wisdom to navigate whatever comes our way. With this newfound trust comes the confidence to make bold decisions, take risks, and pursue our dreams without hesitation or fear of judgment.

The freedom of authenticity also allows us to experience deeper, more meaningful relationships. When we are authentic, we attract people who resonate with our true selves, rather than those who are drawn to a version of us that is based on pretense. These connections are built on mutual respect, understanding, and vulnerability. We can show up as we are, without fear of rejection, and allow others to do the same. This creates a space for genuine connection, where both parties can grow, support one another, and share in the beauty of life's journey.

Living authentically also frees us from the constant pressure to be someone we're not. It's easy to fall into the trap of trying to fit in, especially in a world that often values conformity over individuality. But when we let go of the need to conform, we tap into a power that is uniquely our own. We no longer feel like we're walking a path that was designed for someone else; we are walking our own path, one that is aligned with our soul's purpose. This journey is not always easy, but it is always worth it.

There is a quiet strength in being authentic. It takes courage to stand firm in who we are, to honor our own truth, and to let go of the fear of being misunderstood or criticized. But with each step we take toward authenticity, we create a life that is deeply meaningful and fulfilling. We find that the more we embrace our true selves, the more peace we experience. We are no longer burdened by the weight of others' expectations or the need to prove our worth. Instead, we walk in the freedom that comes from knowing we are enough, just as we are.

So, if you are feeling the call to live more authentically, take a moment to listen to that inner voice. Trust that you are worthy of living a life that is true to yourself. Embrace the discomfort that may come with shedding old identities, and let go of the fear that has held you back. You are the creator of your own life, and in choosing authenticity, you open the door to limitless possibilities. The freedom to be yourself is a gift that only you can give yourself, and once you fully embrace it, you will never look back.

A Call to Action: Step Into Your Truth

The call to live authentically is a call to embrace who you truly are, without fear or shame. It is a challenge to stop hiding behind the roles, the labels, and the scripts that others have written for you, and to start writing your own story. It is an invitation to stand in your truth, to honor your journey, and to show up in the world exactly as you are—flaws, struggles, and all.

If you are reading this and feel the stirrings of this truth inside you, I encourage you to listen. Take a moment to reflect on the life you are living and ask yourself: Is this truly my life? Is this the life I want to lead, or is it a version of success that I've inherited from others? If the answer is no, then it's time to make a change. Start small, take one step at a time, but above all, be brave enough to step into the unknown.

Living authentically is not an easy path, but it is the most rewarding one. It's the path to freedom, to peace, and to true fulfillment. It's the path to becoming the person you were always meant to be. And as you step into that truth, you will not only find your own freedom—you will inspire others to do the same.

So, I call on you today: Let go of the masks. Unlearn the scripts. And step into the fullness of who you were always meant to be. This is your life. Live it authentically.

Why We Stray From Authenticity

From the moment we are born, we are hardwired to seek connection. As human beings, we are inherently social creatures, and the need for love, approval, and acceptance from those around us becomes a fundamental part of our emotional survival. As children, our primary focus is often to be accepted and loved by our caregivers, peers, and society at large. This drive to belong is woven into the very fabric of who we are. Early on, we are taught that fitting in is essential, that the approval of others is the pathway to security. These lessons, whether overt or subtle, are ingrained in us from a young age, shaping the way we view ourselves and the world around us.

As we grow, this conditioning intensifies. Society, in all its complexities, presents us with numerous expectations—standards of beauty, success, and behavior that we are encouraged to follow. We are taught how to act, what to wear, what to say, and who to be. The message is clear: If we conform, we will be loved and accepted. If we do not, we risk being left out, misunderstood, or worse, rejected.

Over time, this social conditioning becomes so deeply ingrained that it begins to feel like an invisible force guiding our every action. We begin to make decisions not based on what we truly desire but on what we believe will gain us approval from others. Slowly, this desire for acceptance can overshadow our own needs, hopes, and dreams. In the process, we lose sight of who we truly are and what we truly want, becoming more concerned with how we are perceived than with the authenticity of our existence.

When we begin to step outside the boundaries of this conditioned behavior—when we dare to show our true selves—something inside us hesitates. A quiet voice within asks, "What if they don't like me? What if they reject me? What if I fail? What if I'm not enough?" This voice is the voice of fear, and it often holds more power over us than the call of our true selves. Fear of rejection, of being misunderstood, and of not measuring up to the expectations of others becomes the invisible chain that binds us to conformity. It paralyzes us, making it difficult to break free and show up as our true selves.

I, too, have known this struggle. For years, I lived in the shadow of fear. Fear of rejection. Fear of being judged. Fear of failing. These fears were my constant companions, shaping every decision I made. I felt like I had to live up to the expectations of others to be loved, to be respected, and to be accepted. I played the role of the "good daughter," the "perfect nurse," and the "ideal mother." I believed these roles defined me. I believed that by fitting into these boxes, I would be worthy of love and approval.

But the truth is, I was suffocating under the weight of these roles. I was living a life that wasn't truly mine. The more I tried to meet the expectations of others, the more disconnected I became from my true self. I had to suppress my feelings, my dreams, and my individuality to please those around me. I became a master at wearing masks, but underneath it all, I felt hollow. I felt like an imposter in my own life. There was a constant sense of dissatisfaction, a gnawing feeling that I was living someone else's life, not my own.

It wasn't until I reached a point of exhaustion—emotionally, mentally, and physically—that I realized something had to change. I couldn't continue to live a life dictated by others' expectations. I had to reclaim my own voice, my own desires, and my own truth. And in that moment, I made a decision: I would no longer live for others. I would no longer hide behind the masks of who I thought I was supposed to be. I would show up as myself, in all my imperfections, with all my dreams and flaws, unapologetically.

The Cost of Conformity

The price of conformity is high. When we live our lives based on the expectations of others, we sacrifice our authenticity. We suppress our true selves to fit into the mold that society has created for us. But the toll this takes is immense. Over time, we lose touch with our passions, our values, and our true purpose. We become disconnected from the very essence of who we are, and in doing so, we invite dissatisfaction, frustration, and a sense of emptiness into our lives.

We may have outward success, we may be fulfilling the roles that others expect of us, but inside, we feel like something is missing. We may have achieved the accolades, the recognition, and the approval we once sought, but none of it feels truly fulfilling. This is because we are living a life based on someone else's script. And when we do that, we can never truly feel whole. We can never experience the deep sense of fulfillment that comes from living in alignment with our true selves.

The more we conform, the more we lose sight of who we were meant to be. We forget the dreams we had before society told us they were impossible. We forget the passions that once fueled us before we became too focused on meeting external expectations. We forget the beautiful, imperfect, and unique qualities that make us who we are. Instead of living life from a place of authenticity, we live it from a place of fear—fear of rejection, fear of failure, fear of being judged.

Breaking Free: The Power of Authenticity

To live authentically means breaking free from the chains of fear and societal expectations. It means rejecting the scripts we've been handed and writing our own story. It means stepping into our power and embracing our unique truth, no matter how messy, imperfect, or unconventional it may be.

Living authentically is not about being perfect. It's not about fitting into any one mold or conforming to anyone's idea of who we should be. It's about showing up as we are—flawed, vulnerable, and human—and accepting ourselves fully. It's about letting go of the fear that holds us back and embracing the freedom to be ourselves, without apology.

When we choose authenticity, we reclaim our power. We stop living for others and start living for ourselves. We stop measuring our worth by external standards and begin to measure it by our own values and truth. This is where true fulfillment lies. It is in the freedom to be ourselves, unapologetically, without the need for approval or validation. It is in living a life that is aligned with our deepest desires, our passions, and our purpose.

The Call to Step Into Your Authenticity

If you find yourself trapped in the cycle of conformity, I encourage you to listen closely to the whispers of your soul. What have you been suppressing? What parts of yourself have you been hiding out of fear? What dreams have you abandoned because you were told they were unrealistic? Now is the time to reconnect with your true self. It's time to let go of the masks, the roles, and the expectations that have been placed on you. It's time to embrace your authentic self, in all its raw, unfiltered beauty.

This is your life, and you deserve to live it on your terms. You don't need to seek validation from others. You don't need to conform to anyone's standards. You are enough, exactly as you are. The world needs you—your true, authentic self—not the version you think people want to see.

So, I challenge you today: Break free from the chains of fear and societal expectations. Step into your authenticity. Show up as you are, without apology, without fear, and without hesitation. The world will be better for it, and so will you.

The Freedom Found in Authenticity

Authenticity isn't just a philosophical concept—it is a way of life, a mindset, and a transformative practice that can change the very core of who we are. To live authentically is to embark on a journey of liberation, freeing ourselves from the heavy burdens of self-doubt, fear, and the expectations of others. It's about peeling away the layers that have been imposed on us over the years—layers of conditioning, societal pressures, and the constant need for approval. What remains underneath all these layers is our true, unfiltered selves, waiting to be embraced. This authenticity is not merely about being true to our ideals or values—it's about being fully and unapologetically ourselves, without the fear of rejection or judgment.

When I began embracing my authentic self, I felt a freedom I had never known. It was as though I had been carrying an invisible weight all my life, and for the first time, I was able to put it down. The constant anxiety of "What will people think of me?" that had dictated so many of my decisions and actions suddenly faded into the background. I stopped allowing the judgments of others to define my sense of worth. I realized that I didn't need anyone's approval to be whole, to be loved, or to be enough. I could trust myself and my choices, knowing that I was enough simply by being me.

This newfound peace, however, didn't come without its struggles. The journey toward authenticity is not an easy one, and it is not one without discomfort. To live authentically means to allow ourselves to be seen—not just in our successes, our strengths, and our triumphs, but also in our vulnerabilities, imperfections, and struggles. It means exposing the parts of ourselves we have spent so long hiding, the parts we fear might make us unworthy or unlovable. To be authentic requires the courage to stand in the face of fear and still choose to show up as we are.

This courage, this willingness to be seen, is deeply connected to vulnerability. Vulnerability is the cornerstone of authenticity. It's about being open to the world, showing the rawness of who we are, and accepting ourselves in all our complexity. When we allow ourselves to be vulnerable, we are no longer hiding behind a mask or pretending to be someone we are not. Instead, we are standing in our truth, no matter how messy or uncomfortable that truth may be. Vulnerability is often met with resistance—it feels unsafe, uncertain, and sometimes downright terrifying. But it is in this very vulnerability that we discover the greatest strength.

When we allow ourselves to be fully vulnerable, we learn to trust not just others, but ourselves. We learn to trust that even in our moments of weakness or imperfection, we are still worthy of love, respect, and acceptance. We learn to let go of the toxic belief that we must be flawless or constantly performing to be loved. We stop seeking validation from external sources, and instead, we create a space of internal validation, recognizing that our worth is inherent, not dependent on the approval of others.

This kind of freedom—freedom from the need to please, to conform, or to wear a mask—is liberating beyond measure. It is the freedom to say, "This is who I am, and I am enough." It is the power to stand tall in our truth, without apology. The moment we stop living for the expectations of others and begin living for ourselves, we step into a powerful sense of agency. This is where true liberation lies: in the acceptance of ourselves as we are, with all our flaws and imperfections, and in the freedom to be unapologetically ourselves.

Living authentically is not about perfection. It's not about fitting into some societal ideal or even aligning with someone else's version of what it means to be "successful" or "worthy." It's about stepping away from the stories we've been told, the roles we've been assigned, and the expectations we've internalized. It's about honoring our own unique journey, and embracing the fullness of who we are, no matter how imperfect that may seem.

The Power of Letting Go

One of the most liberating aspects of authenticity is the power it gives us to let go—let go of the pressure to be everything to everyone, let go of the need to meet society's standards, and most importantly, let go of the unrealistic expectations we place on ourselves. Authenticity calls us to release the stories we've been telling ourselves about who we should be. It invites us to stop comparing ourselves to others and instead, focus on embracing our unique path, however winding or unconventional it may be.

We often hold on to old identities, old stories, and old versions of ourselves out of fear. We fear that letting go of the past means losing our sense of identity or security. But the truth is that holding on to these outdated versions of ourselves only limits our growth. When we embrace authenticity, we make space for new possibilities and new ways of being. We open ourselves up to the richness of life, to the freedom that comes from shedding old skins and stepping into a new chapter, one that is fully aligned with who we truly are.

The Journey Toward Authenticity

The journey to authenticity is not linear. There will be ups and downs, moments of doubt, and moments of immense clarity. There will be times when we falter, when we question whether we're truly on the right path. But each step we take, each moment we choose to show up as ourselves, brings us closer to the freedom we seek. The more we lean into our authenticity, the more we discover our inner strength, resilience, and power.

The beauty of authenticity is that it does not demand perfection—it only asks us to be real. It doesn't require us to have all the answers; it simply requires us to be open to the process, to trust that we are already enough, just as we are. Each day, we have the opportunity to choose authenticity. We can choose to live from a place of honesty, vulnerability, and self-acceptance. We can choose to let go of the masks and be seen for who we truly are.

True Freedom

The true freedom found in authenticity is not just about living a life of ease or comfort—it's about living a life of integrity. It's about aligning our inner truth with our outer expression. It's about being unapologetically ourselves, fully embracing our worth and our uniqueness. Authenticity empowers us to live boldly, to make choices that reflect our true desires, and to create lives that feel genuine, fulfilling, and meaningful.

In embracing authenticity, we step into our power and own our worth. We let go of the need to please others, to conform, or to hide behind a mask. Instead, we embrace the fullness of who we are, knowing that we are deserving of love, respect, and acceptance, just as we are. And that, my friend, is the most powerful freedom of all: the freedom to live authentically, fully, and unapologetically.

When we choose authenticity, we choose freedom—not just freedom from the expectations of others, but freedom from the limitations we've placed on ourselves. We choose to be ourselves, and in doing so, we open the door to a life that is rich with possibility, joy, and fulfillment. So, I challenge you to take that first step today: Let go of the need for approval, embrace the fullness of who you are, and allow yourself the freedom to live authentically. You are worthy, you are enough, and you deserve the freedom to be yourself.

Breaking the Chains of Fear

Fear is a pervasive force in our lives—subtle yet insidious. It often operates in the background, influencing our decisions and behaviors without us even realizing it. It is the ultimate thief of authenticity, the invisible force that keeps us trapped in patterns of self-doubt, insecurity, and limitation. Fear feeds on our vulnerabilities, preying on our deepest fears of rejection, failure, criticism, and judgment. It convinces us that we are unworthy, that our true selves are too flawed or too much to be accepted, and so we bury our authenticity deep within, afraid to let it surface.

Fear is like a heavy cloak draped over our potential, obscuring our vision of who we truly are and what we are capable of. It tells us that we are not good enough, that we don't deserve to be seen or heard, and that the world would be better off if we stayed quiet, small, and invisible. But I have come to realize that fear is a liar. It is a master manipulator, convincing us that we are powerless, that our dreams are out of reach, and that we must play by society's rules in order to survive. Fear is a voice that constantly whispers, "You can't do this," "You're not worthy," "What will people think?"

But here's the truth: Fear only has power if we allow it to. It thrives on our belief in its lies, on our hesitation to challenge its voice. But what if we stopped listening? What if we chose to rewrite the story fear tells us? What if we took the reins and decided, "I'm not going to let fear dictate my life anymore"? That's when fear begins to lose its power. That's when we start taking back control.

Transforming Fear into Growth

Transforming fear into growth requires a shift in how we view fear itself. Rather than seeing it as an obstacle that must be avoided, we must begin to see it as a signal—a sign that we are stepping into unknown territory, growing beyond our current limitations, and expanding into new versions of ourselves. Fear, in this sense, becomes a catalyst for transformation. It's not something that stops us, but something that propels us forward when we choose to face it head-on.

In my journey, I realized that fear would always be a part of my growth, but it didn't have to control me. The key to overcoming fear wasn't to wait for it to go away, but to take action in spite of it. It's easy to get caught up in the narrative that we can't move forward until we feel "ready" or until the fear subsides. But what I learned is that readiness often comes *through* action, not before it. The more I moved toward the things that frightened me, the more I discovered that my fears were not nearly as powerful as they seemed. They were, in fact, often exaggerated stories in my mind, keeping me stuck in a cycle of doubt and inaction.

When I first began taking steps towards authenticity, the fear was deafening. I doubted myself, second-guessed my decisions, and was constantly worried about how others would perceive me. But I made a commitment to show up anyway. I didn't wait for the fear to disappear. I gave myself permission to feel afraid, but I didn't let it control my actions. Instead of avoiding discomfort, I leaned into it, using it as a signal that I was on the right path.

One of the most powerful practices I developed was to speak my truth, even when my voice trembled. At first, it was terrifying to express my feelings and share my story with others. The vulnerability was overwhelming, and I often feared rejection or judgment. But the more I practiced speaking my truth, the less fear had a hold on me. Each time I took a step forward, I felt lighter, more confident, and more empowered. I realized that my truth was a source of strength, not a weakness, and that by embracing it, I was empowering myself to live authentically.

Setting boundaries was another area where fear played a significant role. For much of my life, I had been afraid to say "no" or to assert my needs, thinking that it would cause conflict or disappoint others. But when I began setting clear boundaries, I discovered that it wasn't about shutting people out—it was about creating space for myself, my well-being, and my authenticity. It wasn't always easy, but each time I stood firm in my boundaries, I felt a greater sense of respect for myself and the courage to continue on my journey of growth.

Fear, in many ways, is a teacher. It shows us where we are still holding back, where we still need to grow, and where we still need to trust ourselves. But it also shows us what we are capable of when we face it. The more we take action in the face of fear, the less power it has over us. With each step, we build our confidence, our resilience, and our trust in our own abilities. The voice of fear starts to fade into the background, and in its place, we hear the voice of courage, guiding us toward the life we are meant to live.

As we continue to move forward despite our fears, we create momentum. The more we face fear with courage, the more we expand our comfort zone. What once seemed impossible becomes possible. What once seemed scary becomes an opportunity for growth. Over time, fear no longer holds the same weight. Instead of paralyzing us, it becomes a signal that we are on the edge of something great—something transformative.

It's important to remember that fear is not something to be eradicated. It's a part of the human experience, and it will always be there, especially when we are stepping into new challenges. But rather than running from it, we can choose to transform it. By facing our fears with courage and authenticity, we allow ourselves to grow in ways we never imagined. And with each step we take, we break free from the limits we once placed on ourselves and move closer to the fullest expression of who we are meant to be. Fear, then, becomes not a roadblock, but a stepping stone on the path to personal growth and transformation.

The Courage to Move Forward

Courage is not the absence of fear. It is the willingness to move forward in spite of it, to take action even when doubt clouds our judgment and insecurity whispers in our ears. Courage isn't something we're born with; it's something we cultivate through action. The more we act in the face of fear, the stronger our courage becomes.

As I embraced courage, I noticed a profound shift—not just in how I saw myself, but in how I viewed the world around me. Fear no longer controlled my decisions or actions. By choosing to move forward despite it, I began to reclaim my power. Each time I stepped into fear and chose courage instead of retreat, I grew stronger and experienced greater freedom.

This transformation didn't happen overnight, nor was it easy. But the more I practiced it, the easier it became to face my fears and keep moving forward. Fear, I realized, wasn't an insurmountable obstacle—it was part of the journey. When I chose courage, fear became a stepping stone, not a stumbling block.

This shift in perspective was life-changing. Fear was no longer the enemy; it signaled that I was stepping outside my comfort zone and growing. I stopped letting it limit my potential, instead seeing it as a reminder that I was pushing toward something greater.

With each confrontation with fear, I grew more confident, assertive, and aligned with my true self. Fear didn't go away, but it lost its power over me. I understood that it's okay to feel afraid, but fear doesn't have to stop me from living authentically. Courage became my guide, and each step revealed new depths of strength.

I also realized that courage isn't about feeling fearless—it's about moving forward despite fear. It's about trusting yourself, believing in your ability to navigate the unknown, and viewing every challenge as an opportunity for growth. Even when unsure of the outcome, taking imperfect action strengthens resolve.

As I continued practicing courage, I tapped into a deeper resilience. Each act of courage built a foundation of inner strength, helping me face bigger challenges with greater ease. I no longer waited for perfect conditions or for fear to subside. I kept moving forward, trusting that every step was taking me closer to the person I was meant to be.

Over time, my relationship with fear shifted. It was no longer something that held me back—it became a symbol of progress. Fear was a sign that I was stretching beyond my limits and stepping into new possibilities. Leaning into courage taught me that fear wasn't something to avoid but something to transform.

Each new challenge boosted my confidence in my ability to move through fear and emerge stronger. I no longer let doubt or insecurity hold me back. I used them as fuel to keep moving forward, knowing that every step took me closer to the life I had always dreamed of—authentically, boldly, and fearlessly.

The courage to move forward is a practice. It's built, step by step, choice by choice. The more we choose courage, the more it becomes a part of who we are. We create a life where fear no longer controls us. Instead, we control how we respond to fear—choosing to move forward, choosing to grow, and choosing to embrace the fullness of who we are meant to be.

The Power of Action

One of the most powerful tools in overcoming fear is action. Fear thrives in stillness, in waiting, in indecision. When we stand still and hesitate, fear gains ground. It plants seeds of doubt, feeding on our uncertainty. But when we take action, even in the presence of fear, we take away fear's power. Action is the antidote to fear. It is through action that we begin to break the chains that bind us.

The act of moving forward, even when we're unsure, is what propels us into growth. It is through doing the things that scare us that we build confidence, trust, and resilience. Every time we act in spite of fear, we reinforce the belief that we are capable, that we are worthy of success, and that we can handle whatever challenges come our way. Fear may still show up, but it no longer controls us. It becomes just another hurdle to jump over on our path to growth.

The Liberation Found in Courage

Breaking the chains of fear is not just about overcoming obstacles—it's about unlocking the full potential of who we are. It is about shedding the limitations that fear imposes on us and stepping into a life of freedom, authenticity, and empowerment. The more we choose courage, the more we realize that we are not defined by our fears. We are defined by the actions we take in the face of them.

As we embrace courage and move through fear, we create space for new possibilities, new opportunities, and new versions of ourselves. The freedom that comes from breaking the chains of fear is unparalleled. It is the freedom to live boldly, to make decisions from a place of inner strength, and to pursue our dreams without the shackles of self-doubt.

Fear will always be part of our journey, but it no longer has to be the driving force. By choosing courage, we allow ourselves to step into the fullness of our potential. And when we do, we discover that we are capable of far more than we ever imagined. So, I challenge you: Face your fears, take that step forward, and choose courage. The freedom on the other side is waiting for you.

The Masks We Wear

As humans, we are often taught that in order to survive, we must conform. Society, family, friends, and even our own inner voices impose expectations on who we should be, how we should act, and what we should value. In the effort to meet these expectations, we put on masks—facades that protect us from judgment, vulnerability, and the fear of rejection. These masks allow us to navigate the world without exposing parts of ourselves we believe are too messy, too raw, or too imperfect to be seen.

At first, these masks may seem necessary, helping us fit in and avoid discomfort. They provide a sense of safety, allowing us to avoid the pain of being misunderstood. But over time, something changes. The masks stop being just tools for protection and begin to define us. Instead of simply hiding our true selves, they start to replace them, shaping our identities in ways that no longer align with who we truly are. We become so used to wearing them that we forget what it feels like to be without them.

The problem with these masks is that they can make us lose touch with the parts of ourselves that are most authentic. We stop feeling like ourselves. We start to make choices based on the roles we've adopted—roles that were never truly ours. We may strive for approval, measure our worth by how well we fit into society's mold, or live to fulfill others' expectations rather than our own truth.

The longer we wear these masks, the more we risk losing ourselves. What was once an act of survival can evolve into a trap, one that prevents us from embracing our full potential. Our deepest desires, our real feelings, our vulnerabilities—everything that makes us uniquely us—remain hidden beneath layers of pretense.

But the yearning to be seen for who we really are doesn't disappear. It may grow louder, especially in the quiet moments when the mask begins to slip. These moments of vulnerability can feel frightening, but they are also the opportunities for growth. Letting go of the mask is a courageous act of self-acceptance. It's about allowing ourselves to be seen as imperfect, messy, and beautifully real.

This process of shedding the masks isn't easy, but it's necessary. It's a journey of rediscovering who we are beneath all the layers we've built up. It's about allowing ourselves to show up authentically—not as a polished, perfected version of ourselves, but as we truly are, complete with all our flaws, fears, and hopes. This is where freedom lives—not in being flawless, but in embracing our true, unfiltered selves.

When we let go of the mask, we invite deeper connection—not only with ourselves but with others. In our raw authenticity, we encourage others to drop their own masks. We create a space where vulnerability is welcomed, where we can be loved for who we truly are, without the need to perform or pretend.

The beauty of this journey lies in the fact that, when we finally let go of the masks, we are no longer trapped by the expectations of others. We begin to feel the true freedom of being ourselves—unapologetically, boldly, and authentically.

The Masks of Perfection and Strength

Some of the most common masks we wear are rooted in our desire to appear flawless, to avoid criticism, and to fulfill the roles expected of us. The "perfect" mask is one of the most prevalent. It's the mask of the person who seems to have it all together—never faltering, always in control, and constantly striving for unattainable perfection. We put on this mask to protect ourselves from judgment, to avoid the vulnerability of showing our imperfections, and to make ourselves acceptable to the world around us. But the truth is, perfection is an illusion, and the pursuit of it often comes at the expense of our authenticity.

Another mask that many of us wear is the "strong" mask. This is the mask of resilience, independence, and invulnerability. It is the belief that we must always appear strong, that showing any sign of weakness or need is a failure. It tells us that we cannot lean on others, that we must carry our burdens alone, and that vulnerability is a form of weakness. But what happens when we wear this mask for too long? We exhaust ourselves, we suppress our emotions, and we disconnect from the support and love that others want to offer. We forget that true strength isn't about being unbreakable, but about being able to be broken and still show up, still choose to grow, and still choose to be vulnerable.

The "composed" mask is another common one. This is the mask we put on when we feel the need to appear put-together, calm, and collected—never letting our emotions get the best of us. We wear it to avoid feeling overwhelmed, to avoid showing how much we are struggling inside. But beneath this mask, the emotional weight often builds, creating tension, stress, and anxiety. We deny our emotions, thinking that they are signs of weakness or imperfection, when in reality, they are part of the human experience and deserve to be expressed.

The Masks We Wear in Our Relationships

I can personally relate to wearing many of these masks. Throughout my life, I wore the "good daughter" mask. I thought that being the perfect daughter—obedient, calm, and always striving for approval—was the only way to earn my parents' love and respect. But in doing so, I suppressed my true feelings and desires. I didn't give myself permission to be imperfect, to make mistakes, or to follow my own path. My worth became tied to what I thought they wanted me to be, not who I truly was. I became so focused on fulfilling expectations that I forgot to honor my own voice. The mask I wore kept me small, held me back, and prevented me from truly showing up for myself.

I also wore the "strong woman" mask for many years. I convinced myself that to be strong, I had to be tough—emotionally and physically. Vulnerability, I believed, was a weakness. Asking for help or showing that I was struggling meant I was failing. This belief led me to isolate myself, thinking that if I showed any cracks in my armor, it would diminish my worth. But the truth was, this mask made me more distant from the people who could offer me support. It built walls around me, preventing me from forming deeper, more authentic connections. The pressure to always be strong drained my energy, and I realized too late that strength doesn't mean doing everything on your own—it's about knowing when to lean on others and embrace your humanity.

Then came the "perfect mother" mask. I believed that being a good mother meant sacrificing my own needs, my own identity, for the sake of my children. I convinced myself that I had to put everything aside for them, that my dreams and desires didn't matter as much. While it's true that motherhood requires sacrifice, I lost sight of who I was outside of the role. This mask led me to neglect my own well-being. I stopped listening to my own heart, silenced my own needs, and fell into the trap of trying to be everything for everyone. But in the process, I lost touch with myself. I became so consumed by the roles I was playing that I forgot the importance of nurturing the person I was before I became a mother.

Each of these masks was created with good intentions. I wore them to protect myself, to fit in, and to be loved. But over time, they began to control me. Instead of allowing me to show up authentically in my relationships, they shaped the way I interacted with others. The mask of the "good daughter" led me to suppress my true self in exchange for approval. The "strong woman" mask isolated me, making me believe that I had to carry the weight of the world alone. The "perfect mother" mask forced me to ignore my own desires, making me lose sight of who I was outside of my roles.

The problem with these masks is that, when we wear them for too long, we start to forget who we are without them. We lose the ability to connect with others from a place of true vulnerability, and we begin to rely on these facades to navigate our relationships. But the real magic happens when we take off the mask. When we allow ourselves to be imperfect, to show our struggles, to ask for help, we open the door for deeper connection and healing.

As I've learned to let go of these masks, I've discovered that authenticity is the key to meaningful relationships. I've found that being real—embracing both my strengths and weaknesses—invites others to do the same. In shedding the weight of trying to be perfect, I've allowed myself to be loved for who I truly am, not for the person I thought I had to be. It's not easy, but with each step of shedding these layers, I've come to understand that the best version of myself is the one that shows up fully, without pretense.

In relationships, whether with family, friends, or partners, we all have a tendency to wear masks. We put on faces that protect us, that help us navigate the expectations others have of us. But the truth is, those masks only hold us back from the real connections we desire. When we let go of the masks we've been wearing, we invite authenticity, vulnerability, and deep connection. Only then can we truly be seen for who we are—imperfections and all. And it's in that rawness that we discover the beauty of real, meaningful relationships.

The Cost of Wearing Masks

The cost of wearing these masks is high. The more I wore them, the less I recognized myself. I became trapped in the roles I had created, living a life that was more about fulfilling expectations than about being true to who I really was. I became disconnected from my own desires, dreams, and passions, and in doing so, I lost my peace. The masks I had worn for protection became suffocating. They weren't helping me; they were holding me back. They disconnected me from the people I loved, the life I wanted, and, most importantly, from myself.

In wearing these masks, we often forget that the people around us are not looking for perfection—they're looking for authenticity. They want to know the real us, the flawed and beautiful parts of our story that make us unique. But as long as we hide behind our masks, we deny them the opportunity to love us fully and we deny ourselves the opportunity to experience the love and acceptance we deserve.

Peeling Back the Layers

The journey to authenticity requires us to peel back these layers of masks. It requires us to ask the tough questions: *Why am I wearing this mask? Who am I pretending to be? What am I afraid of revealing?* These are not easy questions to answer. In fact, they can be terrifying. But it is only by facing these questions that we can begin to understand the reasons behind the masks we wear and start the process of healing and self-discovery.

Taking off the masks is a vulnerable act. It requires us to show up in our raw, unfiltered selves—to be seen without the protective armor we've been hiding behind. But this is where the magic happens. When we begin to take off our masks, we expose our true selves to the world, and that's when we begin to reconnect with our authentic power. We stop pretending to be someone we're not and allow ourselves to be fully human—flawed, beautiful, and worthy of love and acceptance just as we are.

The Freedom of Authenticity

The moment we begin to take off the masks, we reclaim our freedom. We no longer have to live in fear of judgment or rejection. We no longer have to uphold impossible standards or try to fit into boxes that were never meant for us. When we show up as our true selves, the world begins to see us for who we truly are: unique, beautiful, and enough. And in that recognition, we find peace. We no longer need to prove ourselves or seek validation from others. We can simply be, and that is enough.

The path to authenticity is not always easy, but it is always worth it. When we take off the masks, we create space for the truest version of ourselves to emerge. And in doing so, we invite the world to embrace us—not the masked version of us, but the real, raw, unfiltered us. The freedom that comes with this authenticity is liberating, and it allows us to live a life that is aligned with who we truly are. We are no longer confined by the roles and expectations placed upon us. We are free to live, to love, and to be ourselves fully.

The Healing Process: Reconnecting With Your True Self

The healing process is not a quick fix or an easy path—it is a profound journey of rediscovery, reclamation, and restoration. It's a journey that takes us deep into the recesses of our heart, mind, and soul, where we must face the wounds, the pain, and the scars that have shaped us. It's a process of reconnecting with the version of ourselves that was buried under years of fear, shame, and expectations placed upon us by others. It's about remembering who we were before the world told us who we should be.

For many of us, the journey toward healing begins with the painful realization that we have spent years—perhaps even decades—neglecting our true selves. We may have forgotten what it feels like to listen to our own inner voice, to trust our instincts, or to honor our desires. We may have allowed the opinions of others to define us, shaping our actions, thoughts, and beliefs around what we thought would make us loved, accepted, and worthy.

But healing offers us the opportunity to undo that damage. It is a process of returning to ourselves—of rediscovering our worth, our voice, and our power. It's about reconnecting with the parts of us that we've silenced or ignored for too long, giving ourselves permission to be who we truly are.

Acknowledging the Pain: Facing What We've Been Avoiding

The first step in the healing process is acknowledging the pain we've been carrying—whether it's trauma from the past, rejection, abandonment, fear, or any other form of emotional or physical harm. We cannot heal what we refuse to face, and healing requires us to look at the parts of our lives that have caused us pain.

We might feel afraid or overwhelmed by this process, but acknowledging the pain is the beginning of breaking its hold over us. When we face our wounds head-on, we no longer allow them to control our present reality. We start to see them for what they are: pieces of our past that no longer need to define us.

This step may involve revisiting painful memories or confronting the narratives we've held onto for so long. We might have internalized the belief that we are not good enough or that we are unworthy of love, success, or happiness. These beliefs often stem from past experiences—whether they're related to childhood, relationships, or societal expectations—that led us to think we were less than, undeserving, or broken. But in confronting these beliefs, we begin to expose the lies we've been telling ourselves.

Letting Go of the Old Stories: Releasing Limiting Beliefs

The stories we tell ourselves shape our lives. We often hold onto old beliefs that are limiting and untrue—stories that tell us we are not enough, not deserving, or not worthy of love and happiness. These stories are a product of our experiences, but they do not define us.

Healing requires us to let go of these old stories. It involves dismantling the negative beliefs we've internalized over time and rewriting them with truth. We must remind ourselves that our worth is not contingent on anyone else's approval, and that we are worthy of love, success, and happiness simply because we exist. Releasing these limiting beliefs isn't always easy, but it is essential. We cannot fully heal if we continue to hold onto the stories that keep us stuck in a cycle of self-doubt and insecurity.

Forgiveness: Releasing Guilt and Shame

Forgiveness is a cornerstone of the healing process. Many of us carry deep wounds from the actions of others—whether it's from betrayal, abandonment, or rejection. We may also carry guilt and shame for the ways we have allowed ourselves to be treated, for the choices we've made that didn't honor our true selves, or for the ways we've compromised our values in search of approval.

But forgiveness is not about excusing the wrongs that have been done to us; it is about releasing the grip that the past has on us. Forgiveness is an act of freeing ourselves from the pain of the past so that we can step into a future of healing and transformation.

Forgiving others is important, but perhaps the most profound form of forgiveness is the one we offer to ourselves. We often carry the weight of guilt and shame for the ways we have allowed ourselves to be shaped by the opinions of others, for the times we've compromised our boundaries, or for the mistakes we've made. But we must remember that healing cannot occur if we continue to punish ourselves for our past choices. We must learn to extend the same grace and compassion to ourselves that we would offer to a loved one who has been hurt. When we forgive ourselves, we release the burden of shame, allowing ourselves to step into the light of our true potential.

The Long, Often Painful Process of Healing

The healing journey is long, and it's often painful. There will be moments when it feels like progress is slow, or when the weight of the past seems too heavy to bear. We may find ourselves revisiting old wounds or confronting aspects of ourselves that we have long avoided. But this is all part of the process. Healing is not linear. It ebbs and flows, and there will be times when it feels like we are taking two steps forward and one step back.

But it is in these moments of discomfort that we are doing the most profound work. Every time we face our pain, every time we let go of an old story or belief, we are moving closer to our authentic selves. Every time we forgive ourselves, we are opening up to the possibility of a new, brighter future.

Rediscovering Our True Selves

Through the healing process, we rediscover our true selves. We begin to reconnect with the person we were always meant to be—the person we were before the world told us who we should be. We reclaim our voice, our power, and our worth. We no longer let external validation determine our sense of self; instead, we learn to validate ourselves, to trust our own inner wisdom, and to honor our desires.

The more we heal, the more we realize that we are enough as we are. We no longer have to seek perfection, approval, or acceptance from others. We are worthy of love, success, and happiness simply because we exist. And as we embrace this truth, we step into a life that is aligned with our deepest values and desires.

The Gift of Self-Love

Perhaps the greatest gift that comes from the healing process is the gift of self-love. As we peel back the layers of pain, fear, and insecurity, we begin to see ourselves through the lens of compassion, acceptance, and kindness. We learn to love ourselves—not because we are perfect, but because we are real, whole, and worthy of love just as we are.

Self-love is not about ego or narcissism; it is about honoring our own worth, embracing our imperfections, and showing up for ourselves in ways that nurture and support our growth. It's about treating ourselves with the same kindness and care that we would offer to a friend or loved one. When we practice self-love, we set the foundation for all other forms of love to flourish—love for others, love for the world, and most importantly, love for ourselves.

Embracing the Present Moment

Healing also invites us to embrace the present moment. Too often, we are trapped in the echo of the past or consumed by the uncertainty of the future. We replay old wounds in our minds, wishing we had done things differently, or we worry about what lies ahead—how we will handle the challenges or what outcomes will come our way. While it's natural to reflect on what has been or to plan for what could be, true healing only happens in the present. It happens when we stop looking back at what we've lost or projecting ourselves into a future that hasn't arrived yet. Healing is a practice of fully engaging with the life that is right in front of us, in this moment, just as it is.

By embracing the present, we liberate ourselves from the chains of regret and anxiety. We let go of the weight of the past, the "what-ifs" that cloud our judgment, and the fear of what might come tomorrow. We allow ourselves to experience the fullness of now—the feelings, the sensations, and the opportunities that exist in the here and now. The present is where our power lies. When we are fully present, we are in a state of acceptance. We accept where we are, who we are, and what we are experiencing. In this space of acceptance, we find peace and clarity.

This doesn't mean we ignore our past or abandon our dreams for the future. Instead, it means we acknowledge both with a sense of balance. The past has shaped us, but it no longer needs to control us. The future holds possibilities, but we can only take the steps toward it by being fully present now. It is in this delicate balance that we find the freedom to heal. We stop running from the pain of yesterday, and we stop rushing toward the uncertain promise of tomorrow. We embrace the beauty of the present moment and allow ourselves to be fully alive in it.

Being present also allows us to be with our emotions without judgment. It's easy to be overwhelmed by pain or discomfort, but when we embrace the present, we give ourselves permission to feel whatever arises. We no longer need to push away or suppress emotions; we allow them to come and go freely, knowing they are part of the healing process. We stop fighting against ourselves, and instead, we meet each feeling with compassion. It's in the space of non-judgment that we truly start to heal.

Healing in the present moment is also about being fully engaged with our surroundings, with the people in our lives, and with the experiences that are unfolding in front of us. How often do we find ourselves distracted, living in our minds rather than in the moment? We might be physically present but mentally absent, thinking about the past or worrying about the future. But when we practice being present, we allow ourselves to fully experience life as it happens. We savor the small moments—whether it's the warmth of the sun on our skin, the sound of laughter shared with loved ones, or the quiet stillness of solitude.

As we embrace the present moment, we also cultivate gratitude. Gratitude for what is, rather than what was or what might be. In each present moment, there is something to be thankful for, even if it's just the breath we are taking or the awareness we have of the world around us. This gratitude grounds us, reminding us that healing is not a destination but a journey. And the most powerful part of that journey happens right now.

True healing happens when we stop resisting the present and start fully inhabiting it. When we engage with life as it unfolds, with all its imperfections and uncertainties, we create the space for transformation. We stop waiting for the perfect moment or for the healing to be complete. We recognize that healing is an ongoing process, one that unfolds with each step we take in the present.

By embracing the present moment, we open ourselves to the possibility of healing. We free ourselves from the constraints of time—no longer bound by the past or controlled by the future. We live fully in the now, where healing begins. And in doing so, we make room for the growth, peace, and freedom that we so desperately seek.

The Journey is Ongoing

The healing process is ongoing. It is not something that has a clear endpoint or a final destination. It is a continuous journey of growth, transformation, and self-discovery. But every step we take toward healing is a step closer to embracing our true selves. And every time we heal a wound, we make room for greater joy, peace, and fulfillment in our lives.

As we heal, we become more connected to the world around us, to the people we love, and most importantly, to ourselves. We learn to live authentically, without the need for masks, without the fear of judgment, and without the belief that we are anything less than enough.

Healing is not an easy process, but it is the most rewarding one. And as we heal, we learn to love ourselves more deeply, embrace our flaws with grace, and live our lives with a sense of peace, purpose, and authenticity that we have never known before.

Reclaiming Your Voice

Reclaiming your voice is not just about speaking—it's about understanding the deep power of your words, your perspective, and your presence in the world. It's the act of embracing who you truly are and expressing that person boldly, without apology. This journey often requires breaking free from the conditioning and influences that have kept you silent for far too long. The society that encourages conformity, the family dynamics that promote silence, and the internal fears that make you question your worth—they all play a role in suppressing your voice.

For many of us, the pain of past trauma, the fear of rejection, or the wounds of judgment from others lead us to silence our true selves. We silence our thoughts and feelings to avoid conflict or to gain acceptance. But as time goes on, that silence becomes a form of self-betrayal. It is like living with a quiet, aching voice inside that longs to be heard but is constantly held back by doubt and fear. The weight of this suppression can take its toll, leading to frustration, resentment, and a deep longing for expression.

Reclaiming your voice is like reclaiming your sense of self. It's acknowledging that you matter, that your opinions are valid, and that your experiences are real and worthy of being shared. It begins with the internal realization that you no longer have to dim your light or hide your truth for anyone. It means breaking free from the script that others have written for you and instead, writing your own narrative. When you begin to speak your truth, you begin to live in alignment with your authentic self.

This process is not instantaneous. It involves vulnerability and courage. At first, speaking up may feel unnatural or intimidating. The fear of judgment or rejection can still be a lingering shadow, but with each word you speak, you become stronger. You begin to understand that your voice has the ability to create change—not just in your own life, but in the lives of others. When you speak your truth, you give others the permission to do the same. Your voice can be a beacon for those who have been silenced by their own fears.

Reclaiming your voice is not just about the big, bold declarations—it's also about the quiet, everyday moments where you express your desires, your needs, and your boundaries. It's in telling the people around you what you need without guilt or shame. It's in standing up for what you believe in, even when it feels uncomfortable. It's in acknowledging your worth and declaring that you will no longer allow others to dictate how you should live, think, or feel.

One of the most powerful aspects of reclaiming your voice is the way it redefines your relationship with fear. Fear often tries to silence us. It tells us that we aren't good enough, that our voices don't matter, or that speaking out will lead to rejection. But when you start speaking up despite fear, you begin to disarm it. Fear no longer has the power to keep you in silence. You become unstoppable because you no longer need the approval of others to feel worthy.

It's important to understand that reclaiming your voice does not mean speaking without consideration. It means speaking from a place of honesty, integrity, and self-respect. It means knowing that your words can be powerful and choosing to use them responsibly, with intention. Your voice is not just for others; it is for you, too. It is the most powerful tool you have in your journey of self-love and self-discovery.

When I began to reclaim my voice, it was a process of trial and error. I made mistakes, stumbled, and faced rejection. But each time, I became stronger, more confident, and more in tune with my inner truth. I realized that my voice was not something to fear, but something to celebrate. It was my right to speak, my right to share my story, and my right to be heard.

And as I reclaimed my voice, I realized something even deeper: my voice is not just a tool for expressing my feelings and opinions; it's a bridge to connection. When I speak my truth, I invite others to do the same. I create space for vulnerability, for understanding, and for authenticity. Through my voice, I am not only reclaiming my power but also helping others to reclaim theirs.

Reclaiming your voice is a lifelong journey. It is not something that happens overnight, but something you build each day through practice, courage, and faith in yourself. The more you speak your truth, the more you realize how strong and powerful you truly are. And the more you speak up, the more you inspire others to do the same.

Remember, your voice is yours alone. It has the power to heal, to inspire, to create change, and to affirm your existence in this world. Don't let anyone—or anything—take it away from you. Speak up. Be seen. Be heard. Your voice matters. It is a part of your unique, authentic self, and it deserves to be shared with the world.

Letting Go of Perfectionism

Letting go of perfectionism is one of the most liberating and transformative acts we can undertake in our lives. Perfectionism is a trap we often build for ourselves, not realizing that the more we try to meet impossible standards, the further we distance ourselves from the joy of living authentically. At its core, perfectionism is about fear—fear of judgment, fear of failure, and fear of not being good enough. It convinces us that our worth is conditional, dependent on how flawless we appear to the world. But this belief is rooted in a lie, and it is this lie that keeps us bound to a never-ending cycle of striving and self-doubt.

For many years, I too believed in the myth of perfection. I thought that if I could be the ideal daughter, the perfect nurse, the ideal mother—if I could perform flawlessly in every role I played—then I would be deserving of love, respect, and success. It seemed like a logical equation: perfect performance equals love and validation. But the more I chased perfection, the more elusive it became. No matter how much I accomplished or how well I performed, it never felt like enough. There was always a new goal to meet, a new achievement to strive for, and with each accomplishment, the feeling of being "good enough" remained just out of reach.

The pressure of perfectionism was exhausting. It led to self-criticism, a constant feeling of inadequacy, and a deep sense of disconnection from my true self. Instead of celebrating my accomplishments, I only saw what I hadn't done yet. Instead of appreciating who I was, I focused on all the ways I fell short. This relentless pursuit of flawlessness took a toll on my mental and emotional well-being, leaving me feeling overwhelmed, anxious, and unfulfilled. It wasn't until I started to examine this belief more closely that I realized perfectionism wasn't helping me; it was harming me.

Perfectionism thrives on the fear of vulnerability. It tells us that in order to be loved and accepted, we must show up perfectly—never showing weakness, never making mistakes, and never failing. But this kind of thinking prevents us from experiencing the fullness of life. The truth is, perfectionism is an illusion. No one—no matter how successful, talented, or accomplished they appear—is perfect. Perfectionism is a shield that keeps us from embracing our humanity. It prevents us from being real, from connecting authentically with others, and from experiencing the beauty in the messy, imperfect moments of life.

The moment I allowed myself to let go of the need for perfection, something remarkable happened: I started to experience peace. Letting go of perfectionism doesn't mean that we stop trying to be our best selves; it simply means we stop judging ourselves harshly when we fall short of impossible standards. We begin to see ourselves through a lens of grace, recognizing that we are worthy not because of how flawless we are, but because of who we are, imperfections and all.

Our imperfections are what make us human. They are the very things that allow us to connect with others on a deeper level. It is through our vulnerabilities, our struggles, and our flaws that we become relatable, compassionate, and real. When we embrace our imperfections, we free ourselves from the pressure of perfection and allow ourselves to live authentically. We stop performing and start being.

Letting go of perfectionism is about shifting our mindset. It's about recognizing that failure and mistakes are not signs of weakness but opportunities for growth. When we fail, we learn. When we make mistakes, we evolve. These experiences shape us into stronger, wiser individuals. By releasing the need to be perfect, we allow ourselves to embrace the messy, beautiful process of being human.

Instead of focusing solely on outcomes, I began to appreciate the journey—the moments of growth, the lessons learned, the progress made, even if it wasn't perfect. I stopped beating myself up for not having it all together, and I started to celebrate the courage it took to show up, even on the days when I didn't have everything figured out. I began to experience more joy, more self-acceptance, and more peace because I wasn't constantly chasing a standard that didn't exist.

The key to letting go of perfectionism is self-compassion. We need to treat ourselves with the same kindness and understanding that we would offer a loved one. It's about recognizing that we are enough, just as we are. It's about knowing that we don't have to be perfect to be worthy of love, success, and happiness. The world doesn't need another perfect person—it needs real, authentic people who are willing to show up as they are, flaws and all.

This process of letting go isn't easy. Perfectionism is deeply ingrained in many of us, often stemming from early childhood messages, societal expectations, or our own inner critic. But each step we take toward embracing our imperfections brings us closer to living authentically. It allows us to release the pressure of being perfect and embrace the freedom of being real.

Letting go of perfectionism is a practice, one that requires patience and ongoing self-reflection. We need to become aware of the thoughts and beliefs that fuel our perfectionism and challenge them. We need to question the standards we've set for ourselves and ask whether they are truly necessary for our well-being. By choosing to let go of perfectionism, we give ourselves permission to live more fully, to embrace our mistakes, to celebrate our successes, and to be proud of who we are—not despite our imperfections, but because of them.

As I continue to let go of perfectionism, I've discovered that my life has become richer and more meaningful. I no longer feel the need to perform for others or live up to unrealistic standards. I've learned that perfection is not the goal—authenticity is. When we let go of perfectionism, we create space for true peace, happiness, and fulfillment. We allow ourselves to be present, to experience life fully, and to love ourselves in all our beautifully imperfect glory.

Embracing Your Own Story

Embracing your own story is one of the most powerful acts of self-love and authenticity you can engage in. It is an invitation to step into your true self, fully accepting who you are, where you've been, and where you are headed. Your story, no matter how imperfect, is yours and it holds immense power. It is a tapestry woven from your experiences, challenges, growth, triumphs, and failures. But often, it is the parts of our stories that are messy, painful, or filled with regret that we are most reluctant to embrace. We carry them like a heavy cloak, not realizing that they are a vital part of our journey and what makes us uniquely beautiful.

For many years, I struggled with embracing my own story. I carried shame and embarrassment about the things I had endured—the trauma, the mistakes, the moments of weakness. I convinced myself that these parts of my past were something to hide, something to be ashamed of. I feared judgment from others, afraid that they would see me as broken or flawed. The weight of my past felt too heavy to bear, and I tried to cover it up, believing that I would only be accepted if I appeared flawless, if I hid the things that had caused me pain.

But as I began to truly embrace my journey, everything shifted. I realized that hiding my story was not protecting me—it was preventing me from healing. It was only when I allowed myself to fully own my past, with all its complexities, that I could step into my authentic self. My story was not something to run from; it was the very thing that had shaped me into the person I was becoming. Every hardship, every mistake, every triumph had contributed to my growth and resilience. It had given me a perspective on life that I could share with others.

Embracing your story is a radical act of courage. It means acknowledging that your experiences—good, bad, and everything in between—are part of who you are, and they are worthy of being shared. There is nothing to be ashamed of in your journey. The pain, the struggles, the moments of uncertainty—these are the things that have made you strong. They are the things that have taught you invaluable lessons about yourself, about life, and about how to rise when you fall.

When I began to accept my own story, I noticed a remarkable shift in my energy. I no longer carried the heavy burden of shame. I wasn't afraid to speak my truth, to share my experiences with others, and to be vulnerable. Instead of seeing my past as a liability, I started to view it as a well of wisdom, something I could draw from to help others who might be facing similar challenges. I began to understand that my story wasn't just about me—it was about connecting with others, offering them a sense of solidarity, and showing them that they were not alone in their struggles.

Your story is not just a series of events—it is a reflection of your strength, your perseverance, and your capacity for growth. When you begin to embrace it, you will see how those difficult chapters have helped shape the person you are today. You will realize that the shame you once felt was only a product of not fully understanding the power in your journey. Each part of your story—the good, the bad, and the ugly—has brought you to this moment. And this moment is where you can truly embrace yourself and all that you have overcome.

The beauty of embracing your own story is that it opens doors to healing—not just for yourself, but for others as well. When you share your story, you create space for others to share theirs. You begin to connect on a deeper level, as you allow others to see the real you—the imperfect, vulnerable, and beautiful human being that you are. It is in this connection that true healing happens. You offer others the chance to see that they are not alone in their struggles, that their stories, too, are worthy of being heard and embraced.

For many of us, the process of embracing our story begins with forgiveness. We must first forgive ourselves for the mistakes we've made, for the times we've judged ourselves too harshly or failed to honor our own experiences. We must also forgive those who have wronged us along the way. This forgiveness is not about excusing behavior or pretending that the past didn't hurt—it is about freeing ourselves from the grip of resentment and regret. When we forgive, we release ourselves from the chains of our past and allow ourselves to move forward.

Once we begin to embrace our story, we open up the possibility for self-acceptance and self-love. It becomes easier to look in the mirror and see ourselves as worthy of love, worthy of success, worthy of happiness. Our story no longer defines us in a negative light; it becomes a testament to our resilience, to our capacity to heal, and to our strength in the face of adversity. We stop seeing ourselves through the lens of shame and begin to see the beauty in our journey.

Embracing your story is not just about accepting the pain—it's about celebrating the growth, the lessons, and the victories along the way. It's about recognizing that you are exactly who you are meant to be, and that your experiences, no matter how painful, have prepared you for the next chapter of your life. Each twist and turn, each challenge faced and overcome, has given you the wisdom and strength to live authentically.

Your story matters. It is unique, and it has the potential to touch others in ways you may never fully understand. When you embrace it, you take away its power to control you and give it the power to heal, to inspire, and to connect. Your story is your gift to the world. It's not something to hide or be ashamed of, but something to be proud of. It is a reflection of your courage, your journey, and your unwavering commitment to living authentically. And in embracing it, you will find that you not only heal yourself but also create a space for others to heal with you.

The Importance of Setting Boundaries

Setting boundaries is one of the most profound acts of self-care and authenticity. It is an essential part of maintaining your mental, emotional, and physical well-being, yet it is often something we overlook or struggle to establish. For so many of us, boundaries can feel like an act of defiance or selfishness, but in reality, they are a clear declaration of self-respect and self-love. Without boundaries, we run the risk of giving away too much of ourselves, becoming drained, overwhelmed, and disconnected from our true selves.

For years, I struggled with setting boundaries. I worried about disappointing others, feeling guilty for saying no, or being perceived as rude or selfish. I was always the one saying yes to every request, agreeing to help even when I was stretched thin, and putting everyone else's needs before my own. It wasn't that I didn't care for others—I did deeply—but I failed to recognize that in constantly prioritizing everyone else, I was neglecting myself. I was so focused on keeping others happy, on being the person everyone could rely on, that I lost sight of my own needs and desires.

It wasn't until I started setting clear boundaries that I realized the immense power they hold. For the first time, I was taking responsibility for my own well-being. I was reclaiming my time, my energy, and my emotions. It wasn't about pushing others away—it was about protecting myself from situations or people that drained me, from things that compromised my values, and from behaviors that made me feel small or undervalued.

Setting boundaries may seem uncomfortable at first, especially if you're not used to saying no or asserting your needs. But the truth is, without boundaries, we allow others to dictate our lives. We are constantly in a state of giving—whether it's our time, energy, or emotional resources—and in doing so, we end up losing ourselves. We forget who we are, what we value, and what we need. This cycle of overgiving leads to burnout, resentment, and emotional exhaustion.

When I began to set boundaries, it was like a weight lifted off my shoulders. I stopped saying yes out of obligation, fear, or guilt. I stopped overextending myself for the sake of others and began to recognize when something didn't align with my values, needs, or goals. Saying no became empowering, not just for me, but for those around me. I learned that when I set boundaries, I was teaching others how to treat me. I was demonstrating that I valued myself, and in turn, others began to respect my time and my energy more.

Setting boundaries isn't about being rigid or inflexible—it's about creating the space you need to live authentically and take care of yourself. It's about making conscious choices that protect your inner peace and well-being, and about recognizing that you are worthy of time, rest, and respect. Boundaries allow you to create the life you want, one that is full of the things and people that truly nourish you, and free from the things that drain you.

It's important to recognize that setting boundaries doesn't mean you are being selfish. In fact, it is the complete opposite. It means you are taking responsibility for your happiness and well-being. It's about valuing yourself enough to say no when something doesn't feel right or when you don't have the capacity to give. It's about understanding that your time, energy, and emotions are precious, and you deserve to spend them on things that align with your values and goals.

One of the most transformative aspects of setting boundaries is that it gives you permission to say yes to the things that truly matter. Instead of being caught up in people-pleasing, you can make conscious decisions about where you invest your time and energy. You can say yes to the relationships that uplift you, to the activities that bring you joy, and to the opportunities that align with your purpose. By setting boundaries, you free yourself from the weight of obligation and make room for the things that truly bring you happiness and fulfillment.

Boundaries also give you the space to grow. When you prioritize your own needs and set clear limits with others, you create the room necessary for personal development, reflection, and renewal. You give yourself the freedom to recharge and replenish your energy, allowing you to show up as your best, most authentic self in all areas of your life.

Setting boundaries doesn't only apply to our relationships with others—it also applies to our relationship with ourselves. It means being clear about the commitments you make to yourself, honoring your own time, and taking the necessary steps to prioritize self-care. It means not allowing guilt to prevent you from taking breaks, seeking support when you need it, or saying no to things that do not serve your well-being.

At first, setting boundaries may feel uncomfortable or even create tension in your relationships. People who are used to you being available or accommodating may feel surprised or even frustrated when you begin to prioritize yourself. But over time, they will come to respect your boundaries, and your relationships will become healthier and more balanced. You will find that when you respect yourself and set clear limits, you are teaching others how to do the same.

The importance of setting boundaries extends beyond just protecting yourself—it's also about creating space for healthier, more fulfilling relationships. When you set boundaries, you encourage mutual respect, understanding, and trust. Healthy boundaries allow for communication, collaboration, and compromise in relationships, without compromising your own well-being.

Boundaries are not just about what you say no to—they are also about what you say yes to. They allow you to create the life that aligns with your true values and desires. Boundaries enable you to protect your time, energy, and emotions so you can invest them in the things that bring you joy, fulfillment, and growth. By setting boundaries, you are taking charge of your life and choosing to live authentically, without sacrificing your own well-being in the process.

When you begin to set healthy boundaries, you will feel a sense of relief and freedom. You will feel empowered, knowing that you are actively protecting your well-being. And you will begin to recognize that, by setting boundaries, you are creating a life that is full of purpose, balance, and authenticity.

8

Chapter 7: Legacy of Love and Strength

A legacy is not just a passing moment; it is the continuation of who we are, even after we are no longer here. It is the imprint of our lives on the world, the traces of our presence that continue to ripple through time. When we think of legacy, too often we focus on what can be quantified—money, properties, or accomplishments—but true legacy goes far deeper than material success. It is shaped by the intangible qualities that define us: the love we gave, the strength we demonstrated in the face of adversity, the kindness we extended, and the wisdom we passed on.

Legacy is the sum of all our actions—the choices we make every day, how we treat others, how we rise after failure, and how we persist even when the road ahead seems uncertain. It is a reflection of our integrity and authenticity. The legacy we leave is not just about the titles we wear, but about the way we show up for the people in our lives, and the impact we have on the hearts and minds of others.

At its core, a legacy is a story—a story told through moments both big and small. It's in the way we lift others up, the way we guide them through their struggles, the way we empower them to be their truest selves. When we act with intention, when we approach the world with an open heart and a mind dedicated to positive change, we build something that outlasts us. Our legacy is the collective experience of how we made others feel, how we empowered them to find their strength, and how we taught them to stand in their own authenticity.

A legacy of love and strength does not come from the accumulation of things—it comes from our ability to touch the lives of others, to leave a piece of ourselves in every meaningful interaction. It is in the heartfelt conversations, the encouragement given in moments of doubt, the love extended in moments of hardship. Our legacy is built in the quiet moments as much as the loud ones—the moments when we chose to be compassionate, when we reached out to someone in need, or when we offered a listening ear. These moments, often unnoticed, hold the greatest power in shaping the future.

This kind of legacy transcends the physical and material realms. It is about the energy we radiate into the world and the values we embody. When we choose to live authentically, we create ripples of inspiration that continue to spread, inspiring others to live in alignment with their own truth. It is through our example, our lived experiences, and the wisdom we pass on that we have the power to shape the world around us.

The most meaningful legacy we can leave behind is one that is centered around love, compassion, resilience, and strength. It is about how we use our unique gifts to inspire change, how we uplift those who feel weak, and how we turn our pain into power that fuels transformation in others. We leave behind not just memories, but a blueprint for others to follow—a path of empowerment, hope, and growth.

When we look at the greatest legacies left behind in history, we see that they were not shaped by wealth or fame, but by the impact people had on others. The legacies of figures like Mother Teresa, Nelson Mandela, Martin Luther King Jr., and so many others, show us that the most lasting influence is not about what we accumulate, but what we give. It is about the love we pour into the lives of others, the way we fight for justice, and the way we lead with our hearts.

This type of legacy is not built overnight, but it is cultivated through intentional actions, consistent values, and a commitment to living authentically. It requires us to be vulnerable, to embrace our imperfections, and to show up even when it feels difficult. It is about embracing our humanity—the pain, the joy, the messiness—and using those experiences to touch others' lives.

When we shift our focus from external accomplishments to internal values, we begin to see that our true legacy is not measured by what we have, but by who we are. It is in the hearts we touch, the lives we change, and the ripple effect of our love, strength, and resilience that continues to reverberate long after we are gone.

As we live each day, let us remember that our legacy is not something that comes at the end of our lives; it is being built right now, in every choice we make, in every moment we live. We don't have to wait for a grand event to leave our mark—we can start today, in the small and simple acts of kindness, love, and authenticity. By living with intention and purpose, we create a legacy that endures beyond time and space, one that speaks to the power of love, strength, and authenticity.

Ultimately, a legacy is the ultimate expression of our life's work, the culmination of our journey, and the mark we leave on the world. It is our story, written not in words, but in deeds and actions—woven into the fabric of those whose lives we've touched and whose hearts we've changed. Let your legacy be one of love, strength, resilience, and authenticity. Let it reflect the power of your true self, and may it inspire others to leave a legacy that echoes through the generations.

The Root of Love: A Legacy That Transcends Generations

Love is the root of all that endures in this world. It is not a transient emotion, but a profound, unyielding force that shapes and transforms everything it touches. True love transcends time and space, leaving an indelible mark on the lives of those who encounter it. It is a legacy that lives on through the generations, passed from one heart to another, creating a ripple effect of compassion, strength, and resilience. This is the legacy I want to leave behind—a legacy built on love that transcends generations, a love that builds, heals, and strengthens.

At the core of this legacy is the deep, unwavering love that a mother gives to her children. A mother's love is powerful beyond measure. It is not simply an emotion; it is a force that propels us forward, guides us through hardship, and provides the foundation for everything we do. The love a mother offers her children is fierce, protective, and selfless. It is the kind of love that can endure pain and loss, that doesn't ask for anything in return, but simply gives, because it knows the transformative power of selflessness.

This love is the greatest gift a mother can offer. It becomes the foundation upon which her children can stand tall, weathering life's storms with strength and resilience. A mother's love is not confined to one moment; it is a lasting, enduring presence that shapes the future. It is passed on in the words of wisdom shared, in the lessons taught, in the actions of care and nurturing. This love endures, long after the mother has passed, as it is carried forward by her children, who continue to share that love with others.

As a mother myself, I know how deep this love runs. It is this love that fuels my desire to leave a legacy of strength, courage, and resilience for my children. I want them to know that they are capable of achieving anything they set their minds to. I want them to feel empowered to face the challenges of life with grace and perseverance. It is my love for them that drives me to create opportunities, to provide them with the tools and lessons they need to succeed. I want to build a future where they stand not only on their own two feet but on the strong foundation of love that I have given them.

But love does not stop with our families. Love is not something we can restrict to just those closest to us. It extends far beyond that, reaching into every corner of the world. Love is what makes us human. It connects us to one another in ways that words cannot fully express. When we show love to others, we inspire them to do the same. When we offer a listening ear, a kind word, a helping hand, we build bridges that connect hearts. This love, when shared freely, has the power to transform not just individuals but entire communities, shaping a world that is more compassionate, more understanding, and more resilient.

This is the love that I want my legacy to represent. It is a love that knows no boundaries, that gives freely without expecting anything in return. It is a love that is not confined to a single person or group of people, but that extends to everyone we meet. It is the love that guides my journey, the love that fuels my desire to make a difference in the world. Every action I take, every word I speak, is rooted in the belief that love is the most powerful force in the world. It is the one thing that can heal wounds, build bridges, and create lasting change.

In my own life, I have seen the transformative power of love. It is the love I received as a child, the love I give to my own children, and the love I share with others that has shaped me into the person I am today. It has been my anchor during times of hardship, my guiding light when the path ahead seemed unclear. It has given me the strength to keep going, even when I felt like giving up. And it is this love that I want to pass on—to my children, to my family, to my community, and to the world.

The legacy of love I leave behind is not something that can be measured in material wealth or worldly success. It is not something that can be seen or touched. It is the unseen force that moves through us all, connecting us to one another, binding us together in a shared humanity. It is the love that continues to grow, long after we are gone, carried forward by those we have touched.

When we live with love at the core of everything we do, we create a legacy that transcends generations. The love we give today will continue to echo for years to come, inspiring others to carry that love forward. And in doing so, we build a world that is stronger, kinder, and more compassionate.

Our legacy is not defined by the things we accumulate or the achievements we reach. It is defined by the love we offer, the love we share, and the love that we inspire in others. That is the true legacy—the one that transcends time and generations, leaving behind a world that is better, kinder, and filled with hope.

As I reflect on the legacy I want to leave behind, I am reminded that it is not something that can be rushed or forced. It is built over time, one small act of love at a time. Each moment, each interaction, each decision is a building block for the future. By living with love at the center of everything we do, we can leave behind a legacy that will endure long after we are gone—a legacy that is rooted in the deepest, most transformative force in the world: *Love.*

Strength: The Power of Rising from Adversity

Strength is not simply a characteristic; it is an evolving force that grows through adversity. It's the power to push forward when every fiber of your being wants to give up, to stand tall when life tries to knock you down. Strength is not just about physical endurance, it is about emotional resilience, mental fortitude, and spiritual perseverance. It is the courage to rise each time you fall, to keep going when the road seems impossibly long and difficult.

I didn't understand this kind of strength when I first entered this world. I wasn't born with a clear understanding of resilience. Like most, I had to learn it the hard way—through hardship, pain, and loss. The journey to resilience is not an easy one; it's often forged in moments of deep struggle, when we feel as though we cannot go on. Yet, it is in these moments that we discover the incredible depth of our own strength.

In the depths of pain, I found my capacity to endure. I realized that every trial I faced had the potential to teach me something. Each obstacle became an opportunity to grow, and with each obstacle, I became stronger. The beauty of strength is that it is not about avoiding the storms of life; it's about learning to navigate them with grace and resilience. True strength is the ability to continue moving forward, even when you feel like you are at your breaking point.

What I've learned through my own experiences is that strength isn't born from perfection or the absence of struggle. It is born in the battle itself. Strength is not defined by the absence of failure, but by the ability to rise after every fall. It's about showing up for yourself, even when it feels easier to stay down. Every setback is a chance to rise again, and in rising, we discover our true power.

This kind of strength is not just for me to keep to myself. I want to pass it on—to my children, to the generations that will come after me. The legacy I want to leave is one of resilience, courage, and the ability to rise, again and again, no matter how many times we are knocked down. It's the kind of strength that teaches us that setbacks are not the end of the story. They are simply chapters in a much larger narrative of growth and transformation.

The most important thing I can teach my children is this: life will not always go as planned. There will be moments of pain, loss, and disappointment. There will be times when they will feel defeated. But the strength to stand back up, to face each challenge with courage, to keep pushing forward when the road is unclear—that is the kind of strength that will carry them through life's toughest moments.

Strength is about mindset. It's about shifting the way we view failure and adversity. Instead of seeing these challenges as insurmountable obstacles, we can choose to see them as opportunities for growth. Each failure is a stepping stone to success, each difficulty a lesson in resilience. The more we experience hardship, the more we come to realize that we have the inner power to overcome anything that stands in our way. It is this unwavering belief in our own strength that helps us face even the darkest of times.

By teaching my children to be resilient, I am not just preparing them for the inevitable challenges of life; I am giving them the tools to shape their own futures. When they face trials, they will know that their worth is not determined by the things that go wrong, but by their ability to rise up again and again. I want them to carry this strength with them throughout their lives, to face each obstacle head-on with grace and determination, and to know that they are never truly defeated as long as they keep going.

This strength is also about self-compassion. It's about recognizing that while we may be tough on the outside, we are allowed to feel our pain and to take care of our emotional health. True strength isn't about suppressing our emotions or pretending we are invincible. It's about acknowledging the pain and still moving forward with purpose. It's about knowing that there is no shame in being vulnerable or seeking help when we need it. Strength is about being honest with ourselves, embracing our humanity, and finding the courage to face whatever comes with an open heart.

It is this strength, this resilience, that I want my children to inherit from me. I want them to understand that life's challenges do not define them. They will face hardships, but those hardships will only add to their strength. I want them to know that even when they feel broken, they are not defeated—they are simply being shaped into the person they are meant to become. I want them to face each setback with the understanding that growth comes from struggle. I want them to trust in their own ability to overcome, to rise from the ashes, and to be better for it.

There will be times when life feels overwhelming, when the weight of the world is heavy upon our shoulders. But it is in these moments that we discover the true depth of our strength. It's in these moments that we find the courage to take one more step, to rise up from the ashes, and to keep moving forward. And it is in these moments that we realize that strength is not just about enduring hardship—it's about growing stronger through it.

The legacy I hope to leave is not one of perfection, but one of resilience. I want my children to know that they can endure anything that life throws at them. I want them to carry the lessons of strength, courage, and resilience into their own lives, passing them on to future generations. This strength is not something we are born with; it is something we cultivate over time. It is something we develop through every challenge we face, every obstacle we overcome. And it is this strength that will carry us through life's toughest moments, allowing us to rise again and again, stronger than we were before.

The Ripple Effect: Empowering Others to Carry the Torch

Building a legacy is not a solitary endeavor; it is a shared experience that ripples outward, touching and uplifting others along the way. While personal growth is vital, it becomes even more powerful when we consider how it affects the people around us. The legacy we leave behind is not defined by what we've achieved for ourselves, but by how we've contributed to the growth and development of others. This is the essence of true leadership: lifting as we rise.

When we dedicate ourselves to becoming the best version of ourselves, we create an invisible thread that connects us to those who are on their own journeys. The progress we make—whether big or small—becomes a beacon of possibility for those around us. It demonstrates that transformation is possible and that no matter where we start, there is always room to rise. The more we develop, the greater the potential we have to inspire and empower others to do the same.

One of the most profound ways to leave a lasting impact is through mentorship. Mentorship is about more than offering advice; it's about offering love, encouragement, and belief in someone else's potential. I often reflect on the women who mentored me, those who saw something in me long before I could see it in myself. They recognized the strength I had inside, and they nurtured it. They didn't just teach me skills—they taught me to believe in myself, to trust in my own abilities, and to pursue my dreams with courage. Their mentorship shaped my journey in ways I could never have imagined, and the impact they had on my life is immeasurable.

I strive to be that mentor for others. Just as those women reached back and helped me along my path, I want to do the same for the next generation. Whether it's through my business ventures, my writing, or simply by being a listening ear, I am committed to sharing the wisdom I've gained throughout my journey. I want to be the person others turn to when they need guidance, when they need someone to help them see their own potential, and when they need inspiration to keep going.

Mentorship isn't just about teaching—it's about creating a space where others feel safe to grow, to make mistakes, and to transform. It's about holding space for people to discover their own power, to unlock the doors to their own potential, and to believe in themselves even when they can't see it yet. A mentor is someone who walks alongside others, helping them navigate the difficult paths, celebrating their successes, and offering support when things get tough. A mentor's impact is not measured by the immediate results they see, but by the long-term ripple effect they create.

A legacy that empowers others is not a static one; it's a living, breathing entity that grows and evolves over time. Every person we help, every life we touch, adds a new layer to the story of transformation. Each individual who steps into their power becomes a part of the greater whole—a community of empowered, resilient people who are creating change in their own unique ways. The beauty of a legacy built on empowerment is that it multiplies. The more we invest in others, the more they can invest in others, and the cycle continues. It is a legacy that doesn't stop with us; it grows and flourishes, impacting generations to come.

When I think about the legacy I want to leave, I realize that it's not just about my children or my personal accomplishments. It's about everyone who encounters my work, my story, and my journey. It's about creating a space for others to tap into their own potential, to see what they are truly capable of, and to be inspired to take action. The more people I can help, the more lives I can touch, the greater the legacy I leave behind.

My work is a testament to the power of mentorship and empowerment. Through my business, I aim to create opportunities for others to thrive, to tap into their own strength, and to build their own legacies. Whether it's offering a job, providing resources, or simply sharing knowledge, I want to be a force that helps others rise. Through my writing, I seek to inspire and empower, sharing my own story of resilience and transformation in the hopes that it will encourage others to embark on their own journeys of growth. Through every interaction, I strive to be a source of strength, wisdom, and love, offering guidance wherever it is needed.

The beauty of a legacy built on empowerment is that it creates a ripple effect that continues long after we are gone. The people we mentor, the lives we touch, the hearts we change—they all become part of the larger narrative of transformation. And as they go on to help others, that ripple grows wider and more profound. In this way, our legacies transcend time and space. They live on in the people we've influenced, in the lives we've helped shape, and in the ripple effect that continues to grow.

When we focus on empowering others, we are not just building a legacy for ourselves; we are helping to build a better world for everyone. A legacy that empowers others is one that creates lasting change—a world where everyone has the opportunity to tap into their own potential and make a difference. This is the kind of legacy I want to leave. A legacy that is not defined by what I've accumulated, but by the people I've helped to rise. A legacy that will continue to grow and transform, impacting lives for generations to come.

Creating a Legacy of Community

Legacy is not a solitary journey. It is a collective effort—a story that is woven from the threads of many lives, interconnected in ways that transcend time and space. While we often think of legacy in terms of individual achievements or the personal impact we have, true legacy is shaped by the communities we build and the relationships we nurture. It is in community that legacy takes on its fullest form, growing far beyond what any single person can achieve alone.

A legacy that has true power is one that lifts others up, creates space for vulnerability, and fosters a deep sense of belonging. It's not just about individual success; it's about the collective strength of a group working together, supporting one another, and growing together. In community, we find the encouragement we need to keep going when we feel weak, the inspiration to push through when we want to give up, and the love that reminds us of our intrinsic worth. A community-built legacy is one that empowers everyone involved, helping them tap into their potential and make a meaningful impact on the world.

I believe wholeheartedly in the power of community. The connections we form within a supportive environment are what fuel us. It is in community that we are seen, heard, and understood. Here, we are reminded that we are not alone in our struggles or in our victories. We find strength in the shared experiences and the knowledge that others are walking alongside us. The bonds we form in community are the foundation for resilience, for growth, and for transformation.

They remind us that we are part of something larger than ourselves, and that our actions have the power to shape the lives of others.

A legacy built on community is one that transcends the individual and creates something much greater. It becomes a network of support—an ecosystem of shared purpose, compassion, and collaboration. In such a community, people are able to show up as their authentic selves, without fear of judgment or rejection. It is in these spaces that we are truly free to be who we are, to express ourselves openly, and to grow without the constraints of perfection or pretense. The beauty of community is that it nurtures us in ways we cannot do on our own. It provides the care and support that we need to overcome challenges, while also pushing us to be better, to aim higher, and to strive for the greatest versions of ourselves.

My vision for the legacy I want to create is deeply tied to building a community of like-minded individuals who are committed to empowering others and making a positive impact. This isn't just about my personal business or success; it's about creating a space where people from all walks of life can come together and share their wisdom, their knowledge, and their strength. In my business, I want to create an environment that feels like a safe haven—where people feel supported, understood, and valued. It's a space where collaboration thrives, where ideas are shared freely, and where everyone is encouraged to reach for their dreams.

But more than that, it's about creating a culture of care and empowerment. I want my business to be a place where people come not just for work, but for connection. It's where relationships are formed, where mentorship is offered, and where everyone feels that they have something to contribute. In this community, no one is left behind. We rise together, supporting each other through the highs and lows, and celebrating our shared successes. This is the true power of legacy—when we realize that we are all connected and that our actions can have a profound and lasting impact on those around us.

I am committed to building this type of community in every area of my life. Whether it's through my work, my personal relationships, or my outreach efforts, I will work tirelessly to create spaces where people can find belonging, encouragement, and empowerment. My goal is not only to build a legacy for my children, but for everyone who enters my circle. I want to create a network of individuals who are bound together by a shared mission to make the world a better place, to lift each other up, and to create positive change. Through mentorship, shared experiences, and collaborative growth, we can create something much larger than ourselves—a legacy that transcends generations.

A legacy rooted in community doesn't stop at the boundaries of a single group. It has the power to spread, to multiply, and to create a ripple effect that touches lives across the world. The more we nurture these connections, the more they grow, touching people in ways we may never even see. As we empower others, we provide them with the tools, knowledge, and strength to do the same for others. It becomes a cycle of empowerment, where every person we touch can go on to empower others, and the legacy we create continues to build momentum.

In the end, the truest measure of our legacy is not in the wealth we accumulate or the accomplishments we achieve for ourselves, but in the impact we have on the lives of others. A legacy rooted in community creates something far more profound than any material possession or personal accolade. It creates a living, breathing network of love, support, and empowerment. It shapes the world in ways we can't even begin to imagine, and it ensures that the work we do today will continue to echo through the generations, inspiring others to rise, to grow, and to build their own legacies of love and impact.

This is the legacy I am working to build—a legacy that thrives in community, a legacy that uplifts others, a legacy that will carry forward long after I am gone. It is a legacy of empowerment, of connection, of belonging—a legacy that transcends time and creates a lasting impact on the world. And it all starts with the relationships we build today.

Leaving Behind More Than Material Wealth

Leaving behind more than material wealth is one of the most powerful aspects of building a lasting legacy. While the accumulation of financial resources, properties, and possessions is often seen as the pinnacle of success, it is crucial to recognize that these are fleeting. They can be lost, spent, or passed down, but their impact is temporary. True wealth, however, is found in the depth of the relationships we build, the lives we touch, and the hearts we uplift. These are the treasures that endure, and they become the foundation of a meaningful and impactful legacy.

When I reflect on the type of legacy I want to leave behind, it becomes clear that it is not the tangible assets I acquire that define my story. It's the intangible—the lessons learned through hardship and perseverance, the strength developed in times of struggle, and the love shared with others. It is the moments of kindness, the encouragement offered during someone's darkest hour, and the inspiration to rise and keep moving forward. These are the elements that truly make a legacy eternal, because they live on in the hearts and actions of others, long after we're gone.

I think about the people in my life who have left an indelible mark on me, not because of their material possessions, but because of their spirit, their kindness, and their resilience. The wisdom they shared, the support they offered, and the love they gave continue to influence me every day. I want to be that person for others—to be remembered not for the wealth I may or may not have accumulated, but for the love and care I gave, for the strength I exemplified, and for the encouragement I offered others to rise up and reach for their dreams.

True legacy is measured not in what we have, but in who we are and how we impact the world around us. The relationships we cultivate, the trust we build, and the way we inspire those around us is where true wealth lies. I want to leave a legacy that transcends time and circumstance. A legacy that speaks not only to the material things I may leave behind, but to the emotional and spiritual gifts that I give to others along the way. These gifts are priceless, because they carry with them the power to transform lives and change the world.

Love is at the center of this kind of legacy. Love has the ability to bridge divides, heal wounds, and spark movements. It's not just about romantic love, but the kind of love that is unconditional and unwavering—the love that sees beyond flaws, the love that believes in the potential of others, and the love that empowers people to be their best selves. This is the love that I want to leave behind: a love that is remembered in every act of kindness, in every encouragement, in every moment of support I offer to those around me.

In the grand scheme of life, when we think about what we want to leave behind, it is the impact we have on others that truly matters. It's the lives we touch and the hearts we uplift that will echo through the generations. I want to leave behind a legacy of transformation—a legacy that not only changes lives in the present but also plants seeds for future generations. I want my children, my family, my friends, and even strangers to feel the strength and love that I offered during my time on this earth, and I want them to pass it on.

My legacy won't be measured in the buildings I own or the money I have, but in the way I inspire others to live authentically, to rise from adversity, and to love unconditionally. These are the things that cannot be taken away—they live on in the hearts of those who were touched by them. And when those people go on to impact others, the ripple effect continues to expand, creating an ever-growing legacy of love, strength, and transformation.

In the end, a legacy that transcends time and generations is one that is built on the core values of love, compassion, and service. It's about making a difference in the lives of others, and it's about teaching others to do the same. When we focus on leaving behind a legacy of positive impact, we create a world that is stronger, more loving, and more resilient. The material things we accumulate may fade away, but the love we give, the lives we touch, and the hearts we uplift will continue to live on, creating a lasting and profound impact for years to come.

So, as I move forward in my journey, I will continue to focus not on the wealth I accumulate, but on the wealth I create in others. I will strive to leave a legacy that is defined by the love I give, the strength I embody, and the impact I make. This is the kind of legacy that will endure—one that transcends time and generations, and that continues to inspire long after I am gone.

Passing the Torch to Future Generations

Passing the torch to future generations is one of the most profound responsibilities we hold when it comes to leaving a meaningful legacy. A legacy is not a static entity; it's a living, evolving force that can only truly thrive when it's shared and carried forward by those who come after us. Our legacy is built not only on what we have achieved, but also on the seeds we plant in the minds and hearts of the next generation, so they can continue the work, build upon it, and take it to greater heights.

One of the most important aspects of passing the torch is ensuring that future generations are not only equipped with wisdom and teachings but are also given the tools, resources, and mindset to create their own legacies. In my own life, I've been shaped by the wisdom and love of those who came before me. Their teachings have been the foundation of my own growth, and now it's my turn to pass that foundation along to those who come after me. This is a cycle of growth and transformation that continues through time, and it's one that I am committed to perpetuating.

I want to provide the resources and opportunities that will allow my children, my nieces, my nephews, and anyone who looks to me for guidance, to not just survive in the world but to thrive. The world we live in is constantly changing, and the challenges of the future will undoubtedly be different from those we face today. However, the core values of resilience, love, strength, and faith remain timeless. These are the values I want to instill in those who come after me—values that will serve as the bedrock upon which they can build their own lives, pursue their own dreams, and make their own unique contributions to the world.

I believe that true empowerment comes from teaching others how to think for themselves, how to problem-solve, how to tap into their own inner strength, and how to live with purpose. It's about showing them that they are not victims of circumstance, but architects of their own lives. By teaching them the mindset of resilience, the importance of hard work, and the value of a strong community, I am giving them the power to create their own legacies—legacies that will continue to transform the world long after I'm gone.

This is not just about leaving behind a set of instructions, but rather about giving them the freedom to explore, to grow, and to create. I want to inspire them to embrace challenges, to seek out opportunities for growth, and to build upon the foundation I've laid. I want them to know that they don't have to start from scratch—they are inheriting a legacy of love, strength, and wisdom that will serve as a compass as they navigate their own paths.

But it's not just about the knowledge we pass on; it's also about the mindset we instill. I want to pass on the belief that they are capable of anything they set their minds to. I want to teach them that failure is not a reason to give up but an opportunity to learn, grow, and rise again stronger. I want them to understand that the world is full of opportunities for those who are willing to work for them, and that they are more than capable of shaping their own destinies. This mindset will empower them to build upon the legacy I leave and continue to create positive change in their own lives and the lives of those around them.

A legacy that is truly passed on does not stop with one generation—it continues to evolve, to grow, and to make an impact in ways we may never fully understand. When we pass the torch, we are not just leaving behind a set of teachings or values; we are setting in motion a chain reaction of empowerment and transformation that has the potential to change the course of history. The work we begin may take many forms as it is passed down, but the core message of love, strength, resilience, and service will remain the same. Each new generation will build upon it, adding their unique contributions, making it their own, and taking it even further.

In my own life, I've seen firsthand how powerful this ripple effect can be. The mentors who have guided me, the lessons I've learned, and the values I've been taught have shaped who I am today. Now, it's my turn to be that guiding force for the next generation. By passing the torch, I am creating a legacy that is not confined to a single lifetime but stretches far beyond it—one that will continue to impact the world for years to come.

It's also important to note that passing the torch isn't just a one-time act—it's a continual process. As I continue to grow, learn, and evolve, I must also pass along the knowledge and wisdom I gain along the way. It's an ongoing cycle, one that never truly ends because the work of transformation and empowerment is never done. As long as there are lives to touch and hearts to uplift, the torch must keep passing, lighting the way for others and creating a ripple effect of love, strength, and positive change.

This is how my legacy will continue to grow and evolve—by passing the torch to those who are ready and willing to carry it forward. It's not about leaving behind a static entity; it's about creating a living, breathing legacy that adapts, transforms, and grows stronger with each generation. I am planting the seeds today, knowing that the fruits of those seeds will grow into something even greater than I can imagine, something that will leave an indelible mark on the world for years to come.

By empowering those who come after me with the tools, resources, and mindset to succeed, I am ensuring that my legacy will never end. It will continue to transform, to impact, and to create a better world for all. Through the torch I pass, I hope to light the way for generations to come, showing them that they too have the power to shape their own destinies and build their own legacies. This is the true essence of legacy—when it transcends one lifetime and becomes a force for good that ripples through the world, touching hearts and changing lives for generations.

A Legacy That Lives On

A legacy that truly lives on is not measured by the material wealth we accumulate or the recognition we achieve, but by the impact we have on the lives of others and the change we inspire in the world. It is about building something that goes beyond personal success, creating a force that continues to empower and uplift others long after we are gone. A legacy like this is not merely a memory; it is a movement—a living, breathing testament to the values, strength, and love we pour into the world. It becomes something greater than ourselves, something that resonates deeply within the hearts of those we touch and influences the course of future generations.

When I think about the legacy I want to leave behind, I think of the ripple effect it can create. The actions I take today, the love I give, the wisdom I share, and the resilience I embody will ripple outward and inspire others to do the same. This is the power of a legacy—it is never confined to one individual or one generation. It spreads, it grows, and it multiplies as it is passed from one person to another, across communities and cultures, over time and space.

The essence of this legacy is rooted in love, strength, and resilience. Love, because it is the foundation of all that we do. It is the love we give to others, the love we show ourselves, and the love that inspires us to be better and do better in the world. Strength, because it is through our moments of struggle, challenge, and hardship that we develop the fortitude to keep going, to push through adversity, and to rise again when life knocks us down. Resilience, because it is the ability to bounce back, to learn from our experiences, and to emerge stronger than before. Together, these three pillars form the backbone of a legacy that has the power to change lives and transform communities.

This legacy will be felt in every life I touch. Whether it's through the guidance I offer, the business ventures I build, or the relationships I foster, I want my presence in the world to leave a lasting mark. I want to be the kind of person who empowers others to find their own strength, to rise above their challenges, and to believe in their ability to shape their own destinies. I want to provide a space for others to feel seen, heard, and understood—a place where they can be their authentic selves and find the courage to step into their power.

As I continue to build my businesses, I aim to create platforms that allow people to thrive—not just financially, but emotionally, spiritually, and mentally. I want my work to reflect the values I hold dear: compassion, integrity, empowerment, and growth. I want to show others that success is not just about the bottom line; it's about the lives we touch, the difference we make, and the legacy we leave behind. My business ventures are not just about profitability—they are about creating a culture of support, collaboration, and collective growth, where every individual feels valued and empowered to reach their full potential.

But my legacy isn't limited to the professional sphere. It extends to every conversation I have, every interaction I share, and every piece of wisdom I pass down. Through my words and actions, I aim to inspire others to live with intention, to take ownership of their lives, and to recognize the power they hold within themselves. I want to teach others that their experiences, both good and bad, are valuable learning opportunities. Every challenge faced is a chance to grow, and every setback is simply a stepping stone toward greater things.

The wisdom I pass down will not only help others navigate the challenges of their lives but also guide them on the path to creating their own legacies. I want to be a mentor, a guide, and a source of inspiration for those who are ready to embark on their own journeys of transformation. I want to show them that they have the power to shape their futures, to rise above their circumstances, and to leave a legacy that will touch the lives of others in meaningful ways.

Ultimately, my legacy will outlive me. It will live on in the hearts of those I've touched, in the businesses I've built, in the communities I've impacted, and in the generations that follow. It will live on in the lives of my children, my nieces, my nephews, and all those who carry forward the lessons of strength, resilience, and love. It will continue to inspire and empower others, sparking a movement that can change the world for the better.

This legacy is not just about what I do—it's about what others can do because of the foundation I've laid. It's about providing the resources, the wisdom, and the encouragement for others to rise and create their own legacies. When we leave a legacy that is based on love, strength, and resilience, it has the power to ignite change that extends far beyond our own lives. It creates a ripple effect that transforms lives, builds communities, and shapes the future.

I am committed to leaving behind a legacy that speaks to these values. I want my journey to be a testament to the power of resilience—the ability to rise from adversity, to grow through pain, and to embrace life with love and gratitude. I want my legacy to be one of empowerment—showing others that they too have the ability to create change, to rise above their challenges, and to leave a lasting impact on the world.

This legacy will be felt in every life I touch, in every business I build, and in every person I inspire. It will continue to live on, growing, evolving, and impacting the world for generations to come. It is not just my story—it is the story of every person who has been touched by my journey and who carries it forward into their own lives. This is the power of a legacy—it lives on, it transforms, and it changes the world.

9

Chapter 8: The Roadmap to Empowerment

In the journey toward transformation, one of the most crucial steps is recognizing the immense power that resides within you. It's easy to underestimate the strength we possess, especially when faced with challenges, but I am here to tell you that the path to empowerment begins with understanding and believing in your potential. Just as I have learned to embrace my own power, I want to guide you through the steps that will empower you to create your legacy.

Acknowledging Your Power: The First Step

The first step toward empowerment is understanding that you are not powerless. No matter where you come from, what you've experienced, or where you are right now, you have the potential to rise, to transform, and to create a life of your own design. Often, we are our biggest barriers. We doubt our worth.

We shrink in the face of challenges, thinking we are too small to conquer them. But within each of us lies the same power that moves mountains, births revolutions, and transforms the darkest moments into triumphs.

It's time to stop questioning your worth. It's time to stop listening to the voices of doubt and fear. Instead, listen to the truth within you—the truth that says, "You are capable. You are worthy. You are powerful."

True empowerment begins within, by honoring the inherent power that lies dormant in each of us. Often, we let the weight of past failures, trauma, or self-doubt obscure this truth. But empowerment is about peeling back those layers to reveal the undeniable strength beneath. When you acknowledge your power, you open the door to infinite possibilities and opportunities. No longer will the external world dictate your limitations. Your inner strength will be your guiding compass.

Emotional Empowerment: Mastering Your Mindset

Emotional empowerment is the cornerstone of personal transformation. To truly step into your power, you must learn to take control of your emotions rather than allowing them to control you. Emotions are valid and important; they provide insight and guide us. However, allowing them to govern your actions without a clear mindset can lead you down a path of self-doubt, regret, and stagnation.

Mastering your emotions means mastering your reactions. By

acknowledging your emotional state without judgment, you free yourself from the need to react impulsively or defensively. Emotional mastery is the ability to pause, reflect, and respond with intention—choosing thoughts and actions that align with your highest self. This pause creates space for clarity and discernment.

To truly master your emotional state, the first action is to practice mindfulness. Become aware of your thoughts and feelings. Acknowledge them without judgment. Only then can you begin to shift your perspective. It is in the stillness of awareness that you can choose how you respond to situations, rather than reacting impulsively. Mindfulness is the foundation of emotional intelligence—it allows you to step out of emotional reactivity and into a more conscious, empowered way of living.

Forgiveness as Freedom

A crucial element in emotional empowerment is forgiveness. Not just forgiving others but forgiving yourself. Many of us hold onto the wounds of our past—grudges, regrets, and guilt—and these emotional weights prevent us from moving forward. Forgiveness doesn't mean excusing the pain caused, but rather releasing its hold on your life. It is an act of liberation. When you forgive, you free yourself to move forward, to grow, and to step into the future with a heart that is light and open.

Forgiveness is not simply a gift to others—it is a gift you give yourself. By forgiving, you release yourself from the emotional prison created by resentment and anger. Holding onto the past only prevents you from moving forward. Forgiveness is the key that unlocks the door to emotional freedom. It is the act of choosing your own peace over carrying the heavy burden of past hurt.

Financial Empowerment: Creating Wealth and Abundance

While emotional and spiritual empowerment are essential, financial empowerment is the practical foundation that allows you to build the life you desire. You must educate yourself about money and wealth-building strategies. Many of us were never taught about money in a way that empowers us. We were told to work hard, save, and retire—but there is more to it than that.

Financial freedom is not just about accumulating wealth; it is about making money work for you. This involves learning how to invest, understanding the power of compound interest, and creating multiple streams of income. Financial empowerment gives you the ability to create opportunities for yourself and others, enabling you to live a life by design, not by default.

- *Investing:* Investing is one of the most powerful ways to build wealth. Start with small steps, such as opening a brokerage account or contributing to a retirement plan. Diversify your investments—stocks, real estate, bonds, and mutual funds all offer opportunities to grow your money. The earlier you start, the more time your investments will have to compound. Investing is not just for the wealthy—it is a tool for building wealth that is accessible to everyone. It's about taking your hard-earned money and allowing it to work for you.

- *Financial Literacy:* Invest time in learning about personal finance. Books, courses, podcasts, and mentors are invaluable tools to educate yourself. When you understand how money works, you can make smarter decisions that lead to greater financial success. Financial literacy is the key to making empowered choices—it's about understanding how to navigate the complex world of money so you can create lasting wealth.

- Passive Income: Seek opportunities for passive income—money that comes in even when you aren't actively working. This could be through investments, royalties, business ventures, or real estate. Creating wealth is not just about earning; it's about positioning yourself in a way where money flows toward you, even when you're not physically present. Passive income is freedom—it allows you to build wealth without trading all of your time for money.

Spiritual Empowerment: Connecting with Your Higher Self

Spiritual empowerment is the anchor that holds everything together. Your connection with God, the universe, or your higher self provides the wisdom, guidance, and strength necessary to stay grounded as you pursue your goals. When you are spiritually aligned, you are able to see beyond the physical world and tap into the deeper wisdom that transcends logic and reason. This connection gives you the courage to trust the path before you, even when the journey is unclear.

• *Faith as Foundation:* Building a solid spiritual foundation is essential for empowerment. Faith gives you the resilience to weather the storms of life. With faith, there is always a sense of trust that things will work out for your good, even when it seems like the odds are stacked against you. Faith is your unshakable belief in the unseen, the confidence that no matter how the journey unfolds, everything is happening for your highest good.

• *Prayer and Meditation:* Practicing prayer and meditation allows you to connect with your spiritual self. These practices are tools for quieting your mind, listening for guidance, and finding peace amidst chaos. Meditation and prayer are the bridges to divine wisdom—they create a space for you to receive insights and clarity that are unavailable through the mind alone.

• *Gratitude and Service:* Gratitude and service are powerful spiritual practices that deepen your connection with the divine. By expressing gratitude daily and serving others, you align yourself with the flow of abundance. The more grateful you are, the more you receive, and the more you give, the more you are blessed in return. Gratitude shifts your energy, making you a magnet for more blessings, while service extends that abundance to others.

Building Your Legacy

Finally, as you step into your power, remember that empowerment is not just for you. It is for your community, your family, and for future generations. You are building a legacy—one that is founded on love, wisdom, strength, and resilience. Your legacy is the blueprint you leave behind for those who come after you. It is the impact you have on your community, the lessons you teach, and the lives you touch.

In order to build a meaningful legacy, you must focus not just on your personal growth but also on the lives you want to uplift. This means investing in relationships, mentoring, creating opportunities for others, and leaving a mark that resonates long after you are gone. Your legacy is not just what you create in this lifetime—it is the impact that ripples out into the future, empowering others to follow in your footsteps.

Action Steps to Empowerment

To bring all of these pieces together and step into your power, here is a roadmap you can follow:

1. *Start with Mindfulness:* Practice being present with your

thoughts and emotions. Recognize when negative patterns emerge and shift them consciously.

2. Invest in Knowledge: Educate yourself financially, emotionally, and spiritually. Seek mentors and resources that empower you to make informed decisions.

3. *Build Multiple Streams of Income:* Look for ways to generate income beyond your day job. Consider side businesses, investments, or creative endeavors that bring in passive income.

4. *Set Big Goals:* Dream big. Set long-term goals that inspire you and align with your higher purpose. Break them down into actionable steps and take consistent action.

5. *Practice Gratitude:* Cultivate gratitude in your daily life. Acknowledge the blessings you have and the lessons learned from challenges.

6. *Serve Others:* Empower those around you. Whether through mentorship, charity, or simple acts of kindness, your impact is magnified when you give back.

7. *Align with Your Higher Power:* Stay spiritually grounded. Trust in your intuition and seek divine guidance to navigate your journey.

The Roadmap to Empowerment is about stepping into the fullness of who you are meant to be. It is about trusting in the process and knowing that each step, no matter how small, is contributing to the greater transformation within you.

Remember, empowerment is not a destination, but a journey. It is an ongoing process of growth, learning, and adaptation. There will be challenges along the way, but each challenge is an opportunity to strengthen your resolve and grow even more into the person you are destined to become.

The Power of Your Story

As you move forward on your path to empowerment, remember that your story matters. Your experiences, your triumphs, your struggles—they are all pieces of the puzzle that make up your unique narrative. Your story is a source of strength and inspiration, not only for you but for others as well.

Embrace your past: The pain, the failures, the moments of darkness—they all serve as the backdrop for your resilience. You are a testament to the strength of the human spirit. Let your story inspire others who are on a similar journey.

Share your journey: Don't be afraid to share your story with the world. Whether through writing, speaking, or simply through your actions, your experiences have the power to change lives. When you open up about your struggles and your growth, you give others permission to do the same.

Your story is your legacy, and the more you embrace it, the more it will empower you to live authentically and unapologetically.

Creating Your Empowered Future

As you build the life you deserve, remember that you are the architect of your future. The choices you make today will shape the reality of tomorrow. Every decision, every action, every moment of self-doubt or confidence is part of your creation process. You are the artist, and the canvas of your life is yours to paint.

To create an empowered future, align your actions with your vision. Keep your dreams in sight, and take steps toward them every day. Remember that even the smallest step forward is progress. It's not about perfection; it's about perseverance.

Trust the Process

As you work toward empowerment, remember that the journey is not always linear. There will be setbacks, moments of doubt, and times when you feel discouraged. But trust the process. Your journey is unfolding exactly as it should, and every experience is contributing to your growth. Keep your eyes on the bigger picture and trust that everything is happening for your highest good.

Stay committed to your vision, take consistent action, and remember that the power to create change lies within you. You are capable of becoming everything you've ever dreamed of and more.

Empowerment is Yours to Claim

Empowerment is not a gift that is given—it is a right that is claimed. It is yours for the taking, and all it requires is the decision to step into your power. Embrace who you are, honor your journey, and trust in the limitless possibilities that await you.

You are stronger than you realize, braver than you know, and more capable than you could ever imagine. The road to empowerment is yours to walk, and I am here to cheer you on every step of the way.

This is your time. This is your moment. Claim your power, and step boldly into the life you were always meant to lead.

10

Chapter 9: Rise Again—Empowering Others

Have you ever felt like the world was against you, pushing you down, only to realize that the strength to rise again has always been within you?

Life has a way of testing our limits, pushing us to the edge, demanding more than we think we can give. But it's in those moments, in the depths of our struggles, that our true power emerges. We find a resilience we never knew we had. The journey is never easy, but it is in the fire of adversity that we become the strongest versions of ourselves.

I want to remind you of something essential: you are capable of rising, and not just for yourself, but for everyone who looks up to you. It's time to break free from the chains that have bound you—whether they are fear, doubt, or the limiting beliefs that have kept you stagnant. You have the power to rise again, to transcend the pain and fear of the past, and to build a future that is more magnificent than you ever imagined.

The First Step: Owning Your Power

The road to empowerment begins with one crucial realization: you have always had the power within you. It is not something that someone else can give you, nor is it something you need to search for outside yourself. It's already there. Hidden in the moments you've fought for your survival, in the tears you've shed, in the nights when you didn't know if you could go on but did anyway. It's in the resilience you've shown even when everything seemed hopeless.

The first step in your rise is acknowledging this power. Own it. Accept that you are enough, that you are strong beyond measure, and that you are destined for greatness.

This is not just positive thinking or empty affirmations. This is a deep, unshakable belief in yourself, grounded in your past triumphs, no matter how small they seemed at the time. Everything you've experienced up until this moment has shaped you for something greater. It was never in vain.

Taking the Leap: Fear is Not Your Enemy

Fear often stands in the way of our greatest potential. It whispers doubts in our ears and creates imaginary barriers that stop us before we even take the first step. But let me tell you something: fear is not your enemy. It is a signal—a sign that you are on the verge of something life-changing.

When you feel fear rising in your chest, don't run from it. Don't shy away from it. Embrace it. Understand that fear only has the power we give it. And when you face it, when you walk toward it with courage and confidence, you diminish its hold over you. Fear becomes your ally, not your adversary.

This is your invitation to take that leap. Step into the unknown. Break through the fear, the doubt, and the limitations that have kept you from stepping fully into your power. Take that first step toward your dreams, no matter how big or small they seem.

It will be hard. There will be challenges. But each obstacle is an opportunity for growth. Every setback is simply a lesson. And every moment of uncertainty is a chance for you to prove to yourself that you are stronger than you ever thought possible.

Rising Together: Empowering the World Around You

Empowerment isn't just about you. It's about those around you, the people who look to you for guidance, support, and inspiration. When you rise, you don't just lift yourself—you lift everyone within your sphere of influence.

By embracing your own journey, you empower others to do the same. Your transformation becomes the beacon for others to follow. They see you rise, and they think, "If she can do it, so can I."

It's in this shared strength, this collective resilience, that we find our true power. We are not alone in this journey. As you rise, bring others with you. Encourage them to step into their own light. Show them the way. Help them break through the barriers that have held them back.

But remember: you cannot empower others unless you first empower yourself. Your own transformation is the key to unlocking the potential in those around you. This is the ripple effect of empowerment. It starts with you, but it spreads out into your community, your family, your friends, and beyond.

The Vision of a New Future

Imagine, for a moment, a world where you are no longer held back by doubt, where every single day is a chance to build something new, something beautiful. A world where you wake up every morning feeling powerful, feeling alive with purpose.

This is not a distant dream. This is the future you are creating right now, through every choice you make, through every step you take toward the person you are destined to become. And as you rise, you create that future—not just for yourself but for everyone whose life you touch.

Picture a life where your success doesn't just benefit you but your family, your community, your legacy. Imagine the impact you will have on those around you when you break free from fear and doubt. Picture the changes you will inspire when you step into your full potential and encourage others to do the same.

This is the vision of the future waiting for you. A future where you are not only rising but lifting others up along the way.

The Call to Action: Your Moment is Now

Now is the time. Right here, right now, you have the ability to take that first step—toward your dream, toward your destiny, and toward becoming the person you were always meant to be. There is no more waiting. No more doubting. No more "maybe one day."

Today is the day you start your journey. Today is the day you take control of your future. Today is the day you rise again and begin to create the life you were always meant to lead.

I'm asking you, right now, to stand up and take that step. Stand in your power. Embrace your fears. Empower yourself so that you can empower others. You have the strength, the courage, and the wisdom to create the legacy you desire. It all begins with you.

The Ripple Effect: Creating a Lasting Impact

As you begin this journey of empowerment, remember that it's not just about the immediate changes you make in your own life—it's about the lasting impact you'll have on others. The people around you will watch you rise, and in doing so, they will find the courage to rise with you.

This is how legacies are built—not in isolation, but in community. The people you empower today will empower others tomorrow, and the ripple effect of your actions will spread far beyond what you can imagine.

Your story has the power to inspire others to break free from their own chains. Your rise has the potential to change lives, communities, and generations. The legacy you create will not just be one of success, but one of love, hope, and the unwavering belief that anything is possible when we rise together.

So, what are you waiting for? It's time to rise. It's time to create a future filled with possibility. It's time to step into your power and begin building the legacy that will endure for generations to come.

Rise again. Your moment is now.

Harnessing the Power of Your Voice

In the journey of rising again, your voice becomes one of the most powerful tools at your disposal. When you speak with conviction, when you own your story, you are not just telling your truth — you are creating a ripple effect that has the power to change the world. For too long, many of us have been told to stay silent, to shrink, to play small. But in this new chapter of life, we must choose to speak up. Not just for ourselves but for those who may not yet have found their voice.

Your voice is an instrument of freedom, a symbol of your authenticity, and a vehicle for your impact. Whether it is through sharing your story, advocating for others, or standing up for what you believe in, your voice has power.

How to Harness Your Voice:

1. *Speak from the Heart:* Authenticity is key. Speak with vulnerability, and allow your true feelings to guide your words.

2. *Be Bold:* Don't hold back. Speak your truth, even when it feels uncomfortable or challenging. You are the one who knows your journey best.

3. *Use Your Platform:* Whether big or small, your platform is an opportunity to influence, educate, and inspire. Leverage social media, writing, or public speaking as avenues to share your message.

4. *Empower Others with Your Voice:* Your words can uplift others and make them feel seen. Share their stories alongside your own, and amplify voices that have been silenced.

The Ripple Effect: Change Beyond You

Empowerment doesn't stop with you. When you rise, you inspire others to do the same. The courage it takes to stand tall in the face of adversity creates a ripple effect that can change entire communities. Your actions, your strength, and your unrelenting pursuit of greatness give others the permission they need to do the same.

Think about the people in your life who have inspired you—what did they do that made you feel empowered? The beauty of empowerment is that it doesn't have to be a solitary journey. As you rise, so do the people around you. It's a collective rising that allows us to overcome challenges, face adversity, and create lasting change.

How to Create a Ripple Effect of Empowerment:

1. *Lead by Example:* The best way to empower others is to live the example. Let your actions speak louder than words.

2. Support Others' Growth: Encourage and nurture those around you. Offer guidance, mentorship, and encouragement to help others rise.

3. *Collaborate:* Strength comes in numbers. Look for opportunities to collaborate with like-minded individuals, creating a network of support, knowledge, and shared vision.

4. *Celebrate Others' Successes:* Empowerment is about lifting others up. Celebrate their victories and share in their joy.

The Vision of a Transformed Future

As we rise, we must also envision the future we are creating. This vision is not just about personal success, but about leaving a legacy that transcends generations. It is a vision of a world where everyone has the opportunity to realize their fullest potential. It's a vision of equity, compassion, and shared growth.

Your legacy will be shaped by the values you live by, the impact you make on others, and the transformative change you leave behind. It will not just be defined by your financial success, but by the love, the courage, and the resilience you impart to the world.

Building the Future You Want:

1. Envision a World of Abundance: Believe that there is enough room for everyone to succeed. Create a world that thrives on collaboration and mutual support.

2. Lead with Compassion: Make decisions based not only on logic but on love and empathy for others.

3. *Create Systems for Others to Rise:* As you build, leave a path for others to follow. Whether it's through mentorship, education, or financial support, ensure that your success allows others to achieve their own.

4. *Leave a Legacy of Love:* Your legacy will be the love you give, the relationships you foster, and the communities you build. It's a legacy that will be remembered long after you're gone.

The Power of Gratitude in Your Journey

Gratitude is not just a mindset; it is a practice that will change the way you experience life. As you rise, acknowledge the blessings, the challenges, and the lessons that have shaped you. Cultivate gratitude for the journey, for the people who have helped you, and for the opportunities that have been presented to you.

Gratitude is a force that propels you forward. It turns every setback into a lesson, every success into a moment of humility. When you practice gratitude, you elevate your energy and your mindset to a place where abundance flows easily into your life.

Gratitude Practices to Empower Your Journey:

1. *Daily Reflection:* Take time each day to reflect on the things you are grateful for. This can be done in a journal, through prayer, or quiet meditation.

2. *Express Your Gratitude:* Don't just feel thankful—express it. Let those around you know how much you appreciate them and the role they've played in your life.

3. *Shift Perspective:* In difficult times, focus on what you've learned and the strength you've gained. Gratitude helps you see the bigger picture, where challenges are stepping stones to growth.

The Final Call to Action—Rise, Reclaim, and Shine

Now, I ask you: what are you waiting for? The time to rise is now. It is time to reclaim your power, to step into the fullness of who you are meant to be. The world needs your gifts, your strength, your voice, and your vision. You are not here by accident; you are here for a purpose.

Your dreams are not just for you—they are for the world. Your story is not just yours; it is part of a larger narrative that we are all writing together. By rising and empowering yourself, you pave the way for others to do the same.

As you take your next steps, remember this: you are not alone. There is a community of dreamers, achievers, and warriors walking with you. Together, we will rise and create the future we are meant to have. So go forth, fearlessly. Own your power, and watch as the world responds.

Your Call to Action:

1. *Embrace Fear:* Fear is not the enemy; it is the signal that you are about to grow. Walk toward it, not away from it.

2. *Own Your Journey:* Your journey is uniquely yours. Embrace every part of it, the good and the challenging.

3. *Inspire Others:* As you rise, lift others. Be the example, the mentor, and the inspiration they need.

4. *Create the Future:* Your actions today will build the world of tomorrow. Do it with purpose, love, and determination.

The world is waiting for you. It's time to rise again and make your mark.

11

Chapter 10: The Power of Your Legacy – Living with Purpose and Empowerment

Legacy is more than a collection of wealth, accolades, or tangible achievements. It is the essence of who you are, the principles you stand for, and the footprints you leave behind in the hearts and minds of others. A legacy is a living testament to the impact you've made and the ways you've influenced the world around you. It is what you give, not just in material terms, but in the love, the wisdom, and the strength you impart to future generations.

Your legacy is built with every decision, every action, and every intention you set forth. It is not simply something you leave behind, but something you actively create as you move through life. This chapter isn't just about the legacy you hope to leave—it's about the active, ongoing process of building that legacy every single day.

Building a Legacy That Transcends Time

A true legacy is not created overnight, nor is it defined by fleeting moments of success. It is defined by the love you pour into your life, the authenticity you embody, and the resilience you demonstrate in the face of adversity. It's the quiet strength you show when no one is watching, and the courage you exhibit when you stand up for others. The legacy you build is deeply embedded in your values and in the way you live those values out loud, unapologetically.

In every decision you make, whether big or small, you are laying the foundation for your legacy. Each moment is an opportunity to create something meaningful that will live on far beyond your lifetime. It's not about what you accumulate in material wealth but what you contribute to the lives of those around you, how you uplift them, how you empower them, and how you help them rise.

Your legacy is a reflection of who you are, of the impact you've made, and of the ripple effects you've set in motion. The beauty of a true legacy lies in the fact that it transcends time. It lives on in the stories passed down by those whose lives you've touched, in the principles and values you've instilled in the hearts of your children and loved ones, and in the changes you've sparked in the world. When you build a legacy, you ensure that the essence of who you are will continue to echo through generations.

The Ripple Effect: How Every Action Builds Your Legacy

Legacy is built not just in grand, headline-worthy moments, but in the small, seemingly insignificant actions you take each day. It's the encouragement you give to someone who's struggling. It's the kindness you show to a stranger. It's the love you express when it feels hard to do so. These actions ripple outwards, creating an effect that touches lives far beyond your own.

What may feel like a small, personal act to you—a smile, a word of encouragement, a helping hand—may serve as a powerful catalyst in someone else's life. You might not realize it at the time, but your actions can change the course of someone's day, their life, their destiny. By showing up with love and intention, you're creating a legacy that can span generations.

Every relationship you nurture, every person you invest in, every act of service, no matter how simple, is a step toward creating your legacy. Each moment is an opportunity to leave an imprint on someone's heart, to give them the confidence they need to move forward, to light a spark of inspiration that will carry them through their own struggles.

Even when you feel like you're doing nothing significant, trust that the seeds you plant today will grow into something meaningful tomorrow. Your influence reaches far beyond the immediate.

The Heart of a Legacy: Love, Resilience, and Service

When we think about legacy, we often focus on material things—the homes, the assets, the bank accounts—but the heart of a true legacy lies in the intangible aspects of life: love, resilience, and service. These are the qualities that define your journey and leave a lasting mark.

- *Love:* It is the foundation of every meaningful relationship, the glue that binds families, communities, and even nations. The legacy of love you leave will ripple out through the lives of your children, your friends, your colleagues, and anyone who crosses your path.

- *Resilience:* It is the ability to overcome challenges and rise from adversity. The struggles you've faced—and the strength you've shown in rising above them—become part of your legacy. These stories of perseverance inspire those around you and teach them that no matter the challenge, there is always the possibility of growth and rebirth.

- *Service:* Your legacy is not just about what you have done for yourself, but what you have done for others. The impact you have through service—whether by offering a helping hand or simply listening—is one of the greatest gifts you can give the world.

When you embody these qualities, you not only live your purpose but also leave a lasting imprint on the world. A legacy grounded in love, resilience, and service is one that will endure forever.

Your Legacy and the Generations That Follow

One of the most powerful aspects of a legacy is its ability to transcend time and continue to shape the world long after you're gone. This is where the true power of your legacy lies—in how it influences the lives of those who come after you.

Your legacy is the gift you give to your children, your family, and your community. It is the example you set and the lessons you teach. It is the strength you demonstrate and the love you offer freely. As you build your legacy, you must consider not only the present but the future—how your actions today will impact the lives of those yet to come.

You may not be able to control every aspect of the future, but you can certainly influence it. By living authentically and intentionally, by living in alignment with your values, you are setting the groundwork for the future generations to follow. Your legacy becomes their blueprint for life.

Imagine your children growing up with the tools, wisdom, and values you've instilled in them, equipped to make their own mark on the world. Picture your community flourishing because you dedicated yourself to lifting others up. That is the power of legacy—a living, breathing force that continues to change the world long after you're gone.

Living Your Legacy—Now, Today, In Every Moment

Creating your legacy doesn't have to be a long-term, far-off goal—it can be something you live every day. Every decision you make, every action you take, is part of the foundation for the legacy you are building. Legacy isn't something that can be postponed until tomorrow; it is something you actively create today.

Live with intention. Live with authenticity. Live with love. When you make conscious choices to live in alignment with your values, you are building your legacy in real time.

You don't need to wait for a certain moment or milestone to start. Your legacy is created with every act of kindness, every word of encouragement, every sacrifice you make for the good of others. When you live with love and purpose, you begin to see the impact of your legacy unfold before your very eyes.

The Roadmap to Building Your Legacy

You have within you the tools to build a legacy. It starts with:

- *Understanding Your Values:* What are the principles that guide your life? Define them clearly, and let them serve as the foundation for every decision you make.

- *Building Relationships:* Legacy is built in the connections you cultivate, the people you help, and the ways you serve others. Nurture these relationships with intention, knowing they will become part of the legacy you leave behind.

- *Living Authentically:* Be true to yourself. Don't let societal pressures, fear, or doubts hold you back. Live the truth of who you are, knowing that your authenticity will be the greatest gift you can offer the world.

- *Taking Action:* It's not enough to dream of a legacy—you must take action. Whether it's through financial success, acts of kindness, or mentoring the next generation, each step you take creates your legacy.

Embrace Your Legacy—Now

It's time to step into your legacy. You don't need to wait for the perfect moment. You have everything you need inside of you. You've been preparing for this your whole life.

By embracing your true self, living with intention, and acting with love and authenticity, you will create a legacy that speaks for itself. This legacy will continue to grow and flourish, shaping the lives of those who come after you, and leaving a mark on the world that will never fade.

Rise up.

Step into your power.

Create the legacy you were always meant to build.

The world is waiting for you.

12

Chapter 11: The Infinite Power of Faith and Belief

In the journey to self-empowerment, building a legacy, and embracing authenticity, there is one element that holds the power to transform everything: faith. Faith in ourselves, faith in our purpose, and faith in something greater than ourselves. This chapter will dive deeply into the transformative power of faith and belief, showing how these forces guide us when the road is unclear and when the weight of the world feels too heavy to bear. Faith is not a passive quality—it's an active force that shapes our decisions, our resilience, and our legacy.

The Essence of Faith

Faith is not just a religious concept. It's a principle that transcends religious boundaries and touches every aspect of our lives. It's about believing in something that cannot always be seen, touched, or proven, yet knowing it is real. Faith fuels courage when fear tries to paralyze us, and it propels us forward when doubt seems insurmountable. Faith can be found in the belief that your story matters, that you are meant to achieve greatness, and that your path, even though difficult, is leading you to where you are meant to be.

Without faith, the journey is longer and more daunting. With it, obstacles become stepping stones, and the impossible becomes possible. It's the silent force behind every successful endeavor, every dream achieved, and every moment of resilience in the face of adversity.

The Role of Belief in Building Your Legacy

Our beliefs shape who we are. What we believe about ourselves dictates what we achieve. Belief in your own worth, your capability, and your potential is not a luxury; it's a necessity. If you do not believe in your worth, no one else will either. The first step toward building the legacy you desire is the unwavering belief that you are worthy of the journey ahead, the success you seek, and the happiness you deserve.

Belief also plays a critical role in overcoming self-doubt. Too often, we are our own harshest critics. We listen to the negative voices in our head, telling us we aren't enough or we can't accomplish our goals. But belief is the antidote to that self-sabotage. By actively cultivating a strong belief in our potential, we can silence the doubts and focus on the truth: you are capable of achieving your dreams. Your legacy is not determined by the obstacles you face, but by your response to those obstacles, and your belief in your ability to rise above them.

The Power of Believing in Others

As we build our legacy, we must also nurture the belief in others. No one achieves greatness alone. Surrounding yourself with people who believe in you, support you, and challenge you to be better is just as important as believing in yourself. Empowering others by lifting them up and nurturing their belief in themselves is one of the most profound ways we can leave a lasting legacy. You help create a ripple effect, where belief becomes contagious and others begin to understand their own power and potential.

Just as belief in others can empower them, it also has the power to inspire reciprocity. When you believe in people, they tend to believe in you too. You begin to build a community of mutual respect and trust that propels each of you forward, working together to create something bigger than yourselves.

How Faith and Belief Empower Resilience

Resilience is the ability to bounce back from setbacks, adapt to challenges, and keep going despite the circumstances. But resilience is not an innate trait—it is something that is cultivated. Faith and belief are the pillars that hold up your resilience. Without them, resilience becomes much harder to tap into, and the road feels impossible.

Faith allows us to see beyond the present difficulty. It allows us to believe that, no matter how difficult the situation, there is something greater waiting for us on the other side. Belief in our purpose and in the possibility of a better future gives us the strength to keep going when the going gets tough.

The Intersection of Faith, Action, and Destiny

Faith without action is simply a dream. Belief in something greater than yourself must be coupled with tangible actions to make it real. In other words, faith must be put into practice through the decisions we make, the steps we take, and the consistency with which we pursue our goals. It's not enough to believe; you must act on that belief to bring about the change you seek.

Faith is what allows you to take action even when the outcome is uncertain. It provides the courage to step into the unknown and trust that each step will bring you closer to the life you desire. Without action, faith remains an idea, an abstract concept. But when paired with consistent effort, faith and belief are what guide you to your destiny.

Faith in the Unseen: Trusting the Process

There will be moments in your journey when the path ahead is unclear. You may not know how you will get from where you are to where you want to be. You may question whether it is even possible to achieve your dreams. This is when faith becomes essential.

Faith is what allows you to trust the process, even when you cannot see the outcome. It's about knowing that each moment, each challenge, and each victory is part of the larger picture. Even when things seem uncertain, you must trust that your faith will lead you to where you are meant to be. Trust the process. Trust the steps that are unfolding in front of you, and believe that every part of the journey is preparing you for the greatness that awaits.

Turning Challenges into Stepping Stones

Challenges are inevitable. Life will throw obstacles in your path, some that may seem insurmountable. But with faith, those challenges can become opportunities for growth and transformation. Every hardship you face has the potential to teach you something important, to strengthen you, and to prepare you for the next phase of your journey.

Faith gives you the courage to face those challenges head-on and the strength to keep moving forward. Each obstacle you overcome adds to your resilience and your belief in your ability to succeed. These challenges are not roadblocks; they are stepping stones, guiding you to the next level of greatness. With faith as your foundation, you will find that no obstacle is too great to overcome.

The Legacy of Faith: A Ripple Effect Across Generations

As you build your legacy, one of the most profound gifts you can give to future generations is the gift of faith. It's not just about the material wealth you leave behind; it's about the belief systems, the courage, and the resilience that you instill in those who follow in your footsteps. By teaching others to believe in themselves, trust the process, and have faith in something greater than themselves, you pass on a legacy that will last far beyond your lifetime.

This faith is the foundation of a lasting impact, not just for your own family, but for your community and the world at large. The ripple effect of one person's faith can change the course of history, inspiring others to rise above their own struggles and step into their own greatness.

Living a Life of Faith and Belief

To live a life of faith and belief is to live in alignment with your highest self, knowing that you are capable of achieving your dreams and leaving a lasting legacy. It's about embracing the unseen and trusting that the journey will take you where you need to go. It's about believing in your own worth and empowering others to do the same. Faith is the thread that weaves through everything we do, giving meaning to our lives, purpose to our struggles, and strength to our resilience.

In the end, faith is what makes the impossible possible. It is the force that drives us to keep going, even when the road is difficult. It is what empowers us to rise, to transform, and to create the legacy we are meant to leave behind. Faith is not just an idea; it's a powerful, life-altering force that guides us toward our highest potential.

As you move forward on your journey, remember that faith is the key. Believe in yourself. Believe in your purpose. And most importantly, believe that you are capable of achieving everything your heart desires. With faith, there is no limit to what you can accomplish.

Embracing the Infinite Possibilities

Faith, as the driving force in our lives, not only helps us overcome challenges, but also opens the door to an infinite array of possibilities. When you operate with faith, you open yourself up to opportunities that you may have previously dismissed. Faith clears the fog of uncertainty and allows you to see the path that was always there, yet hidden from your view due to fear or doubt. With this clear vision, you are empowered to pursue dreams that once seemed unattainable.

This is where true transformation happens: when you stop limiting yourself based on what you can see, and start trusting in what you feel, what you know deep within your soul. Faith is the bridge between your present circumstances and your greatest potential. It enables you to step into the unknown, unafraid and ready to create new possibilities for your life, your family, and your community. The universe, or whatever higher power you believe in, is always conspiring for your highest good—but it is your faith that activates this force.

Faith in Action: Manifesting Your Vision

The most powerful aspect of faith is that it is not passive. Faith in yourself, in your purpose, and in your destiny must be accompanied by action. It is in the act of doing, of stepping forward with confidence, that faith truly reveals its power. Without action, faith becomes nothing more than a wish, an idea floating in the ether. But when faith is combined with action, it transforms into something real, something tangible. It becomes the energy that propels you toward your goals, every single step of the way.

When you believe that your legacy matters, that your dreams are possible, you must take the necessary steps to make them a reality. Whether that means taking risks, learning new skills, making difficult decisions, or trusting in the timing of the universe—action is the key that unlocks the doors of opportunity. The universe responds to your belief by aligning opportunities, but it's your actions that bring those opportunities to fruition.

Transforming Fear into Faith

One of the most powerful tools in your journey of faith is the ability to transform fear into faith. Fear will always be present, especially when you step into new and unfamiliar territory. But rather than allowing fear to paralyze you, you can choose to use it as fuel for your faith. Fear is simply a sign that you are stretching beyond your comfort zone, and that's where growth happens.

When fear rises, it's not a signal to retreat; it's an invitation to trust. Trust that you are strong enough to handle what comes next, trust that the path will be revealed, and trust that the lessons embedded in the challenges will only make you stronger. Every time you face your fears and take a step forward, you strengthen your faith, proving to yourself that you are capable of doing hard things. You begin to realize that the very fears you once feared are the ones that hold the greatest lessons and rewards.

Faith as a Catalyst for Healing

Faith is also a powerful force in the healing process. Whether it's emotional, physical, or spiritual healing, faith is the catalyst that accelerates recovery. It's easy to become discouraged when you face setbacks in life, especially if you've experienced trauma, loss, or heartbreak. But with faith, you can begin to heal. Faith allows you to believe that you can overcome pain and that you are worthy of love and joy, no matter what you've been through. It's in those moments of deep vulnerability and trust that you find the strength to rise again.

Healing through faith doesn't mean ignoring the pain; it means accepting the pain and trusting that it will serve a purpose in your growth. As you heal, you will be able to offer your experiences, wisdom, and compassion to others who are going through their own struggles. This healing, coupled with your faith, becomes part of the legacy you leave behind. You create a ripple effect of hope and encouragement for others to follow.

The Legacy of Faith: Passing the Torch

The ultimate legacy you can leave is one built on faith. Not just the faith you have in yourself, but the faith you inspire in others. The way you choose to live, the way you rise after every fall, the way you face challenges with grace and strength—these actions become the living example of what faith can achieve.

This legacy is passed down to future generations, not through words alone but through actions. When you walk in faith, you show others the way. Your children, your family, and your community begin to believe that they too can walk in that same faith. You help them see that they are capable of overcoming the impossible, that their dreams are worth fighting for, and that with faith, anything is possible.

Imagine the impact of this legacy: a family, a community, a generation of people who live boldly, who act with purpose, and who have the unwavering belief that they can create the world they want to see. It starts with you, and it continues for generations to come. This is the power of faith—a gift that transcends time, a gift that will echo through the hearts and minds of those you touch.

Faith as the Foundation of Your Destiny

Faith is not just a part of your journey; it is the foundation on which everything else is built. It is the fuel that ignites your passion, the strength that supports your resilience, and the light that guides your way through darkness. As you continue to build your legacy, step into your power, and create the life you were meant to live, remember that faith is the invisible force that makes everything possible.

The power of belief is infinite. With faith, there are no limits. With faith, there are no obstacles that cannot be overcome. With faith, you can rise above any challenge, manifest any dream, and leave a lasting legacy that will inspire generations to come. Trust the process, believe in yourself, and know that your faith will always lead you to the place where you are meant to be.

In the end, it is your faith that will shape your destiny. It will carry you through the trials, the triumphs, and the moments of uncertainty. It will give you the courage to rise again, every single time. So, hold fast to your faith, for it is the key to everything you desire. With faith, your legacy is unstoppable, your potential is limitless, and your future is bright beyond measure.

13

Chapter 12: The Infinite Power of Self-Love

In a world where external validation often holds so much weight, the most profound and life-altering power lies within: self-love. It is a force that not only transforms the way you see yourself but also the way you interact with the world around you. It serves as the foundation of every achievement, every relationship, and every triumph. Without it, everything you accomplish may feel incomplete, as if you are seeking external validation to fill an internal void.

Self-love is not about narcissism or selfishness—it's about recognizing your own worth and treating yourself with the same kindness, respect, and compassion you would extend to a beloved friend. It is the recognition that you are enough, just as you are. This profound acceptance and love for yourself are vital, as they form the very core from which your inner power radiates.

The Power of Self-Acceptance

Before we can love ourselves, we must first accept ourselves—every part of us, even the aspects we have hidden away or deemed unworthy. Self-acceptance is the gateway to self-love. It's about embracing your flaws, recognizing your strengths, and giving yourself grace in moments of imperfection. So often, we are our own harshest critics, pointing out every mistake and flaw without acknowledging our incredible resilience and beauty.

To truly love yourself, you must first accept who you are in this moment. You are not the person you aspire to be one day, nor are you the person you were in the past. You are exactly who you need to be right now. In all your humanity—your strength, your struggles, your victories, and your vulnerabilities—there is greatness. Accept yourself fully and completely, without reservation. Embrace the parts of you that have been wounded, for they hold the keys to your healing and growth.

I remember a time when I looked in the mirror and couldn't see anything worth loving. All I saw was failure, pain, and pieces of myself I thought were too broken to be whole again. But in the silence of that moment, something whispered, "You're still here." That whisper became a roar. That day, I began the slow, sacred journey of loving the version of me I had once abandoned.

Self-Love as the Foundation of Empowerment

Self-love is not passive; it is the root of all empowerment.

When you love yourself deeply, you become impervious to the opinions and judgments of others. You stop seeking validation from external sources, realizing that the only validation you need is from within. You begin to set healthy boundaries, prioritize your well-being, and make choices that honor your needs. This empowers you to pursue your dreams with unwavering confidence, knowing that your worth is not contingent upon anyone else's approval.

When you stand firm in self-love, you become unstoppable. You are no longer afraid of rejection or failure, because you understand that these do not diminish your value. Instead, they are simply opportunities for growth. Each experience—whether perceived as a success or a failure—becomes an essential part of your journey. With self-love as your anchor, you will rise each time you fall, stronger, wiser, and more compassionate toward yourself and others.

Rewriting the Narrative: Overcoming Self-Doubt

Self-doubt is a universal struggle, one that holds countless people back from living their true potential. It's easy to get lost in the stories we tell ourselves about our inadequacies or our limitations. These narratives can be rooted in past failures, societal expectations, or the hurtful words of others. But self-doubt is nothing more than a lie we've been conditioned to believe. It's a reflection of our fears, not our truth.

Rewriting the narrative begins with recognizing that these thoughts do not define you. You are not your past mistakes or your perceived shortcomings. You are not the negative words that were spoken to you. You are a powerful being, capable of achieving far beyond what your mind may try to limit you to. Each day, challenge the stories of self-doubt by affirming your worth, your ability, and your inherent greatness. Every time the voice of doubt arises, counter it with affirmations of self-love, and soon, the narrative will shift.

Practicing Radical Self-Care

Self-love goes hand-in-hand with radical self-care. Caring for yourself in a way that nourishes your body, mind, and soul is an act of love and respect. It's not about superficial indulgences or fleeting comforts. It's about creating space in your life for what nurtures and replenishes you, allowing you to show up fully for yourself and for others. Radical self-care means prioritizing your health, setting boundaries, saying no when necessary, and giving yourself the rest and peace you need to thrive.

It's easy to get caught up in the demands of life—work, relationships, societal pressures—and neglect our own needs. But radical self-care requires a shift in mindset: It is not selfish to care for yourself. In fact, it's essential. You cannot pour from an empty cup. The more you nourish and care for yourself, the more you have to give to others. When you practice radical self-care, you are honoring your body, your mind, and your spirit, giving them the respect and attention they deserve.

Self-Love Ritual: Begin each day by placing your hand over your heart. Say out loud: "I am worthy. I am loved. I am becoming." Repeat this three times—until your soul believes it. This is how you train your nervous system to receive what you've always deserved.

Healing through Self-Love

Self-love is not just about how you treat yourself in moments of success or joy. It is also how you treat yourself during times of pain, struggle, and heartache. It's easy to love yourself when everything is going well, but true self-love shines brightest when you are in the midst of healing. In times of hardship, when you feel broken or lost, it is even more critical to show yourself compassion and patience. Healing is not linear—it takes time, and it requires tenderness. Don't be too hard on yourself when things don't go as planned or when you experience setbacks. Embrace the process of healing with love, knowing that every step forward, no matter how small, is a victory.

When you heal through self-love, you not only mend your own heart but also the hearts of those around you. Your healing journey becomes an example for others who are also struggling. You become a beacon of hope, showing that it is possible to rise above the challenges and emerge stronger than before.

The Ripple Effect of Self-Love

When you embody self-love, you create a ripple effect that extends far beyond your own life. Your self-love radiates out into the world, inspiring others to embrace their own worth and value. You teach those around you that they, too, are deserving of love and respect, no matter their past, their mistakes, or their circumstances. This ripple effect extends into every area of your life—from your relationships to your career to your community.

Self-love is contagious. When you love yourself, you encourage others to do the same. You empower them to step into their own power, to believe in their potential, and to embrace the fullness of who they are. Imagine a world where everyone lived with self-love as the foundation. A world where people are not afraid to be their authentic selves, to pursue their dreams, and to care for their own well-being. This is the world we can create when we make self-love a priority.

The Journey of Self-Love

Self-love is not a destination—it is a journey. It is a lifelong process of growth, healing, and empowerment. Each step you take on this journey brings you closer to the fullest, most authentic version of yourself. Through self-acceptance, self-care, and healing, you will find the strength to rise above your challenges and live a life of purpose and impact.

As you continue to cultivate self-love, remember that it is the foundation upon which everything else is built. It is the root of your power, your resilience, and your ability to create a lasting legacy. When you love yourself, you unlock your true potential and create a ripple effect that can change the world. Love yourself deeply, radically, and unconditionally, for you are worthy of all the love and success life has to offer.

Embrace your own power, and remember—self-love is the key to everything. It is the starting point for everything you want to achieve, the driving force behind every dream you pursue, and the foundation of the legacy you will leave behind.

The Legacy Vow: A Declaration of Self-Love

I, [Name], vow to love myself—fully, deeply, and unconditionally.

I vow to accept every part of me,

even the parts I once rejected,

even the stories I once buried in silence.

I vow to speak to myself with kindness,

to honor my needs without guilt,

and to nourish my mind, body, and soul without apology.

I vow to rewrite the lies that told me I was not enough.

To rise every time I fall.

To believe that healing is holy, and rest is sacred.

I vow to stop waiting for someone else to see me.

I already see me.

I am already whole.

I vow to walk in love—

not just for the world,

but for the mirror I face every day.

This is not just a vow.

This is my return.

This is my revolution.

This is my legacy.

Signed: ______________________________

Date: ________________________________

Guided Reflection: Mirror Work Journal Prompts

1. **When was the last time I truly saw myself without judgment?**

What did I feel? What did I hide? What do I need to hear from me now?

2. **What do I need to forgive myself for to love myself more fully?**
Write it down. Release it. Make peace with it.

3. **What boundaries do I need to set to protect my peace and power?**
Where am I giving too much and receiving too little?

4. **What does radical self-care look like for me—not as a trend, but as a way of life?**
List 3 non-negotiables I can start practicing this week.

5. **If my self-love created a ripple effect, who in my life would be impacted first—and how?**
Describe the shift. Then commit to being that mirror for them, too.

And every time you forget who you are, whisper this truth to yourself:

"I am worthy of love, even before I become who I'm becoming."

14

Chapter 13: The Courage to Dream Big

The Power of Unstoppable Dreams

There is a quiet power in the act of dreaming big—a power that transcends the limitations of our present reality. Dreams are not mere fantasies or passing whims; they are the guiding forces of our lives, pushing us toward the life we are meant to create. A dream, when nurtured and fueled by passion, becomes more than just a wish—it becomes a vision, a calling, and a driving force that propels us forward. It is in those expansive dreams, those seemingly impossible desires, that the seeds of greatness are planted, ready to grow into something transformative.

Dreaming big is not an act of mere imagination—it is an act of defiance against the forces that tell us we are too small, too unworthy, or too ordinary to achieve anything extraordinary. Dreams challenge us to look beyond the walls we've built around ourselves, to envision a future that far exceeds the limits of our current circumstances. But to dream big, we must be willing to release the self-doubt and limitations that often plague us.

The path to greatness, however, is not always clear. There are obstacles—emotional barriers, societal expectations, and the harsh realities of life—that seek to keep us rooted in mediocrity. These challenges often come disguised as fear, insecurity, and criticism. We may face doubt from others who cannot see the magnitude of our vision or, worse, doubt from within ourselves. It's easy to let these obstacles keep us from taking that first step toward our dreams. But I want you to understand that it is precisely through facing these challenges head-on that we find our greatest opportunities for growth.

In every moment of doubt, there is a lesson. In every setback, there is an opportunity to rise stronger. It is through the challenges, the obstacles, and the difficulties that we develop resilience, courage, and strength. When we dare to dream big, we awaken the untapped potential within us—potential that is lying dormant, waiting for the right moment to rise to the surface.

The beauty of dreaming big is that it forces us to confront our own limitations. When we set our sights on something that seems far beyond our reach, we are compelled to grow, to evolve, and to transform. Dreaming big is not just about achieving external success—it's about expanding our internal capacity to believe in ourselves, to trust in the process, and to embrace the discomfort that comes with growth.

The truth is, we are often our own biggest obstacle. We allow our fear of failure, our fear of judgment, and our fear of the unknown to hold us back. But the only way to break through these barriers is to push past them—to step into the unknown with confidence and courage. When you begin to dream fearlessly, you free yourself from the shackles of doubt and limitation. You open yourself up to the possibilities that lie just beyond your comfort zone.

One of the most powerful things you can do to unlock your dreams is to shift your mindset. Instead of seeing obstacles as reasons to quit, begin to see them as stepping stones toward success. Understand that every successful person has faced challenges—they are not exceptions. What sets them apart is not that they were immune to failure or hardship, but that they chose to keep going despite it. When you adopt this mindset, you begin to see every challenge as an opportunity to grow stronger, to learn, and to take one more step toward your dream.

In my own journey, I learned that the road to my dreams was not straight or smooth. I encountered plenty of obstacles along the way—some external, and some within myself. There were times when I wanted to give up, when I doubted my ability to succeed. But in those moments, I reminded myself of the power of my dream. I reminded myself that the discomfort, the fear, and the struggles were all part of the process. I held fast to my vision, and slowly but surely, the path began to clear.

Taking the first courageous step toward your highest aspirations requires both belief and action. It's about making the decision to move forward, even when you don't have all the answers. The key is to trust in the journey, knowing that the steps you take today will create the foundation for tomorrow's success. Every small action you take toward your dream—whether it's making a phone call, writing a plan, or reaching out for support—brings you one step closer to the life you envision.

As you embark on the journey of dreaming big, remember that no dream is too big. The size of your dream is not determined by your current circumstances; it is determined by your willingness to pursue it with all of your heart. You have the power within you to create the life you desire. It may take time, and the road may not always be easy, but if you stay committed to your vision and take inspired action, your dream will become your reality.

Your dreams are unstoppable because they are uniquely yours. They are a reflection of your purpose, your passion, and your potential. The world needs your vision. The world needs you to step into your greatness and to share your gifts with others. So, dare to dream big. Embrace the challenges, trust the process, and take action every day toward the life you know you are meant to live.

Dreaming big is not just about having a vision for the future—it's about awakening the power within you to make that vision a reality. It's about stepping into your greatness and unleashing the full force of your potential. Don't wait for permission to dream big. Don't wait for the perfect moment.

The moment is now. The power to change your life is in your hands. So, dream boldly, act fearlessly, and live with purpose. The world is waiting for your unstoppable dreams to come to life.

Overcoming the Invisible Chains: Breaking Free from Limitation

We are all born with the natural ability to dream—just as children dream of becoming astronauts, artists, or leaders of nations. As children, our imaginations are boundless, and we have an innate belief that anything is possible. However, somewhere along the way, we learn to temper those dreams. We start to consider what is "realistic," what is "practical," and what is "possible." Slowly, but surely, the vivid, bold dreams of childhood are replaced with a more limited vision. These limitations are often self-imposed and come from the beliefs we internalize based on our circumstances, upbringing, or societal expectations.

For much of my life, I too was bound by these invisible chains. My dreams felt too big, too audacious, too unattainable. I had been conditioned to settle for what I thought was possible. I was told that certain things were out of my reach—that because of my background, my financial status, or my past mistakes, I would never achieve the greatness I secretly desired. The fear of failure, judgment, and rejection held me back. I was afraid to fail because I thought it meant that I wasn't good enough. I thought that being ordinary was just the way it had to be. But the turning point came when I realized that what society deemed impossible was not a truth—it was merely a perception, a limiting belief that I had the power to shatter.

In order to break free from this mental prison, I had to redefine what was "realistic." I had to challenge the assumptions I had made about my own potential. I had to challenge the voices—both internal and external—that told me I wasn't enough, that I didn't have what it takes. I had to shift my mindset from one of limitation to one of possibility.

It wasn't easy. There were many moments of self-doubt and fear. I questioned whether I was capable of achieving the dreams I had. I faced criticism from others who believed my aspirations were too lofty. And yet, with each doubt, I made a choice. A choice to press on. A choice to keep dreaming. A choice to silence the voices that told me "no." Slowly, I began to peel back the layers of fear and insecurity that had been placed upon me.

As I slowly chipped away at these limiting beliefs, I began to see a new world of possibilities open before me. The more I recognized that the barriers I thought existed were not as strong as I once believed, the more courage I found to move forward. I began to see that the world is full of opportunities—opportunities that are not reserved for a select few, but for anyone who is willing to break free from the chains that hold them back. The first step toward dreaming big is recognizing the chains that have held you back. These chains are not physical, but they are often more powerful because they exist in your mind.

Our minds are powerful forces. The beliefs we carry shape the actions we take and, ultimately, the life we create. When we allow ourselves to be confined by fear, by doubt, or by the limitations of others' opinions, we are giving away our power. These chains may not be visible, but they are incredibly strong. They can keep us from reaching our full potential if we let them. Once you become aware of these chains, you can begin the process of unshackling yourself from the constraints that have kept you small.

The process of breaking free isn't always a linear one. There will be times when you take two steps forward and one step back. There will be moments when the weight of your fears and doubts feels heavier than ever. But every time you challenge a limiting belief, you weaken the chain. Every time you take a step toward your dreams, you break free a little more. It may take time, but with every conscious choice to believe in yourself and your potential, the chains will weaken, and the vision of your dream will become clearer.

I realized that the only limits that exist are the ones I place on myself. This awareness changed everything. I started setting bigger goals, ones that terrified me, because I understood that fear was not a sign to stop—it was a sign to go. I began to embrace discomfort and uncertainty, knowing that they were signs of growth. The more I took risks, the more I started seeing results. The more I believed that I was worthy of success, the more success I attracted.

Breaking free from limitations is not just about achieving external success. It's about a shift in identity. It's about seeing yourself not as someone who is bound by their past, their circumstances, or their limitations, but as someone who is capable of extraordinary things. When you begin to see yourself as capable, as deserving, as powerful, the world around you will begin to reflect that new belief. Your actions will be fueled by confidence, not fear. You will begin to act with purpose, knowing that you are worthy of every success that comes your way.

I look back at my journey and realize that every obstacle I faced, every challenge I overcame, was an opportunity to break free from another invisible chain. Today, I stand stronger, more confident, and more capable than ever. And the beauty of it is that anyone can do the same. The key is to recognize the chains, to challenge the beliefs that limit you, and to take action—no matter how small—toward your dreams.

The road to breaking free from limitations is not always easy, but it is worth every step. Once you break free, you'll realize that the only thing standing between you and your dreams is the courage to believe in yourself. The only thing holding you back is the belief that you cannot do it. So, take that first step today. Let go of the limitations, challenge the beliefs that have kept you stuck, and embrace the possibility of what could be. You are capable of more than you ever imagined. And it's time to start living the life you were meant to live.

Break the chains. Dream big. Live boldly.

Building the Vision: Seeing Beyond the Present

A dream is not just a wish—it is a vision of what could be, a picture of your life painted with the brush of possibility. But in order to live out that vision, you must be able to see it clearly, even when the world around you tells you it's impossible. Visionaries are not simply people who can see beyond their present circumstances; they are those who choose to focus on what could be, rather than what is.

When I first began to dream big, the vision I held for my life was hazy. I knew I wanted something more than what I had, but I couldn't quite picture what that looked like. My life felt ordinary, and my desires felt far-reaching. But as I sat in those quiet moments, reflecting on my deepest aspirations, I realized something profound: I had the power to shape my own future. The key was not in simply dreaming but in *visualizing.*

I began the practice of visualization, a technique that would forever change the way I approached my goals. I made it a habit to meditate on my future. Each day, I would close my eyes and see myself living the life I desired. I visualized the life of success, the freedom to create, the joy of helping others, and the fulfillment of my deepest purpose. I saw myself as a successful entrepreneur, a woman who had broken through every barrier and was now living with purpose and freedom. I envisioned every detail—from the way I dressed to the people I served, from the atmosphere around me to the inner peace I felt.

But the power of this practice lies not just in the act of imagining, but in *feeling* what it would be like to live that life. It's one thing to think about your dream, but it's an entirely different experience to *live it* in your mind and soul. Imagine every sense coming alive—hear the sound of your accomplishments, see the smile of those you've helped, feel gratitude, and most importantly, experience the emotions of living your best life. The more vivid and real your vision becomes, the more it anchors itself into your subconscious mind.

This is where the magic happens.

The act of visualization helps you *align your mind and emotions* with your desires. When your vision feels real, when you can feel the sensations of your success, your mind begins to operate as if that success is already here. This creates a powerful shift. It becomes easier to make decisions, take risks, and persevere through challenges because your vision is no longer a far-off dream—it becomes a present reality in your mind.

Once your vision is clear and deeply rooted within you, the universe begins to conspire in your favor. Opportunities arise in unexpected ways. Doors begin to open, connections are made, and the synchronicities you once thought were coincidences start to show up regularly. The more you align your thoughts, actions, and feelings with your vision, the more the world around you seems to respond. The energy you put out returns to you in the form of opportunities, ideas, and people who will help bring your dreams to life.

I remember the first time I noticed the subtle signs that my visualization practice was working. I would think of a new idea, and within days, someone would mention it or a new resource would appear. I would set a goal, and somehow, the exact person or tool I needed would show up at just the right moment. At first, I thought it was a coincidence. But as it continued to happen, I realized that this was not a mere chance. My vision was creating momentum, and the universe was responding to my faith, my clarity, and my actions.

But don't let this process be one that happens only in the quiet of your mind. Visualization is powerful, but without action, it remains just a beautiful picture. The key is to combine *inspired action* with your vision. Once you see the life you desire, start taking tangible steps to move toward it. These steps might not always be large or bold at first, but the more you take action, the more the universe will align with your purpose.

Sometimes, when we dream big, we feel that we need a "perfect" plan in place before moving forward. But the truth is, action creates clarity. It is by taking one step toward your dream that the next step will reveal itself. Trust the process. Even if you don't have all the answers right away, keep moving forward with confidence, knowing that you are actively building the life you envision.

In those moments when doubt creeps in, when the vision feels distant or unattainable, remember that every great dream takes time. Even the most successful individuals didn't get to where they are by rushing through the process. They understood that great things take patience, perseverance, and consistent effort.

Your vision is a seed. And just as a seed needs time to grow and develop roots, your dreams need time, space, and consistent nurturing to flourish. Water your dreams with optimism, and feed them with intentional actions. Watch them grow over time, knowing that with each step you take, you're bringing that dream closer to reality.

Start today.

Visualize the life you desire—see it clearly, feel it deeply, and believe in its possibility. And as you do, take inspired action every day. Know that the universe is working with you, not against you, and that everything you need is already on its way. Your vision is not a distant dream—it is a *blueprint* for the future. Hold onto it tightly, and let it guide you every step of the way.

Dream big, but more importantly, *see* big. Your future is waiting for you.

Actionable Strategy:

- *Set aside time each day for visualization.*

Close your eyes and vividly imagine your life as if you've already achieved your biggest dreams. How do you feel? What are you doing? Where are you? The more details you can add, the more real it will feel.

The Courage to Fail: Embracing the Risks

To dream big requires courage—courage to face the fear of failure. In the pursuit of big dreams, there will inevitably be failures along the way. But failure is not the end; it is the beginning of growth, of learning, and of transformation. Those who achieve greatness do not do so by avoiding failure—they do so by embracing it as a natural part of the process.

For years, I feared failure. I feared that I would try and fall short, that my dreams would be crushed under the weight of unmet expectations. But one of the greatest lessons I have learned is that failure is not a reflection of my worth. It is simply a lesson in disguise—a feedback mechanism that helps me adjust, grow, and rise higher. Failure is not a failure of you as a person; it's a failure of the approach, the timing, or the circumstances. When you understand this, it becomes easier to rise from the ashes of disappointment and forge ahead.

I've learned that those who dare to dream big are the ones who have experienced the most failure. The people we look up to—those who have achieved extraordinary success—have often faced the most daunting challenges and setbacks. The difference between them and those who give up is that they have learned to use failure as a stepping stone, not a stumbling block.

When I started my journey toward becoming an entrepreneur, I failed many times. I launched projects that didn't work. I faced setbacks that seemed insurmountable. But with each failure, I learned something valuable. I learned resilience. I learned persistence. And most importantly, I learned to trust in the process. The road to success is never linear, but those who stay the course, despite the inevitable failures, are the ones who will ultimately achieve their dreams.

Failure, in many ways, is a powerful teacher. When something doesn't work out, it forces you to reevaluate, adjust, and pivot. You must ask yourself: What can I learn from this experience? What went wrong, and how can I improve? Sometimes, failure is a reminder that there's an even better path waiting for you—one that you would never have found without taking that first leap. It's the universe's way of redirecting you to a new, better opportunity, even though it might not seem that way at first.

One of the hardest things to accept when pursuing big dreams is that not every step will be a success. In fact, the more you push forward, the more you are likely to fail. But that doesn't mean you're not moving in the right direction—it means that you are growing, learning, and evolving. Failure forces you to get up, dust yourself off, and keep going. And with every step, you build resilience and strength that will serve you well in the long run.

Another important lesson I've learned is that failure does not define you unless you let it. I've seen many people give up on their dreams after facing a setback, telling themselves that they just weren't meant to succeed. But the truth is, you only fail when you stop trying. If you keep going, even in the face of failure, you are moving forward. It's not the failure itself that matters, but your ability to keep going despite it.

Failure also teaches humility. It keeps us grounded and reminds us that we are all human, imperfect and constantly learning. It's easy to get caught up in the success stories of others and forget that behind every achievement is a series of failures, mistakes, and lessons learned. These stories of failure are often left out of the narrative, but they are crucial to understanding what it truly takes to achieve great things.

I've also learned that failure is a sign of courage. It takes courage to step out of your comfort zone, to try something new, and to risk failure. People who play it safe rarely fail, but they also rarely experience success. It's only those who dare to dream big, to risk failure, that achieve the extraordinary. The greatest accomplishments in history were born from people who were willing to fail and learn from it.

So, how do you overcome the fear of failure? First, shift your perspective. Instead of seeing failure as something negative, see it as an opportunity to learn and grow. Recognize that each setback brings you closer to your ultimate goal, even though it may not feel that way at the time. Understand that failure is an inevitable part of the journey, and the more you embrace it, the stronger and more successful you will become.

Next, be kind to yourself. Failure can feel personal, especially when it's something you've worked hard for. But remember, it's not about you as an individual—it's about the process, the effort, and the lessons learned. Don't be hard on yourself for making mistakes or facing setbacks. Instead, celebrate your courage to try and keep going. Failure is not the opposite of success; it's part of the path toward success.

Finally, take the time to reflect and adjust. When things don't go as planned, take a step back and evaluate what went wrong and what can be done differently. Often, failure is simply a sign that you need to pivot and try a new approach. Learn from your experiences and use them to refine your strategy. This is how you move from failure to success.

The courage to fail is one of the most important attributes you can cultivate on your journey to realizing your dreams. Failure is not something to be feared or avoided—it is a necessary part of the process. The most successful people in the world have faced numerous failures along the way, but they didn't let those failures define them. Instead, they used each setback as an opportunity to grow, learn, and move closer to their goals. So, when you face failure on your journey, remember that it's not the end—it's simply the beginning of a new chapter in your story. Keep going, keep learning, and keep dreaming. Your big dreams are within reach.

Actionable Strategy:

- *Failure Reframed:* The next time you fail, rather than seeing it as a defeat, ask yourself: What can I learn from this? How can I use this experience to grow and improve?

Aligning with Purpose: The Power of a Bigger Why

Dreams are not just about achieving goals—they are about fulfilling a higher purpose. When you align your dreams with your purpose, your vision becomes more powerful. It is no longer about material gain or personal success, but about contributing something meaningful to the world.

When I first started dreaming big, I was focused on success for the sake of success—on financial freedom, recognition, and status. But as I evolved, I realized that true fulfillment comes from serving a greater purpose. My dreams are no longer just mine; they are a vehicle for change, for healing, and for uplifting others. This alignment with purpose gives my dreams an unshakable foundation. It becomes a force that drives me forward, not because I want something for myself, but because I want to make an impact that transcends my personal achievements.

Aligning your dreams with your deeper purpose shifts the entire lens through which you view your journey. Suddenly, success is no longer measured just by the numbers in your bank account or the titles you hold; it's measured by the lives you touch, the people you inspire, and the way you contribute to the world around you. When you are driven by purpose, the path becomes clear. The work feels less like a burden and more like a mission.

The power of a bigger "why" lies in its ability to give you unwavering direction. When your dreams are rooted in purpose, you have something far greater to strive for than personal success. You are working towards making a difference, whether that's through creating jobs, helping others, fostering healing, or inspiring future generations. The ripple effect of living a purpose-driven life is profound. It goes beyond your immediate goals and impacts communities, families, and societies as a whole.

When you are clear about your purpose, your dreams become

unstoppable. The challenges you face will seem smaller, the obstacles less daunting, because you know that your dream is not just for you—it is for the world. And that knowledge will keep you going, even when the road gets tough. There is a certain fuel that comes from knowing that your work is tied to something much bigger than you. Every setback becomes just a small part of the journey; it's not a failure, but a lesson, and every success is celebrated not just for what it brings to you, but for how it contributes to the world at large.

The beauty of aligning with a bigger "why" is that it removes the fear of failure. When your purpose is crystal clear, setbacks feel more like stepping stones than barriers. You understand that every obstacle is part of a bigger story, one that is shaping you into the person who is equipped to fulfill this higher calling. This mindset shifts your perception of challenges—they are no longer roadblocks but opportunities for growth, learning, and resilience.

Purpose also helps you prioritize. It allows you to say no to distractions and focus on what truly matters. When you are aligned with your purpose, it's easier to distinguish between what will bring you closer to your dreams and what will pull you away. You become more intentional with your time, energy, and resources. Each action you take, each decision you make, is filtered through the lens of your purpose, ensuring that everything you do is in service of your bigger vision.

Moreover, living in alignment with your purpose attracts the right people into your life. People who share similar values and are also committed to making a difference will naturally gravitate toward you. They will see the passion and authenticity behind your actions, and they will want to support you. Surrounding yourself with like-minded individuals who share your purpose creates an environment where collective dreams can grow, and collaboration becomes a powerful force for change.

But aligning with your purpose is not always easy. It requires deep introspection and sometimes a period of trial and error. The world can easily distract us with its definitions of success—money, fame, and status—but it's important to remember that true fulfillment lies in answering a call that resonates with your soul. It might take time to discover what that call is, but once you do, everything changes.

Purpose can be found in every aspect of life. It may be in your career, but it can also be in your relationships, your hobbies, your daily actions, and the way you impact those around you. It's not about one grand gesture or single achievement; it's about living each day with intentionality, knowing that your actions are aligned with your deeper values and vision.

When you align with your purpose, your dreams are no longer just about reaching a destination—they are about the person you become in the process. You start to realize that the pursuit of your dreams is not just for the end goal but for the growth, evolution, and impact that occurs along the way. This shift in perspective allows you to embrace the journey with open arms, knowing that every step forward, no matter how small, is part of something greater.

Aligning your dreams with a greater purpose is the most powerful force you can harness. It gives your dreams meaning and significance, turning them into a lifelong mission. It shifts the way you approach challenges, celebrates your victories, and fuels your determination. When your "why" is bigger than you, it becomes an unshakable source of motivation. It reminds you that your dreams are not just for your own benefit, but for the benefit of others, and this realization has the power to propel you beyond anything you could have imagined. So, ask yourself: What is your bigger why? What is the purpose that drives your dreams? And once you find it, let it guide you, shape you, and fuel your journey to greatness.

Actionable Strategy:

- *Purpose Reflection:* Take some time to reflect on the bigger picture behind your dreams. Why do you want to achieve this? Who will benefit from your success? Write down your purpose and connect it to every action you take.

Taking Inspired Action: The Key to Manifestation

Dreaming big is powerful, but it is in the actions we take that our dreams come to life. Once your vision is clear and your purpose is aligned, it's time to take inspired action. This is the part where many people falter—they wait for the perfect moment, the perfect plan, or the perfect conditions. But the truth is, there is no perfect time. The key is to take consistent, intentional action, even when the path ahead is unclear.

When I started my journey, I didn't have all the answers. I

didn't know exactly how things would unfold, but I had a deep trust in my ability to figure it out along the way. I took one step, then another, and another. And every time I moved forward, even in small ways, the universe responded. Opportunities opened up, people showed up, and circumstances began to align in ways I never could have predicted. This is the magic of inspired action—when you take that first step, the universe begins to conspire in your favor, providing the resources, people, and opportunities that you need, even when you don't have the full picture.

Taking inspired action means stepping out of your comfort zone and trusting that the next step will reveal itself as you move forward. It's about embracing the unknown and having the courage to take action despite the fear and uncertainty that often accompany the process of manifestation. Many people think they have to have everything figured out before they can take the first step, but the truth is, clarity comes with action, not before it. The more you take action, the more clarity you gain. Each step you take brings you closer to the next step, and with every action, you gather momentum.

It's also important to recognize that inspired action doesn't always have to be big, dramatic moves. It's often the small, seemingly insignificant actions that lead to the most profound changes. Whether it's sending an email, making a phone call, or taking a moment to learn something new, these small actions accumulate over time and create a ripple effect that propels you forward. Sometimes the hardest part is simply getting started, but once you do, you begin to gain momentum, and that momentum begins to carry you toward your dream.

One of the most important aspects of taking inspired action is alignment. It's about listening to your intuition and trusting that the actions you're taking are in alignment with your vision. If something feels right, do it. If something doesn't feel right, don't. When you're in alignment with your true purpose, your actions become more fluid, more intentional, and more powerful. You don't have to force things to happen; you simply have to trust that the right opportunities and people will show up as you stay aligned with your vision and purpose.

Manifestation is not just about thinking positive thoughts or hoping for the best; it's about taking the steps that bring you closer to your goal. It's about doing the work, even when it's challenging, even when it feels like progress is slow. Taking inspired action is an ongoing process, and the more you commit to it, the more you'll begin to see the results you desire. You can't expect things to fall into your lap without putting in the effort, but when you combine intention with action, you create a powerful force for change.

It's also important to remember that taking inspired action requires patience. The results may not come right away, but that doesn't mean your efforts aren't working. Trust that every action you take is a step in the right direction. Even if things don't unfold as quickly as you'd like, remember that the universe is working behind the scenes to support you. Every small step you take is one step closer to your dream, and even the challenges along the way are part of the process of manifestation.

Finally, the key to taking inspired action is to not overthink things. Many people get caught in analysis paralysis, waiting for the perfect plan or the perfect set of circumstances before they take any action at all. But the truth is, there is no such thing as a perfect plan or perfect conditions. Life is messy, unpredictable, and ever-changing, and if you wait for everything to be just right, you'll never move forward. Instead, take action with the knowledge that you're constantly learning, adapting, and evolving. Trust that you are being guided toward your highest good, and take each step with faith and confidence.

In the end, taking inspired action is about trust—trust in yourself, trust in the process, and trust that the universe has your back. It's about moving forward with courage, even when the path is unclear, and knowing that each step is bringing you closer to the manifestation of your dreams. As you take inspired action, you align yourself with the flow of life, and the universe begins to respond in ways that exceed your expectations. With each step, you're not just getting closer to your dreams; you're becoming the person capable of bringing those dreams to life.

I remember the moment my first big dream came true. It wasn't loud—it was quiet, still, sacred. I stood in the room I once prayed for, serving the people I once dreamed of helping. And in that moment, I realized the power of every tear I cried, every night I doubted, and every small step I took anyway. That moment didn't just confirm the dream—it confirmed me. Your moment is coming too. Keep moving toward it.

So, take that first step today, no matter how small it may seem.

The universe is waiting for you to take action, and when you do, the doors will open in ways you never imagined. You are the creator of your own destiny, and the power to manifest your dreams lies in your willingness to take inspired action, one step at a time.

Actionable Strategy:

- *Daily Steps:* Take one small step every day that brings you closer to your dream. Whether it's researching your next move, reaching out to a potential mentor, or simply writing down your goals, action is the bridge between your dreams and reality.

Building Momentum: The Power of Consistency

Consistency is the secret ingredient in turning big dreams into reality. It's easy to be motivated at the start of a new endeavor, but the true test comes when the initial excitement fades, and the work becomes routine. This is when many people give up, but it's also when the greatest transformation occurs. Consistent action builds momentum, and momentum, over time, can move mountains.

I've often heard it said that success isn't about taking giant leaps—it's about taking consistent, small steps every day. The key is to show up, day after day, even when the results aren't immediate. The little things you do today lay the foundation for tomorrow's success. Consistency not only builds momentum, but it also builds character. It strengthens your resolve and fortifies your belief in your own ability to make your dreams a reality.

When you remain consistent, even through the mundane or difficult days, you create a habit, and habits form the backbone of success. Think of a muscle that gets stronger with every repetition, no matter how small. The more you practice the art of consistency, the more ingrained it becomes in your mindset, and the less you have to rely on motivation or inspiration. It's no longer about having the energy to push forward; it's about the discipline of showing up, day after day, no matter the circumstances.

Sometimes, we measure success in terms of big milestones, but often the most profound achievements come from the accumulation of seemingly small victories. Over time, these incremental steps start to add up, creating compound growth. The key is not to get discouraged by the pace. The days when you feel like nothing significant has changed are often the very days that set the stage for a breakthrough. Keep going, even when you feel like you've hit a plateau—consistency will eventually propel you forward.

Consistency also allows you to adapt and evolve. As you keep moving forward, you start to see patterns and gain insights. You learn what works, what doesn't, and how you can improve your approach. You're not just building momentum in your actions but also in your mindset. This continuous process of learning and adapting helps you stay on track, even when the path is not always clear. It cultivates resilience, grit, and the ability to navigate through challenges with confidence.

To build momentum, it's also important to celebrate the small wins. Recognizing and appreciating your progress, no matter how minor it seems, reinforces the habit of consistency. It acts as a reminder that every step is important, and it keeps the fire of motivation alive, even during the tough times. Small wins add up to big victories, and as you start to notice how much you've accomplished, it can reignite your passion and drive.

In a world where instant gratification is often the norm, consistency is a powerful antidote. It's a commitment to the process, rather than focusing solely on the outcome. This commitment creates a sense of purpose that goes beyond achieving a goal—it transforms the journey into a meaningful experience. The work itself becomes as rewarding as the result, and as you embrace consistency, you begin to trust the process and realize that success is a byproduct of staying the course.

The true power of consistency lies in its ability to compound over time. The steady progress you make today will yield exponential results in the future. It's easy to get discouraged when you don't see immediate results, but remember: every drop fills the bucket. With enough consistent effort, you will eventually reach a place where the momentum you've built carries you further than you ever imagined.

So, keep showing up. Keep putting in the effort. Even on days when it feels like progress is slow or nonexistent, trust that the work you are doing is laying the foundation for something extraordinary. With consistency, your dreams will no longer just be dreams—they will be a living, breathing reality that you've created through persistence and unwavering dedication.

In the end, it's not about the destination—it's about the strength you develop along the way and the person you become in the process. Momentum, fueled by consistency, is the key to unlocking your potential and creating the life you've always dreamed of. Keep moving forward, step by step, and you'll be amazed at how far you can go.

Actionable Strategy:

- *Daily Habits:* Identify three daily habits that will move you closer to your dream. It could be reading, writing, exercising, or networking. Commit to these habits, no matter what, and watch how they compound over time.

The Role of Support: Surrounding Yourself with Like-Minded Dreamers

Dreaming big requires more than just inner strength; it demands the right support system. The people you surround yourself with play an integral role in your success. In the face of adversity, it can be easy to let the negativity of others dampen your spirit, especially when your dreams seem beyond reach. This is why surrounding yourself with people who uplift, encourage, and challenge you to stay true to your vision is crucial to achieving greatness.

Like-minded dreamers do more than provide positive energy—they offer insight and innovative ideas that can propel you forward. Their shared experiences can serve as invaluable lessons, teaching you what works, what doesn't, and what pitfalls to avoid. These individuals have often traveled the road you wish to take, and their wisdom can make all the difference in your journey. They understand the sacrifices, setbacks, and rewards involved in chasing big dreams, which makes them powerful allies as you work toward your own goals.

An essential component of a strong support system is accountability. When you are surrounded by people who are equally committed to their own growth and success, they will encourage you to stay focused, remind you of your goals, and gently challenge you when doubts arise. The beauty of this dynamic is that these individuals become your mirrors—helping you see your potential and strengths even when you struggle to recognize them in yourself. They will celebrate your achievements, no matter how small, and help you learn from your failures, transforming every setback into a stepping stone on the path to success.

Support goes beyond emotional encouragement. During times of uncertainty, the people you trust can provide tangible help, whether through sharing resources, making connections, or simply lending a listening ear. Their presence allows you to voice your concerns, seek advice, or talk through your fears. This process not only gives you clarity but also affirms that you do not face challenges alone.

One of the greatest gifts of surrounding yourself with like-minded individuals is the energy and momentum that comes from being part of a community. When you belong to a group that shares similar aspirations and values, an unspoken bond forms—a collective drive to push everyone toward their goals. Success becomes a shared victory, motivating each person to continue striving for more. This spirit of collaboration nurtures growth, where everyone's unique strengths are celebrated and contribute to the group's collective advancement.

In the pursuit of your dreams, the people you choose to keep close are vital. They can either propel you toward success or hinder your progress. It's important to intentionally curate your circle—ensuring that those around you lift you up, not hold you back. A supportive network of like-minded dreamers not only reminds you that you're not alone but also demonstrates that, together, extraordinary achievements are possible.

Reflection Prompt: The Dream That Refuses to Die

Take a moment to write down the dream that keeps whispering to you, even when the world gets loud.

- What does it look like?
- Who does it serve?
- Why does it matter to your soul?

Now, write down one action you can take this week to water that dream—no matter how small.

You owe that dream your courage.

15

Chapter 14: The Harmony of Wholeness – Embracing the Journey of Integration

Wholeness is not merely a state of being—it is a dynamic journey, a lifelong practice of integration. It's a call to embrace every aspect of ourselves, acknowledging both the light and the shadow, the joy and the pain, the victories and the defeats. Each fragment of who we are, though distinct, is part of a greater whole—a greater story that is unfolding, shaped by resilience, transformation, and grace. Living as a whole person is a journey of profound discovery—one that requires us to honor all parts of ourselves, to reclaim our power, and to step into a future that is not defined by perfection but by authenticity and courage.

This chapter delves into the sacred work of integration—how we unite the disparate parts of our lives into a symphony of wholeness. It's not just about accepting who we are; it's about recognizing the value of every experience, every emotion, and every part of ourselves. The work of integration is ongoing, and it is the key to living with purpose, alignment, and peace.

The Essence of Wholeness: A Journey of Integration

Wholeness is often misunderstood as something we attain at a particular moment—a finish line to cross, a summit to reach. But wholeness is not a destination; it is a continuous unfolding of who we are. It is about integrating the various parts of our life—the ones we celebrate and the ones we hide, the joyous and the painful, the strengths and the weaknesses—into a harmonious, authentic life.

Wholeness begins within. To embrace it, we must first look inward. This process often starts with acknowledging the parts of ourselves that we have ignored or rejected. For many, these are the painful memories, the failures, the vulnerabilities, and the fears that we often bury in the depths of our psyche. Yet, it is precisely these parts of us that hold the keys to our greatest growth. In facing our wounds, we discover our power. In confronting our shame, we unlock the door to self-love. In embracing our weaknesses, we find our truest strength.

The Power of Acknowledgment

The first step in embracing wholeness is acknowledgment—

acknowledging every part of your being as it is. This is not about labeling your life as good or bad, but rather about seeing yourself in full, without distortion. This step requires courage. It's easy to acknowledge the things we're proud of, the accomplishments that make us feel strong and capable. But to truly embrace wholeness, we must also look at the parts of our life that we tend to hide.

Consider the moments in your life that have been painful, or the experiences that made you feel small or insignificant. These are not merely instances of suffering; they are catalysts for transformation. They carry lessons—lessons that are often disguised as hardship or struggle. If we can see them as opportunities for growth, we can begin to integrate them into our lives as powerful teachers.

Your scars are not marks of defeat. They are symbols of your resilience, your strength, and your ability to heal. They are the threads woven into the tapestry of who you are, adding depth and richness to your personal story. Embracing them, rather than running from them, is the path to true wholeness.

Living Authentically in Wholeness

True wholeness is not just about acceptance—it is about living authentically. Living authentically means shedding the masks we wear for the world and stepping into the raw, unfiltered truth of who we are. It requires courage—the courage to let go of external validation, to stop seeking approval from others, and to trust that your worth is intrinsic and not dependent on anyone else's perception of you.

Authenticity is the highest form of self-respect. It is honoring your own truth, regardless of how it might be received. And the more you live authentically, the more you create space for others to do the same. In this way, your journey toward wholeness becomes a gift not only to yourself but to everyone around you. By living authentically, you give others permission to be their true selves as well.

It's important to remember that living authentically doesn't mean living perfectly. Imperfection is a key part of being whole. It's not about becoming flawless; it's about embracing the full spectrum of who you are—your strengths, your vulnerabilities, your triumphs, and your setbacks. You are not a finished product. You are a masterpiece in progress.

The Dance of Dualities

One of the most profound aspects of wholeness is the ability to hold space for dualities. Life is filled with contradictions—strength and vulnerability, fear and faith, joy and sorrow. Wholeness is about embracing these dualities and learning to live in harmony with them.

Many of us are taught to view life in black-and-white terms: things are either good or bad, strong or weak, happy or sad. But the truth is, life is much more complex. Wholeness exists in the gray areas. It's about learning to hold space for both the light and the dark, knowing that both are necessary for growth.

Take, for example, fear and faith. Fear is not something to be avoided or denied. It is a natural, human emotion that serves as a reminder of our vulnerability and our capacity for growth. Faith, on the other hand, is the force that pulls us beyond our fears, encouraging us to step into the unknown with courage and trust. Together, fear and faith form a powerful partnership. When you face your fears with faith, you discover inner strength you never knew you had.

Similarly, vulnerability and strength are not opposites—they are partners in the journey of integration. It takes strength to be vulnerable—to open yourself up, to be seen for who you truly are, with all your flaws and imperfections. And it takes vulnerability to be truly strong—to admit when you need help, to ask for support, and to lean into the discomfort of growth.

Building a Legacy Through Wholeness

Wholeness is not just for your own benefit—it is the foundation of the legacy you leave behind. A legacy built on wholeness is one of authenticity, love, and resilience. It is not about perfection; it is about impact. The way you live—your choices, your values, the love you share—becomes a lasting imprint on the world.

As you continue on your journey of integration, you become a beacon of light for others. The more whole you become, the more you empower others to do the same. Your wholeness becomes a catalyst for transformation in the lives of those you encounter. It creates a ripple effect, as others see your strength and are inspired to embrace their own.

Ask yourself:

What kind of legacy do you want to leave?

What do you want to be remembered for?

The legacy of wholeness is one that touches lives and creates a ripple effect of love, authenticity, and transformation.

Let your wholeness shine through in every interaction, every decision, every moment of kindness. By doing so, you not only build a legacy of personal fulfillment but also contribute to a world that is more connected, compassionate, and authentic.

Practical Steps Toward Integration

The journey of integration is personal, but there are some practical steps you can take to move toward wholeness. These steps require patience, compassion, and dedication—but they will guide you on the path to becoming the person you are meant to be.

1. *Self-Reflection:* Take time to reflect on your journey. What parts of yourself have you been hiding or denying? What parts of your story have you been afraid to embrace? Self-reflection is key to understanding where you are on your path and what needs to be integrated.

2. *Forgiveness:* Forgiveness is a powerful tool for integration.

Forgive yourself for past mistakes and release the guilt and shame that may be holding you back. Forgive others, too, for their transgressions. Forgiveness frees you to move forward without being weighed down by resentment.

3. *Gratitude:* Practice gratitude daily. Gratitude transforms pain into wisdom and allows you to see the beauty in every experience, even the difficult ones. Celebrate your strengths and the lessons learned from your struggles. Gratitude shifts your perspective from lack to abundance.

4. *Connection:* Surround yourself with people who support your journey. Seek out communities that celebrate authenticity and growth. True connection nourishes your soul and reinforces your commitment to living as your whole self.

5. *Mindfulness:* Mindfulness is essential for integration. Practice being fully present in each moment. By living in the present, you allow yourself to experience life as it is, without clinging to the past or worrying about the future. Mindfulness opens the door to deeper self-awareness and integration.

The Symphony of Wholeness

Your life is a symphony, a masterpiece in progress, where each note—whether harmonious or dissonant—contributes to its beauty. Wholeness does not mean flawlessness or perfection; it is the art of embracing the messy, the incomplete, and the ever-evolving nature of life. The discordant moments, the struggles, the times of uncertainty—all of these are as vital to your composition as the triumphs, joys, and serene interludes.

To be whole is to recognize that you are not a static being. You are a dynamic, evolving masterpiece—a living canvas painted with the vibrant hues of growth, change, and discovery. Every experience, no matter how challenging, is a brushstroke that adds depth and dimension to your life. The cracks and imperfections you perceive are not flaws but features of your uniqueness, places where the light of authenticity and resilience shines through most brightly.

Your journey toward integration—the weaving together of all aspects of yourself—is not just a personal pursuit. It is a profound gift to the world. By embracing your wholeness, you show others that it is possible to rise above challenges, to honor every piece of their story, and to live authentically. Your openness, strength, and courage become a beacon, lighting the way for others to step into their own power.

As you walk this path, know this: You are already whole. In your wholeness, you possess an unstoppable force—a quiet, steady power that no obstacle can diminish. It is this wholeness that empowers you to live with purpose, to love with depth, and to face life's uncertainties with grace. Your legacy is not in achieving some imagined ideal of perfection but in embodying the truth of who you are—beautifully imperfect, endlessly resilient, and deeply authentic.

Let your life be a testament to the power of resilience. Show that rising from adversity does not mean erasing the past but embracing it as part of your narrative. Let your story be one of transformation, where pain becomes strength, and fear gives way to courage. Live boldly, not in spite of your scars, but because of them. They are the proof of battles fought and lessons learned, the marks of a life truly lived.

In the symphony of your life, let love, grace, and courage guide your every movement. These are the qualities that sustain the melody, that ensure your legacy will resonate in the hearts of those who witness your journey. The legacy you leave is not in the things you accumulate or the titles you earn but in the lives you touch, the hope you inspire, and the authenticity you embody.

So rise as someone beautifully whole, a living testament to the transformative power of resilience and the profound beauty of authenticity. Take each step with confidence, knowing that your journey has meaning, that your story matters, and that you are enough—just as you are. This is your symphony, your masterpiece, your legacy. Live it boldly, with love, grace, and courage, and let the music of your life inspire others to embrace their own symphony of wholeness.

16

Chapter 15: The Phoenix Within

As we close the final chapter of this journey, let us return to the essence of who we truly are: powerful, resilient, and capable of rising anew from the ashes of our past. You are not the same person who started this journey. You are more evolved, more empowered, and more aligned with your true self than ever before. This chapter, The Phoenix Within, is a celebration of the transformation you have undergone and the infinite potential that lies ahead.

But let's pause for a moment and reflect: the journey doesn't end here. This is not the final destination but rather a new beginning. Your personal transformation is part of something far greater, a universal shift that is unfolding right before our eyes. You are a part of a greater movement—a collective of individuals, each on their own path, but all contributing to the same powerful wave of change. You are not alone in this journey.

The Power of Rebirth

The Phoenix is a symbol of rebirth, of rising from the ashes of its own destruction to become something even more magnificent. This mythical creature is a powerful reminder that from our most painful experiences, our most challenging moments, we have the ability to rise again—stronger, wiser, and more powerful than before. You, too, are a Phoenix. No matter the hardships you have faced, no matter the obstacles that have tried to break you, you possess the innate ability to transform your pain into power, your suffering into strength.

Each time you face a setback, you are being prepared for a grander version of yourself. Each challenge is an opportunity to shed the old, outgrown parts of you, like the Phoenix shedding its old feathers. With each rebirth, you grow into a higher expression of your true self. You are continuously evolving, continuously becoming more aligned with your soul's purpose.

But remember, the Phoenix does not rise overnight. Its transformation takes time. It faces the fire, undergoes the burn, and comes out renewed. So, too, do you face your struggles, but understand that every trial you overcome adds to your strength and wisdom. Every setback, every moment of despair, is part of your metamorphosis. You are not being destroyed; you are being refined.

You Are Not Alone in Your Journey

One of the most important realizations you can have on your journey is that you are not alone. It may feel like you are walking a solitary path, but know this: there are countless others walking alongside you, sharing similar experiences, facing similar challenges, and rising in the same way. The universal energy that connects all of us is undeniable. Every time you rise, you are not only empowering yourself but also contributing to the collective energy of the world. Your transformation sparks a ripple effect that reaches far beyond your own life.

When you face difficulties, remember that your growth is interconnected with the growth of others. You are part of a global transformation, a movement of individuals awakening to their full potential. Whether consciously or unconsciously, the work you do on yourself affects those around you. The love, strength, and resilience you cultivate within yourself are reflected outwardly, influencing the lives of your family, your community, and even the world at large.

It is easy to feel like we are alone in our struggles, but when you look at the bigger picture, you will see how many souls are undergoing their own trials, fighting their own battles, and seeking to rise just like you. You are part of a collective force—a global awakening of people choosing to rise, to heal, and to transform. When you rise, you help others rise. When you heal, others heal with you. Your journey is never isolated; it is deeply connected to the broader tapestry of humanity.

The Greater Universal Transformation

This is where your story transcends the individual. You are not just transforming for yourself, but for humanity as a whole. The personal work you do—the inner healing, the breaking of generational cycles, the release of fear and limiting beliefs—is part of a much larger process of collective evolution. You are contributing to the universal transformation taking place, one person, one action, one choice at a time.

The world is undergoing a shift. People are awakening to their true potential, and the barriers that once divided us are crumbling. Your journey is part of this larger awakening. As you heal, grow, and expand, you contribute to the greater collective consciousness. Every time you rise, you help raise the vibration of the world around you. You are helping to bring about a future where love, authenticity, and empowerment are the foundation of everything we do.

This universal transformation is not something happening to you—it is something happening with you. Your healing is intertwined with the collective healing of humanity. When you forgive, you inspire others to forgive. When you release negativity, you create space for positivity to flourish in the world. Each step you take toward becoming your true self amplifies the energy of transformation, creating a wave of change that ripples through every corner of the earth.

The Ripple Effect of Your Transformation

Your personal transformation is not just about you. It is about the lives you touch, the people you inspire, and the legacy you create. Every choice you make, every action you take, reverberates out into the world, impacting those around you in ways you may never fully comprehend. When you choose to rise, to shed the past, and to step into your true power, you give others permission to do the same.

This ripple effect is powerful. Think about the people in your life who have inspired you, who have made an impact on your journey. These individuals didn't do it because they were perfect—they did it because they dared to rise. They dared to transform. And now, it's your turn to do the same for someone else.

You may not always see the immediate impact of your actions, but rest assured, every step you take toward your higher self has a far-reaching impact. You are paving the way for those who will follow in your footsteps. Your legacy is being built not only by the successes you achieve but by the way you uplift others as you rise.

When you heal, you invite healing into the world. When you forgive, you release the burden of resentment and make room for love to blossom. When you stand in your power, you give others the courage to stand in theirs. The more you embrace your authentic self, the more the world embraces authenticity.

Embrace Your Infinite Potential

In the final moments of this chapter, I want to leave you with a reminder of the infinite potential that lies within you. You are a Phoenix, and your potential is limitless. No matter what you have faced, no matter what you may face in the future, you have the power to rise above it. You are capable of transforming your pain into purpose, your setbacks into comebacks, and your challenges into triumphs.

The Phoenix within you is always waiting to be awakened. It is never too late to rise, to transform, and to step into your true power. The universe is constantly conspiring in your favor, and every step you take toward becoming your highest self is a step toward creating a world of love, unity, and strength.

But remember, rising is a continual process. It is not about one grand moment of transformation—it is about many moments, many choices, and many actions that build upon one another. Each time you face a challenge, you have the choice to rise again. And each time you do, you grow stronger, more resilient, and more aligned with your purpose.

You are limitless. You are powerful. And the Phoenix within you will continue to rise, again and again.

Reflection Prompt: "The Fire That Refuses to Die"

Take a quiet moment with yourself.

Breathe deeply. Place your hand over your heart. And ask:

- *What have I risen from that once threatened to destroy me?*
- *What part of me has been reborn through the flames?*
- *What truth within me refuses to die, no matter how many*

times life tried to silence it?

Write your answer down—not just with ink, but with intention.

Because that fire?

That's your power. That's your legacy. That's the Phoenix within you.

A Final Reminder

As you continue on this journey, remember that you are never alone. Your transformation is part of a greater, universal shift, one that is happening in the hearts and minds of people around the world. You are a part of this collective awakening. Each time you rise, you lift others with you, and together, we create a world filled with love, empowerment, and authenticity.

So, rise again, and rise with purpose. Embrace the Phoenix within you, for you are limitless, and your potential knows no bounds. You are part of something greater than yourself, and your journey is a powerful thread in the vast tapestry of human transformation. The world is waiting for you to soar—so spread your wings, and let the fire within you ignite the world.

Your legacy begins now.

17

Chapter 16: The Final Rise – Embodying Your Legacy

Embrace the Eternal Flame

The journey you've embarked on throughout these pages has been nothing short of transformative. You have walked through trials, faced the shadows of your past, and emerged stronger, wiser, and more resilient than ever before. But, this is not the end of your journey. It is merely the beginning. You now stand at the threshold of greatness, the flames of your inner Phoenix burning brighter than ever.

In the chapters that preceded this one, you discovered your strengths, your vulnerabilities, your purpose. You learned to embrace your authentic self, to rise above past struggles, and to build a legacy of love, strength, and empowerment. But now, you must do more than just reflect on what you've learned. You must step into your new reality with the full force of your willpower and determination. You must fully embody the lessons you have gathered, and let them become the foundation of the legacy you will leave behind.

The Phoenix within you is not a fleeting spark. It is an eternal flame, and it is within your power to keep that fire burning brightly for the rest of your life. You have the strength to rise, again and again, from any setback. Your journey is a constant evolution, and every challenge you face is an opportunity to step further into your full potential.

Your Legacy — A Living Testament

Building a legacy is not just about creating wealth, fame, or recognition. It's about creating something that transcends your individual existence. Your legacy is the mark you leave on the world — the ripple effect of your actions, your wisdom, and your love. It is the impact you have on the people around you and the world at large.

As you move forward, remember that your legacy is not something you achieve once and for all. It is something that is constantly being shaped and molded. Every day, with every decision you make, you are contributing to the story that will be told about you long after you're gone. And what will that story be?

It will be a story of resilience, of love, of authenticity. It will be a story of someone who was not afraid to show the world their raw, unfiltered self. Someone who loved fiercely, who empowered others, and who never backed down from the challenges of life.

Your legacy will not only be shaped by your actions but also by your ability to uplift those around you. Remember, true power lies in the ability to empower others. As you build your legacy, continue to be the beacon of light for those who may be lost in the darkness. The world is in desperate need of more leaders who will shine brightly, helping others find their own path.

The Call to Rise

This chapter is not just the end of a book. It is the beginning of the next chapter of your life. A chapter where you are fully alive in your purpose, where you are unstoppable, and where you are creating a future that is beyond your wildest dreams.

The world needs you, more than ever, to step into your power. We are living in a time of transformation — a time where each of us has the opportunity to rise and shape the future. And your rise is one that will inspire others to do the same.

What will your rise look like? What kind of legacy do you want to leave? How will you step into your greatness and make an indomitable impact on the world?

As you reflect on your journey and everything you've learned throughout this book, remember that you are not alone. We are all connected. Every step you take in your growth is part of a larger, universal transformation. When you rise, you inspire those around you to rise as well.

You Are the Phoenix — The Flame of Transformation

From this point forward, your life will never be the same. You have unlocked your true potential, and you now understand that everything you have gone through, every hardship, every heartbreak, has been preparing you for this moment.

The Phoenix within you has been awakened. The flames of transformation are burning brightly, and you have the power to transform not only your own life but the lives of those you touch. This is the most powerful force in the universe: the ability to change, to grow, and to rise above the ashes, again and again.

The life that awaits you is one filled with possibility, love, and boundless opportunities. You are no longer bound by your past or limited by your fears. You are free. You are limitless. And now, you are ready to make your mark on the world in ways you never thought possible.

The journey ahead will be filled with challenges, but you have everything you need within you to overcome them. The road will not always be easy, but you are strong enough to walk it. Keep going. Keep rising. Keep transforming.

The Legacy You Will Create

You are not just a person — you are a movement. A force of nature. A living testament to the power of transformation, resilience, and love.

As you move forward into this next chapter of your life, remember that you are in control of your destiny. You hold the pen to your story, and every choice you make is a stroke on the canvas of your future.

Let this chapter be the start of your greatest adventure yet. And let it remind you that you are, and always will be, the Phoenix — rising from the ashes to create a life of limitless possibilities.

Reflection Prompt: "Your Moment to Rise"

Pause right here.

Ask yourself with brutal honesty and beautiful grace:

- What is one fear I must finally release to rise fully?
- What truth have I been too afraid to embody?
- What does it look like to walk, speak, and live as the Phoenix I've become?

Now write it down—and promise yourself:

No more shrinking. No more silence. No more waiting.

The fire is here. The moment is now. Rise.

18

Final Thoughts

Your Moment to Rise and Claim Your Power

As you stand at the precipice of this chapter in your life, I want you to take a moment and breathe. You've made it to this point for a reason. Every word you've read, every idea that has stirred within you, has led you here—exactly where you need to be. And now, as you approach the closing of this book, it's not the end. It is a new beginning, a gateway to a future brimming with possibility and opportunity. This is your time.

The journey you've taken through these pages was never meant to simply inform you; it was meant to ignite something within you. It was meant to awaken the fire that has always been within you, waiting for the right moment to blaze. That moment is now. The question is, what will you do with the power that you hold inside of you?

You have everything you need to create the life you desire. You are not here by accident. You have not made it through every trial and tribulation only to fall short of your greatness. Every experience, every hardship, every setback has prepared you for this moment—the moment when you can stand up, claim your power, and start living the life you were always meant to live.

You see, this book is not an ending. It is the starting point of a radical transformation. It is a reminder that you are the creator of your own story. Your past, with all its trials and tribulations, does not define you. It has shaped you, yes—but it has not had the final say. You have the power to rewrite your story.

The journey you are on is not a one-time event; it is an unfolding process. Life is not about finding a destination—it is about the continual evolution of becoming. You are in a constant state of becoming. And this becoming, my friend, is where the magic lies. It is in the moments of doubt, of fear, of challenge, that you are sculpting the person you are meant to be. Every setback is an opportunity to rise.

When I say you have the power to transform, I mean it. You have the ability to completely shift your mindset, your actions, and ultimately, your life. The person you were yesterday does not have to be the person you are tomorrow. And you are not required to remain stagnant in the face of challenges. You can choose to move forward. You can choose to heal, to grow, to rise higher.

You are worthy of your dreams.

I want you to understand that right now. You don't need to prove your worth to anyone—not to your past, not to your family, not to society. Your worth is intrinsic. It is woven into the very fabric of who you are. The universe does not make mistakes. You were born for greatness. And now, you get to decide if you are going to step into that greatness or shrink back into the shadows of doubt.

he power that you seek? It's not outside of you. It's already in you. You don't need anyone's permission. You don't need to wait for the perfect time. The time is now. And you don't need to wait for a sign, because this is it. This book, this moment, these words are all the affirmation you need to take that first bold step.

But, let me be clear: the road won't always be easy. There will be days when you feel like you're not making progress. There will be times when you question whether you're on the right path. That is normal. Progress is not always linear. It's not always clear. But remember this: You have the strength to weather every storm that comes your way. You have already overcome so much to get here. The challenges you face are not insurmountable. They are simply part of your growth. They are building the resilience, the wisdom, and the strength that you need to rise higher.

In those moments of doubt, in those moments when you wonder if you have enough left to keep going, I want you to remember that you are not defined by your struggles. You are defined by how you respond to them. Your power lies not in avoiding challenges, but in your ability to rise every time you fall. You are unstoppable. That's who you are.

The truth is, you are the only one who can hold yourself back. Your success, your growth, your greatness—they all begin with the decision you make today. The decision to take control of your life, to stop waiting for permission, and to boldly step into your power.

I want you to ask yourself: What will you do with this power? Will you keep hiding? Will you keep waiting? Or will you rise?

The world needs your light.

Not because it's perfect, but because it's uniquely yours. Your voice, your perspective, your truth—it's all part of the magic you bring into this world. You are not here by chance. You were meant to be here, to share your gifts, to make an impact. Your journey is just as important as anyone else's. You don't need to wait for someone to tell you that you matter. You matter.

The power you hold is the key to your future, and the future is waiting for you. There is no need to wait for someone else to tell you that you're ready. You are ready now. Every step you take from this moment on will be a step toward the life you've always dreamed of. And remember, the life you create is yours to define. Don't let anyone—family, friends, society—tell you what that should look like. You are the creator of your story.

So, what will you do? Will you let fear hold you back, or will you embrace your greatness? Will you step into the unknown, trusting that you have everything you need to succeed? Will you choose to rise, no matter the obstacles in your way?

The choice is yours. And I believe in you. I believe in your strength. I believe in your ability to rise higher than you ever imagined. Now, go claim your power.

Rise with purpose. Rise with passion. Rise with the fierce knowledge that you are capable of achieving everything you desire. Your story is far from over. It is only just beginning.

You are destined for greatness. Now, rise.

Reflection Prompt: "The Legacy I Choose"

Take one final moment of stillness.

Write down the legacy you choose to leave behind—not one built by fear, survival, or silence, but one carved in purpose, power, and truth.

- What do you want your life to echo long after you're gone?
- Who will feel your rise and be changed by it?
- What choices must you make now to honor that future?

Let this be the vow you carry forward.

Made in the USA
Columbia, SC
16 June 2025

b96edd5f-e0e6-4c11-8ed7-10d4a4ab188aR01